*Studies in German Literature, Linguistics, and Culture:*
*Literary Criticism in Perspective*

## About *Literary Criticism in Perspective*

Books in *Literary Criticism in Perspective*, a subseries of *Studies in German Literature, Linguistics, and Culture*, and *Studies in English and American Literature, Linguistics, and Culture*, trace literary scholarship and criticism on major and neglected writers alike, or on a single major work, a group of writers, a literary school or movement. In so doing the authors — authorities on the topic in question who are also well-versed in the principles and history of literary criticism — address a readership consisting of scholars, students of literature at the graduate and undergraduate level, and the general reader. One of the primary purposes of the series is to illuminate the nature of literary criticism itself, to gauge the influence of social and historic currents on aesthetic judgments once thought objective and normative.

*Franz Werfel and the Critics*

*Drawing of Werfel in 1934.*
*Courtesy of the Austrian Cultural Institute,*
*New York.*

# Jennifer E. Michaels

# Franz Werfel and the Critics

## Camden House

Copyright © 1994 by
CAMDEN HOUSE, INC.

Published by Camden House, Inc.
Drawer 2025
Columbia, SC 29202 USA

Printed on acid-free paper.
Binding materials are chosen for strength and
durability.

ISBN:1-879751-99-2

Library of Congress Cataloging-in-Publication Data

Michaels, Jennifer E.
    Franz Werfel and the critics / Jennifer E. Michaels.
    p.    cm.    --   (Studies in German Literature, linguistics, and
culture. Literary criticism in perspective)
    Includes bibliographical references and index.
    ISBN 1-879751-99-2 (alk. paper)
    1. Werfel, Franz, 1890-1945--Criticism and interpretation.
I. Title.  II. Series
PT2647.E77Z66       1994
833' .912--dc20                                                94-7698
                                                             CIP

# Acknowledgments

I wish to thank Professor Hans Wagener of UCLA for reading my manuscript and for his helpful suggestions, and the Austrian Cultural Institute in New York for allowing me to use the drawing of Franz Werfel.

# Contents

# 1: Introduction

DURING HIS LIFE, Franz Werfel was an extremely popular author whose works were translated into many languages. After his death, however, he was virtually forgotten by the reading public. Werfel gained fame early for his lyric poetry, and many considered him to be one of the most important German expressionist poets. Today he is still remembered for this early poetry and for his contributions to expressionism. Increasingly, however, more recent critics have taken a fresh look at Werfel's neglected dramatic works and have also begun to appreciate once again the evocative power of the novels that had attracted his earlier readers. Some believe, in fact, that the novels and stories are Werfel's lasting achievement (Steiman 1989, 311).

Werfel was born on 10 September 1890 in Prague and died as an exile on 26 August 1945 in Beverly Hills. His life spanned some of the most momentous events of this century—the First World War, the inflation and depression of the 1920s, the rise of fascism, and the Second World War—events that he confronted in several of his works. He spent the first decades of his life in Prague, where he got to know other members of the Prague circle of Jewish writers such as Max Brod and Franz Kafka. Memories of his childhood in Prague pervade many of Werfel's works, even those he wrote at the end of his life. Although he was born into a Jewish family and raised as a Jew, he became attracted to Catholicism, which exerted a strong influence on him throughout his life, especially in his later years. In many of his later works, Werfel was preoccupied with the relationship between Judaism and Christianity and the special role that he believed Jews were ordained to play in the divine plan. He served briefly on the eastern front during the First World War, although not in the front lines, but he was transferred to Vienna to work in the Military Press Bureau in 1917. There Werfel participated in the revolution of 1918, but he soon became disillusioned with radical politics, a disillusionment that was encouraged by his relationship with the conservative Alma Mahler, whom he met in 1917 and married in 1929. Although Werfel continued to write verse during his years in Vienna, he turned his attention increasingly to drama and the novel. He was a prolific author who gained artistic and popular success during these years. In 1927 he was awarded the Schiller Prize and the Czech State Prize. At this time Werfel was considered to be one of the most renowned and respected writers in the German language. As Hans Wagener (1993) points out, when the literary magazine *Die schöne Literatur* polled its readers on 7 July 1927 Werfel received more votes than Gerhart Hauptmann, Stefan George, or Rainer Maria Rilke (8). With the rise of Nazism, Werfel's literary fortunes in Germany changed radically. In 1933 he was expelled from the Prussian Academy of the Arts, and his novel *Die vierzig Tage des Musa Dagh* was banned in Germany in 1934. At the time of the *Anschluß*, Werfel was in Capri. He and Alma Mahler-Werfel found refuge first in France. As the German troops advanced, they fled, like many other German exiles, to Marseilles, where they desperately sought a visa to escape from France. With the help of Varian Fry of the Emergency Rescue Committee, they crossed the Pyrenees on foot and made their way through Spain to Portugal, where they boarded a ship for New York. Shortly after their arrival in New York on 13 October 1940 they moved to the Los Angeles area, where Werfel remained for the rest of his life.

Despite his popularity—or perhaps because of it—critical interest in Werfel's works waned after his death, although he was never completely ignored. Responses to his work have ranged from enthusiastic and uncritical admiration and respect to sharp criticism and rejection. For many critics, Werfel was the greatest and most original lyric poet of expressionism. Others, however, complained that his verse was sentimental and often too derivative, and they objected to his overuse of abstraction, hyperbole, and ecstatic rhetoric. Many critics admired what they saw as the deeply ethical and religious foundation of his work and his sense of his mission as a poet, while others sharply rejected his religious views and called his philosophy opaque. Many praised his novels, several of which became best-sellers, for their imaginative power, realistic depiction of characters, and well-told stories, while others complained that Werfel was merely a scribbler who often worked carelessly and hastily. Many admired him as a social critic, while others rejected his views as superficial and reactionary. Even today critics do not agree about how to evaluate Werfel as a writer and thinker, and there is no consensus among them about the literary quality of his works.

Werfel initially became known for his lyric poetry but he later made a name for himself as a dramatist and novelist. His first volume of verse, *Der Weltfreund* (1911), quickly made him famous in German-speaking countries. His contemporaries considered him to be the leading expressionist poet—a view that was reinforced by the verse collections he published in the following years, up to *Der Gerichtstag* in 1919—and such writers as Kafka and Rilke greatly admired many of his works and viewed him as an important writer. After 1919, however, his collections were virtually ignored. Werfel first became known as a dramatist through his successful adaptation of Euripides' *Die Troerinnen*, which was performed in 1916. His later dramas, most of which premiered on important stages and several of which were directed by Max Reinhardt, established his reputation as a respected dramatist, though his dramas did not enjoy the nearly unanimous praise that reviewers accorded his early lyric poetry. The popular success of his first novel, *Verdi* (1924), established his reputation as a novelist in German-speaking countries, and some of his later novels enhanced it. The standing Werfel enjoyed as a poet, dramatist, and novelist came abruptly to an end in Germany, where his books were banned after Hitler came to power, and in Austria when he was forced into exile in 1938 after the *Anschluß*.

As an exile, Werfel did not have to suffer the oblivion to which most exile writers were consigned in their country of refuge. His celebration as a writer in German-speaking countries, in fact, was not only repeated but even intensified in the United States. Before he was forced into exile in the United States, Werfel was respected in this country as a dramatist and a novelist, but not as a poet. Though poetry was the genre that had initially made him famous in Germany and Austria, Americans were not familiar with Werfel's poetry because very little of it was available in English before the collection *Poems*, translated by Edith Abercrombie Snow, appeared in 1945. This collection, furthermore, was not widely read, despite some positive reviews. By 1945 Werfel's early lyric poetry no longer seemed to have the freshness and originality that had so impressed earlier readers; it appeared to many to be outdated. Werfel first became known in the United States when his play *Goat Song* was produced by the Theater Guild in New York in 1926, after which a "veritable Werfelmania erupted" (Steiman 1987, 55). Despite his success as a dramatist in the United States, it was as a novelist that Werfel was best known here. His novels, which were quickly translated into English, had a wide readership and were reviewed in leading magazines and newspapers. The novels with which he established his fame in the United States, *The Forty Days of Musa Dagh* (1934), *Embezzled Heaven* (1940), and *The Song of Bernadette* (1942), were all Book-of-the-Month-Club selections. *The Song of Bernadette* sold over a million copies in the United States. It was so commercially successful that it became a comic strip in the San Francisco *Herald Examiner*; it inspired a hit song and a soap statuette of Bernadette that was marketed all over the country (Jungk 1987, 216). The successful 1944 Broadway production of *Jacobowsky and the Colonel* further reinforced Werfel's standing in the United States. Several of his works were turned into films, another indication of his popularity. The movie *The Song of Bernadette* (1943), for example, won five Academy Awards. The films based on Werfel's works have been a neglected area of Werfel criticism. While the popular success he enjoyed made his life financially secure if not luxurious in comparison to that of other exiles and gave him an acceptance in his host country that few other exiles enjoyed, it also made critics doubt that he was a serious writer; some suspected that he was successful only because he pandered to public taste.

From early on, critics had noticed certain weaknesses in Werfel's works, particularly his lack of concern with form. As Werfel became more outspoken in the 1930s about his political and religious beliefs, more controversy arose. Some reviewers in Germany and Austria and later in the United States complained about what they considered his reactionary political and religious views. The liberal press in the United States, which regularly reviewed works by exiled authors, was particularly incensed by Werfel's political views. The publication of "An Essay upon the Meaning of Imperial Austria," which he wrote as introduction to his story collection *Twilight of a World* (1937), confirmed for them that Werfel was a reactionary writer. Several Jewish critics viewed his sympathies for Catholicism as apostasy. This was all the more disturbing to them because of Hitler's persecution of the Jews in Europe at the time, and some even accused him of anti-Semitism. Some Catholic critics thought that Werfel distorted Catholicism, although the majority of them enthusiastically accepted his works, especially *Embezzled Heaven* and *The Song of Bernadette*, and admired the deep faith they perceived to be expressed in them. Reviewers' own ideological, religious, and political views, together with the historical context of the war, often made it difficult for them to assess Werfel's political and religious views objectively or to appreciate their importance for his development as a writer, and they were apt either to accept his views enthusiastically or to reject them sharply. Other reviewers pointed out the uneven quality of Werfel's works. While many were impressed with his powerful imagination and his strong storytelling skills, others condemned the sloppiness in form and style that in their view often marred Werfel's writing.

Several critics have tried to account for the rapid decline in critical interest in Werfel immediately after his death in 1945. Günther (1960), for example, believes that after the first surprise and enthusiasm for his works, there followed a disenchantment if not a disdainful turning away (740); and Politzer (1949) accounts for the decline in interest by noting the unevenness of Werfel's work, a quality he attributes to Werfel's exuberant boyishness, which gave his works their immediacy but also made him disregard form (285-86). Werfel's friend and admirer Adolf Klarmann (1969), whom Guy Stern and Peter Schönbach (1992) call the Nestor of Werfel scholarship (187) and who was one of the most influential of the early Werfel scholars and the editor of Werfel's *Gesammelte Werke* (1948-75), believes that there were three main reasons for the decline in interest in Werfel after his death. Klarmann notes that it is common for authors to be forgotten right after their death, although critical interest in their works often resumes later. Another important reason for the critical neglect, he posits, is that Werfel was too successful in a popular sense, and this made many critics wary of him. Finally, Klarmann argues that, at the time Werfel was writing, critics had become more interested in the analysis of form in literary works and less interested in their content and ideas, which, in Klarmann's view, were Werfel's great strengths. Klarmann sees Werfel as a prophet, as the conscience of his time, a role that he believes no longer appealed to a more skeptical generation that had lost its belief in message and mission (410).

Although interest in Werfel in the 1940s and 1950s was not overwhelming, there was a steady, if modest, flow of critical literature devoted to his works, led especially by Klarmann, whose main focus was Werfel's philosophical and religious thinking. In the 1960s, and increasingly in the 1970s and 1980s, interest in Werfel revived, as Klarmann had predicted it would. This renewed critical activity was sparked in the 1970s by the growing attention given to exile studies and has continued to the present. The recent centennial of Werfel's birth gave rise to symposia and several studies on Werfel, such as the collection of essays edited by Huber (1989a); the special edition of *Modern Austrian Literature*, which devoted an entire issue to Werfel in 1991; and the collection *Franz Werfel im Exil* (1992), edited by Wolfgang Nehring and Hans Wagener, which contains eleven essays based on papers given at the International Werfel Symposium at UCLA in October 1990. Hans Wagener's monograph *Understanding Franz Werfel* (1993) is a valuable new contribution to Werfel scholarship because it provides the best English-language introduction to Werfel's works. In 1991 Karlheinz Auckenthaler organized a Werfel conference in Szeged, Hungary, and subsequently published the papers presented there in *Franz Werfel: neue Aspekte seines Werkes* (1992a). In addition, the centennial of Werfel's birth gave rise to special Werfel exhibitions such as the one organized by the Adalbert Stifter Verein in Munich, which was shown in Munich in 1990 and in Regensburg and Düsseldorf in 1991 (Abels et al. 1990). In Germany Werfel's most famous works have been reissued in paperback by Fischer and have sold well. As Schmitz (1987) notes, however, despite the success of the paperback sales, Werfel is not yet enjoying a literary renaissance (330).

Much of the early criticism on Werfel, such as the monograph by Richard Specht (1926), was laudatory and uncritical. In fact, in his analysis of Werfel's works, Specht uses a kind of hymnic language similar to that which he admired so much in Werfel's poetry. Specht, the biographer of Gustav Mahler, interviewed Werfel for this book in 1925. Jungk (1987) complains about the worshipful tone and lack of criticism in Specht's book and writes that it was "remarkable mainly for its stylistic excess and bitter invective against Werfel's contemporaries" (110). Jungk's comment points out some of the many shortcomings in Specht's monograph. Specht did not, however, claim to give a definitive interpretation of Werfel's works; he acknowledged that it was too early for him to determine the direction that Werfel would take, and on occasions he pointed out some of his shortcomings. Although we should be cautious with Specht, his study is still useful since it typifies both the reactions of the time and many of the excesses common to the early critical responses to Werfel.

Following the example of Klarmann, such critics as Annemarie von Puttkamer (1952) in the early years after Werfel's death were particularly interested in Werfel's religious and philosophical ideas, elements of his work that continue to interest some critics today. Karlheinz Auckenthaler, for example, is presently at work on a study of Werfel's religious thinking that should appear in the next couple of years. Although such studies have been important for elucidating Werfel's philosophy of life, which is central to his works, they often ignore their literary aspects and thus run the danger of reducing them to philosophical tracts. This sort of approach has been a weakness in much Werfel criticism, at least until recently. Another weakness has been that critics have often tended to treat Werfel's works reverently: many of the early critics in particular were apt to regard their work as a kind of exegesis.

In the 1950s and 1960s, some critics explored the cultural and geographic forces that, in their opinion, shaped Werfel's work, such as the influence of Prague and Czechoslovakia that Hyrslová (1958) was one of the first to discuss in detail, and this interest has continued today. Other critics were interested in literary influences, such as Walt Whitman's impact on Werfel's early poetry and Werfel's debt to Dostoyevsky (Turrian 1950, Pachmuss 1963). Monographs by Braselmann (1960) and Zahn (1966) took an uncritical biographical approach and summarized rather than analyzed Werfel's plots. Although these two works are not useful today, at the time they were written they helped those who were unfamiliar with Werfel reconstruct his life and works.

Another aspect of Werfel's works that has interested critics is the development of his political thinking. Lea (1968) was one of the first to investigate thoroughly Werfel's attitude to political activism. The interest in Werfel's political views continued to be expressed in articles by Williams (1970, 1974) and Pfeifer (1971) and, more recently, in Steiman's (1985) provocative study, which is one of the most perceptive sources for an understanding of Werfel's political and religious thought.

One of the most important books on Werfel in the 1970s, by Foltin (1972), provided the first reliable information on Werfel's life and works. Foltin contributed significantly to Werfel scholarship, both through her basic research on his life and works and in her more analytical articles. From the 1970s and 1980s until the present there has been continued interest in the exile aspects of Werfel's works. Critics have come to recognize Werfel as an important figure in German exile literature. Since the late 1980s in particular, the focus of some of the criticism has changed. Although some critics are still interested in the religious and philosophical aspects of Werfel's works, increasingly more are exploring their literary aspects and Werfel's connection to his literary tradition. Nowadays critics tend to avoid the pitfalls of much of the early criticism, with its propensity for either enthusiastic and reverent acceptance or sharp rejection, and favor a more critical and balanced weighing of the evidence. Critics no longer function as an advocate for Werfel, a role that many of the earlier critics assumed.

Although there is renewed interest in Werfel today, the Werfel scholar still faces certain problems. In 1972 Foltin pointed out that research on Werfel was still in its early stages. Lippelt (1984) agreed and noted that over a decade later, when he was writing, Foltin's comment was still pertinent. He complained that critics continued to neglect much of Werfel's work: Werfel the artist of form, the ironist, the political thinker, and the novelist, he remarked, was like a stowaway of literary criticism (291). Steiman (1985) addressed the neglect of Werfel the political thinker, and there has been more interest recently in Werfel's novels; but Werfel the artist, the creator of literary works, is still neglected.

The Werfel scholar has to contend not only with many neglected areas in the critical response but also with surprising gaps in basic research on Werfel. Until now, scholars have still not adequately treated much of the material in the Werfel archives at the University of California at Los Angeles and the University of Pennsylvania. For example, the publication of Werfel's diaries and notebooks, contained in the archives at UCLA, would be an extremely valuable resource to Werfel scholars, as Karlheinz Auckenthaler has recognized. He is presently at work on a two-volume edition of Werfel's diaries and notebooks that will be published by Fischer in 1995 and 1996. Another extremely useful resource would be a new critical edition of Werfel's complete works. Although the *Gesammelte Werke*, edited by Adolf Klarmann (1948-75), was a valuable addition to Werfel scholarship when it was published, it does not contain all of Werfel's works, and it also lacks an adequate critical commentary. Klarmann was a staunch advocate for Werfel's works and thus did not always have the necessary critical distance from them. Another obvious area of neglect is Werfel's correspondence. To date, there is no edition of his collected letters. An indication of the state of Werfel research is that, so many years after his death, the special Werfel issue of *Modern Austrian Literature* in 1991 devoted three of its eight articles, and by far most of its pages, to discussions of Werfel's correspondence and to publishing some of his letters for the first time. There is also no comprehensive study of Werfel's essays. Buck (1961) and Foltin and Spalek (1969) provide useful overviews, and Steiman (1985) perceptively analyzes Werfel's most important essays in the context of his religious and political thinking. In his recent monograph, Wagener (1993) begins his discussion of Werfel with an analysis of his major essays and aphorisms and a recognition of their significance for an understanding of his literary works. Werfel's essays on literature and music have, however, been neglected. Clark (1989) analyzes Werfel's view of the theater as expressed in his essay "Die Bühne von Hellerau" (1913), but most other critics, such as Bauer (1978), have mentioned such essays only in passing. Although there has been progress in Werfel scholarship since Foltin and Lippelt made their comments—for example, Jungk's biography of Werfel (1987) and Abel's *Franz Werfel mit Selbstzeugnissen und Bilddokumenten* (1990) begin to address the lack of a comprehensive Werfel biography that Foltin noted—there is still much to be done.

Reich-Ranicki (1965) observes that it is difficult to reduce Werfel's works to a common denominator because of the enormous number of different and uneven works in all genres—novels, stories, poems, poetic sketches, dramas, scenic fragments, essays, lectures, and adaptations—that make up his oeuvre. Such versatility does not lend itself easily to neat categories. Reich-Ranicki aptly remarks that Werfel belongs to those writers and poets who make life difficult for literary critics (229). Similarly, the critical response to Werfel is also extremely varied and not easy to fit into a neat pattern, a characteristic that presented organizational problems for this discussion of Werfel criticism. Critical responses include discussions of individual works, general studies of Werfel's life and works, analyses of Werfel's political and religious thought, studies of the geographical and literary influences on his works, thematic studies, biographical approaches, and occasional Marxist and psychoanalytical approaches as well as studies that are concerned with the aesthetic aspects of Werfel's works. Unlike the critical response to many writers, the history of Werfel criticism is not characterized by a succession of schools of criticism. Instead, various approaches exist side by side. So far, however, Werfel has not aroused the attention of postmodern schools of literary criticism, and feminist critics have not found him an appealing topic.

To try to show the different trends in these varied responses, I adopted the following organization. In the first chapters of this study, I focus on the critical response to Werfel's works, organized according to genre. It has often been pointed out, most recently by Wagener (1993, 27), that Werfel's creative life can be divided into three periods. In the first, poetry was the predominant genre. In his second period he turned to the drama and finally, in his third, to the novel. There is considerable overlap, because Werfel continued to write in all three genres throughout his life—for example, in his third period he wrote not only novels but also his most successful play, *Jacobowsky und der Oberst*, as well as poetry. Nevertheless, such an organization follows chronologically both Werfel's development as a writer and the growth of his reputation. I first discuss Werfel's lyric poetry, with which he established his fame, and then move to his dramas and novels, for which he later became famous. Within each chapter I deal chronologically with Werfel's works and the critical response to them to show both the variety of responses and also the development of responses to a particular work. In order to synthesize the critical response, I highlight topics that have been of special interest to critics. Since a lot of critical interest has focused on such aspects of Werfel's works as geographical and literary influences, his exile, and his political and religious thinking, these trends in criticism are dealt with separately in later chapters of the study. For the most part, analysis of Werfel's essays has taken place in the context of discussions of his religious and political thinking, and this is an approach that I follow here.

Like other books in the series *Literary Criticism in Perspective*, this study of Werfel and his critics, a task that has not been undertaken before, does not attempt to be all-inclusive but rather traces the most influential and important criticism. One of my criteria for selectivity has been to focus on those works by Werfel in which there has been at least a reasonable amount of critical interest, with the exception of neglected works that influential critics have seen as central to Werfel's development. Thus such quite neglected works as the novel *Der Abituriententag* (1928), the play *In einer Nacht* (1937), and most of Werfel's stories, to which Wagener (1993) has recently drawn attention, are mentioned only briefly. Like other books in the series *Literary Criticism in Perspective*, this one focuses primarily on published works of literary criticism—that is, critical essays and monographs that deal in whole or in part with Werfel. The many reviews of Werfel's works are mentioned only in passing. I do not include unpublished dissertations, although Werfel continues to be a topic of modest interest to graduate students and their advisors, as Terry Reisch's recent dissertation, "Franz Werfel's Exile Works: Analysis and Annotated Bibliography of Their Reception" (SUNY–Albany, 1992), demonstrates. In my discussion of Werfel and his critics, I have attempted to point out aspects of Werfel's works that have aroused critical interest and to show the various trends in Werfel criticism that have shaped his reputation as a writer and a thinker. I also hope that this study will indicate areas of research that still need to be explored.

# 2: Franz Werfel's Lyric Poetry

WERFEL'S FIRST COLLECTION of lyric poetry, *Der Weltfreund* (1911), was the greatest literary sensation of 1911 (Guthke 1978, 71). It established its author as the leading German expressionist poet. The first edition of 4,000 copies sold out immediately, and the book was quickly reprinted. Poets such as Rilke, Hofmannsthal, and Kafka admired Werfel's lyric poetry and regarded him as a serious poet, and contemporary reviewers were not only positive but frequently enthusiastic about this collection. Not surprisingly, much of the later criticism of Werfel's poetry has been concerned with this first volume; the tone of much of this criticism, especially the earlier part of it, has been as enthusiastic and uncritical as the reviews at the time of its publication. Later, however, critics such as Thomke (1972) pointed out what they saw as the many deficiencies in the collection and evaluated it negatively. Such recent critics as Wagner (1989) have taken a more balanced view and tried to assess its strengths and weaknesses. Some critics still believe that *Der Weltfreund* is one of the most important texts of German expressionism, and a few still consider it to be one of Werfel's best works.

Several critics speculated about why *Der Weltfreund* seemed to Werfel's contemporaries like a miracle and a revelation. Specht (1926), who like many early critics regarded Werfel as a genius, as a poet in whom mission lived, believes the poems in *Der Weltfreund* were the voice of the new youth; he argues that no other poet of the time struck the heart of his generation with such power. Specht's enthusiastic language indicates his worshipful, reverent approach to Werfel, which is typical of much of the early criticism. Siemsen (1945) testifies to the almost religious impact of *Der Weltfreund* on her and on Werfel's contemporaries when she calls the collection their favorite prayer book and its poet their apostle (157).

This reverent approach to Werfel is also typical of Klarmann (1961) who believes that the collection's impact was so great because the younger generation saw in Werfel their advocate. In his view, Werfel, more than any other poet at the time, expressed for this generation a fresh attitude to the world, an attitude that rejected naturalism and aestheticism and yearned for a new order that would bring about change in the relationship between people, between people and the state, and between people and God (12). In a later article (1969), Klarmann follows in the tradition of Specht when he calls Werfel a prophet: for his generation and the next, he was the voice, the conscience of his age (410).

Williams (1974), whose article reflects the growing interest in Werfel's political thinking, beginning in the late 1960s, believes that Werfel's contemporaries, disillusioned with the materialistic values of their age, found *Der Weltfreund* attractive because of what they perceived as Werfel's freshness, his lack of sophistication, and his powerful expression of emotion. Another quality of the collection that attracted them, according to Williams, was Werfel's message of love for mankind and his sharp criticism of society and authority, most evident in his depiction of the conflict between father and son (60). Williams does not share the early critics' view of Werfel as prophet. Later critics such as Wyatt (1983), however, find it hard to understand why readers at the time saw in this collection a new form of poetic expression. Wyatt thinks it was probably Werfel's directness of expression that moved them so deeply and made them willing to overlook the author's triviality and the constantly simmering ecstatic (252-53).

Typical of much of the critical response to this collection and, in fact, to Werfel's works as a whole is a focus on the ideas and themes that Werfel expresses in his poetry rather than on imagery, language, and form. There has thus been a tendency to neglect the literary aspects of Werfel's lyric work. In this first collection, critics were interested in particular in the theme of childhood, Werfel's love of the world, and the religious and philosophical content of his poetry.

From the beginning, many critics were fascinated with Werfel's use of childhood as a motif, and they generally agreed that this was central not only to his early lyric poetry but also to many of his later works. One of the early critics, Jacobson (1927), points out that the memories of a lost childhood reflect Werfel's longing to return to the purity of childhood and the unity and purity of the childlike soul (338). Schumann (1931) argues that Werfel believed the child had an imaginative and magical attitude to its world. The loss of childhood, therefore, meant for him the loss of a direct and intense relationship with the world (29-30). According to Puttkamer (1952), the child's openness and receptivity were especially significant for Werfel (4). Later critics such as Merlan (1961) and Thomke (1972) see in Werfel's use of the childhood motif an expression of his deeply felt alienation from his world and its values. Merlan argues that Werfel expresses this alienation by dreaming of his childhood and wishing for friendships and relationships that do not exist (26-27). Thomke, whose perceptive if negative analysis of Werfel's expressionist poetry helped usher in a more critical approach to his early verse, contends that Werfel's frequent use of childhood and childhood memories reveals an impressionistic stance to the world. Like Merlan, he points out that the loss of childhood in this collection signifies loneliness and the loss of the original unity of the child's soul (223-24).

Werfel's emphasis on love of the world and mankind in this collection also aroused a great deal of critical interest and admiration. Like many early critics,

Kaufmann (1927) argues that Werfel's love for mankind was his deepest and most essential experience, the foundation on which Werfel's philosophical system rested. Kaufmann notes that this ethos of love is not only the main theme of Werfel's early poetry like *Der Weltfreund* but is also central to his work as a whole (428), a perception with which Grenzmann (1955) agrees. As several critics such as Schumann (1931) point out, Werfel's optimism and his strong affirmation of life in the collection stem from this ethos of love. Critics such as Braselmann (1960) see in Werfel's love of the world a longing for harmony and a desire to be one with the world and all people. Puttkamer (1952), for example, observes that Werfel's openness to the world in this collection is so great that it dissolves his identity (5), and Grenzmann (1955) also calls attention to the poet's readiness to give up his own self (267). Several critics praise Werfel's strong sympathy with all human beings, especially with the suffering and the oppressed (Grenzmann 1955, Arnim 1961). Merlan (1961) in particular develops the ethical message of this theme. For her it is an expression of Werfel's philosophy that all people and things are manifestations of the same spirit. In these poems, Merlan argues, Werfel hopes that if people can recognize their close spiritual relationship, they will love one another and all creation (29), a philosophy that, in her view, accounts for the strongly optimistic tone of the collection.

Wyatt (1983), however, has a different explanation for Werfel's use of the childhood motif, his love of the world, and his urgent desire to share with others. In one of the few psychoanalytical studies of Werfel's early poetry (and, in fact, one of the very few psychoanalytical studies of Werfel's works at all), Wyatt argues that in his early poetry Werfel was not influenced so much by the classical Oedipal conflict as by a deep dependency on the early childish imago of his mother. According to his thesis, the early identification with the imago of the mother, the phallic desire of the small boy for her, and the resulting denial of this desire brought about a system of rules and limits that the ego created and that influenced his character for life. This, Wyatt contends, shaped Werfel's psychological position in his early poetry (267-68). Although Wyatt can be perceptive in his analysis of Werfel's early poetry, the argument discussed above demonstrates the limitation of such a psychoanalytical approach, which sheds little light on the creative works themselves.

From the beginning, critics have stressed the ethical, religious, and philosophical aspects of *Der Weltfreund*, a focus that is still evident today. For Schumann (1931), Werfel's attempt to overcome individuation, which he considers the central concern in *Der Weltfreund*, is deeply ethical (31), and Bithell (1939) likens Werfel in *Der Weltfreund* to Schiller because of the high moral and ethical fervor shared by both poets (423). Many critics, such as Arnim (1961), call attention to the religious feelings that they find central to the poems, but they do not attempt to define in any detail the nature of Werfel's religious beliefs at the time.

Until Thomke (1972) most critics admired Werfel's ethical and religious views in these poems. Thomke's, however, is a loud voice of dissent. Although he admits that Werfel's sympathy for the weak and suffering has some ethical content, he argues strongly that these expressions of sympathy are all too often merely an enjoyment to the full of his own feelings. Thomke accuses Werfel of being weakly sentimental and self-indulgent in this collection (225).

In a recent article, Wagner (1989) agrees with earlier critics that religion is central to *Der Weltfreund*, but he analyzes more thoroughly than others the nature of Werfel's religious beliefs in this early collection. According to his argument, Werfel's central concern here is the relationship between the poetic self and its world: he wants to kindle an attitude of piety to God's creation. Werfel's main spiritual concern, not only in this collection but in all his works, is thus religious, Wagner observes, since he wants to bring about a new awareness of existence in the world. Wagner points out that although this is clearly a religious goal, which Werfel's frequent references to God underscore, his religious beliefs here are not closely linked to any established theologies (39-41).

Although most critics, with the exception of a few like Thomke (1972), generally treated Werfel's ideas in *Der Weltfreund* respectfully, evaluation of the work's aesthetic qualities, which aroused more attention than is usual in Werfel criticism, was much more controversial. Like many of the early critics and reviewers, Specht (1926) stresses enthusiastically the freshness and originality of the poems, which he sees as direct expressions of the creative spirit. In Specht's view, Werfel's hatred of the beautiful form, the decorative and falsifying word, and any artistic perfection led him to create a poetic language that was totally new. Specht acknowledges that, if one applies earlier aesthetic criteria, some of Werfel's poems, such as "An den Leser," could be considered unpoetic because, until the reader discerns their rhythm, they appear to be irregular and to stumble (90). Although Specht recognizes some imperfections in the poems, he rushes to defend Werfel. He explains away any aesthetic problems by declaring that they were caused by Werfel's genius. A poet like Werfel, who was concerned only with the landscape of his soul, could not be expected to worry himself about aesthetic rules, Specht argues; the strength of the poems lies in their spiritual intensity, in an inner glowing that makes them into a "crematorium of ideas" (92). Despite Specht's partisan position, he nevertheless sheds light on Werfel's innovations in this collection. He was also one of the first critics to recognize the importance of musicality in these poems, a characteristic of Werfel's poetic style that such later critics as Klarmann and Puttkamer rearticulated and developed.

Specht's enthusiastic response to Werfel's style shaped much of the later debate about *Der Weltfreund*. Puttkamer (1952), for example, closely follows Specht in her discussion of Werfel's language. Like Specht, she notices imperfections in Werfel's style, but she dismisses them as inconsequential. Like his generation, she writes, Werfel shared a dislike for the beautiful word and for the polished form and therefore often destroyed the music and the imagery of his verse by using a sloppy conclusion or a weak or even tasteless turn of phrase. She glosses over these aesthetic problems, however, by arguing that, for Werfel, the highest demand was the truthfulness of the poetic statement, even at the cost of the beautiful and melodious sound (3). Although Grenzmann (1955) generally praises Werfel's poetic style, he has reservations about some of Werfel's language, which, despite its vividness, is in his view often coarse and offends aesthetic limits (267). In an essay that draws closely on Puttkamer's work, Fox (1964) points out that Werfel's everyday turns of phrase, his use of journalese and foreign words, and his deliberate sloppiness and tastelessness often mar the musicality of his verse, but he defends Werfel by arguing that he could wring new meanings out of incongruous or even grotesque word clusters. Although parts of the collection, in his view, could be labeled antipoetry, Werfel did not intend to shock. Instead, Fox believes, the jarring elements of Werfel's style suggest the disparity between wish and reality (108-9). Trost (1967) was another critic who admired the hymnic quality of Werfel's poetry. In his estimation, Werfel successfully created a hymnic language to serve the new pathos (313).

Although early critics did not deny Werfel's various aesthetic problems in *Der Weltfreund*—even the generally positive Braselmann (1960) acknowledges that the poems in the collection were put together in an arbitrary fashion (17)—they tended to dismiss them by attributing them to genius or to Werfel's concern with spiritual intensity and poetic truthfulness. The aesthetic problems were not significant for these early critics and in no way caused them to reassess their evaluation of Werfel as a major poet. Thomke (1972), however, took a much more negative position and radically questioned the early reverent approaches. Unlike most of the previous critics, who stressed the freshness and originality of *Der Weltfreund*, Thomke disputes the accepted wisdom that the collection is an innovative and pioneering work and concludes instead that many of the poems are trivial and insipid, a view that Wyatt (1983) shares. Neither in its style nor in its content, Thomke argues, is *Der Weltfreund* an expressionist work but rather a loose, cyclical, and impressionistic series of optical and acoustic impressions (221-23). Thomke's study is particularly valuable for his observation that the theatrical, the rhetorical, and the grotesque are an integral part of Werfel's poetry. Although critics of Werfel's dramas often pointed to Werfel's love of the theatrical and the rhetorical, few applied this to Werfel's poetry. Thomke also gives perceptive insights into Werfel's use of the grotesque, which he believes the author employs to express the dubiousness of human existence (230-33).

Thomke's work reflects the more recent trend in Werfel criticism to view *Der Weltfreund* more negatively. In an article in which he questions Max Brod's claim that he played a leading role in the publication of the collection,

Guthke (1978) remarks that, despite their freshness of tone, these poems now seem rather childish and enraptured in their emotional joyfulness. He points out that many of the poems are uneven and that, on occasions, the belletristic, the ostentatious, and an artistic lack of discipline are all too apparent. Yet despite this criticism, Guthke still follows such critics as Specht in attributing these failings to the creative nature of the genius. According to him, most of the poems in *Der Weltfreund* display a genuineness of tone and a perfection of creation (72).

Recent critics have agreed that nowadays the formal aspects of the collection no longer appear innovative or even expressionistic. Wagner (1989), for example, questions the freshness and originality of the poems since he agrees with Thomke that because of its clear debt to impressionism, symbolism, and *Jugendstil*, much of the collection is traditional and conventional. Yet he believes that in some of the poems there is a very different note. In a poem such as "Aufschwung," for example, he argues that Werfel creates a powerful tension between the "strict discipline of the sonnet form and the expressive force of language argument," a tension that reflects "the dichotomy in human (and poetic) existence which the author feels so keenly" (40). Wagner thus suggests that far from being unconcerned with form, which early critics had assumed to be the case, Werfel was actually acutely sensitive to the formal aspects of his verse—at least in some of his poems. Wagner's article is representative of more recent Werfel criticism in its analysis of the interdependence of content and form instead of the overemphasis on content that characterized much of the early criticism. It also typifies another development in Werfel criticism in that Wagner avoids the pitfalls of advocacy that often afflicted the early critics and gives a more balanced evaluation of Werfel's strengths and weaknesses in this collection. Wagener (1993) agrees that many of the poems in *Der Weltfreund* seem rather conventional and traditional today. In his view, what is really innovative in this collection is not its formal aspects but rather "the new relation of the poetic self to its world, the poet's loving attitude toward the world" (29).

Reviews and reactions at the time to Werfel's next collection of poems, *Wir sind* (1913), were also remarkably positive, although this collection did not make the same sensational impact *Der Weltfreund* had made. Critics were interested in what this new collection indicated about Werfel's development as a poet, and much of the interest centered around the development of Werfel's philosophical and religious views. As with *Der Weltfreund*, however, critics tended to favor a discussion of themes and ideas and to mention Werfel's poetic development only briefly.

Werfel's concern for the underprivileged and the oppressed, so evident in *Der Weltfreund*, was again a focus for critics in this new collection. Jacobson (1927), Drake (1928), and Grenzmann (1955), for example, stress Werfel's sympathy for the humble and the rejected and his pity for the misery of all creatures. Fox (1964) considers Werfel's awareness of personal responsibility for others and their suffering to be the center of the cycle (110). Recent critics such as Wagner (1989) agree with these earlier assessments. Wagner argues that Werfel's belief in universal love, especially his love for the underprivileged and neglected, aims to join humanity together. For Werfel, Wagner stresses, this love for everyone is an important concept because it signifies people's link with the universe and thus with the divine (44).

The development of Werfel's religious and spiritual philosophy in *Wir sind* was also a central focus of the critical discussion of this collection. For Specht (1926), the poems express a divinity in the cosmos that includes even the most miserable creatures, and he stresses Werfel's belief in the connectedness of all creatures (106). Another early critic, Drake (1928), was struck by Werfel's longing for the coming of good into the world and his half-mystical feeling of the poet's personal responsibility for all of mankind's weaknesses. Drake argues that Werfel speaks here with a new spiritual voice and emerges as a prophet of spiritual renewal (30-31). In contrast to the optimism of *Der Weltfreund*, Schumann (1931) discerns a new note of painful tension and pessimism that comes, he thinks, from the poet's realization that individuation separates people from each other and most importantly from God. He detects a loss of innocence between *Der Weltfreund* and *Wir sind* since, in his view, Werfel had become conscious of guilt and evil (34-36). Puttkamer (1952) also focuses on this loss of innocence. In her estimation, Werfel had come to believe that just by living people incur guilt, and she attributes this strong sense of guilt not to Werfel's Jewish origins but rather to his contact with Slavic thought (6). Like Schumann, Merlan (1961) saw a development in Werfel's philosophy in this collection. Although Merlan points out that Werfel's belief in the spiritual relatedness of all people is still evident, she argues that the dividedness of people and their separation from others, which Werfel had already suggested in *Der Weltfreund*, is more apparent here. In her view, the tone of the poems had become more pessimistic, but despite the pessimism, Merlan believes that the prevailing mood is hopeful since Werfel was convinced that people could overcome the barriers between them through love and suffering: by suffering the pain and sorrow of the meanest creature, people could attain complete understanding (31-32). Wagener (1993), also struck by the different mood in this collection, points out that people are bound by their individuation, unable to free themselves (32).

Although most critics dealt respectfully with Werfel's beliefs in *Wir sind*, Thomke (1972) finds these same ideas highly problematic and calls Werfel's philosophy in this collection opaque. Thomke agrees with earlier critics that the poems show a struggle for religious renewal. But he strongly disagrees with critics who praised Werfel's humane concern for the poor and the oppressed. Thomke argues here that Werfel's boundless undifferentiated love has little to do with a sense of social pity but is rather an indication of Werfel's own longing for love and his convulsive attempts to overcome alienation. According to him, Werfel was concerned with the outcasts of society only because he thought they were less limited by conventions and morals than bourgeois society. Thomke complains that, despite the religious emphasis in this volume, the transcendental remains empty and undefined. In his view, Werfel's hymnic poetry here is nothing more than a despairing attempt to rescue himself from nihilism. His new ethic, Thomke believes, lacks a humanistic or theistic foundation. Instead, it rests on a completely detached cosmic openness that leads to an ethical anarchism of sympathy. Thomke points out that Werfel later realized the dubiousness of this attitude and abandoned it (244-65).

Metzler (1988) notices a strong turn to religion in these poems since a belief in God has replaced the abstract pathos of belief in mankind that characterized *Der Weltfreund* (323). From his Marxist perspective, however, he does not view Werfel's increasing emphasis on God as a positive development but complains that it mars Werfel's entire work. Metzler's essay is valuable not so much because of the light it sheds on Werfel's works but rather because it is one of the few examples of a Marxist approach in Werfel criticism. Marxist critics on the whole have not been attracted to many of Werfel's works. Although they have appreciated such works as *Die vierzig Tage des Musa Dagh*, they have tended to dismiss others as politically reactionary.

Although most critics focused on Werfel's ideas in *Wir sind*, several were interested in how the poems in this collection reflected Werfel's development as a poet. Most agreed that there was a clear development from the impressionistic poems in *Der Weltfreund*. Specht (1926), however, disagreed. In this collection he finds the same tone, the same celebration of life, and the same musicality of the verse as in *Der Weltfreund*. He likens the verse in *Wir sind* and *Einander*, Werfel's next collection, to powerful chords of a booming organ (106). As in *Der Weltfreund*, however, he thinks that Werfel destroyed the beauty of some of his verse by curious flourishes and an incomprehensible lack of taste. At times Specht even detects, to his dismay, what he terms an atavistic, rhetorical tone of a young Schiller (111). Despite these weaknesses, he admires the collection's poetic quality.

Later critics, however, stressed how Werfel had matured as a poet in *Wir sind*. Puttkamer (1952), for example, notices a difference between the impressionism of some of the poems in *Der Weltfreund* and the expressive surge of feeling in *Wir sind* (8). Some poems in the collection remind Grenzmann (1955) of the expressionist art of Picasso. He argues that, like Picasso, Werfel shows that freezing in a mask hides the soul but does not destroy it. In his view, Werfel wants to let the soul be seen through the mask, to find the human being again despite misery and disfigurement (267-68). More recently, Wagner (1989) concentrates on the development of Werfel's hymnic style in this collection, which, in his view, marks Werfel as one of the leading representatives of expressionism. He concludes that Werfel's style has now lost most of the traditional features that were still evident in *Der Weltfreund* and tends to the abstraction, hyperbole, and metaphorical density so typical of expressionist poetry (44).

Thomke (1972), as usual, inserts a critical note into the reverent reactions to the volume. In his discussion, he points out that the cyclical structure of the collection is loose and not always logical (244). In contrast to what he saw in *Der Weltfreund*, he notices here a heightened subjectivity and a moving away from Werfel's impressionistic early collection. Thomke argues that Werfel is less concerned here with aesthetics than with the intensity of his ecstatic experience, but this ecstatic feeling is, he believes, an end in itself. Thomke is critical of Werfel's tendency to mix images, a result, in his opinion, of Werfel's concern with intensity and not plasticity. He also points out how the grotesque continues to be an important part of Werfel's poetry, a characteristic of the poetry that has been neglected and merits further analysis. Most of all, Thomke is disturbed in this collection by what he sees as Werfel's irresponsible use of language (244-58).

Most studies of Werfel's poems tend to be broad surveys of an entire collection or collections. Few studies have been devoted to individual poems. One that has is Foltin and Heinen's 1970 analysis of "Als mich dein Wandeln an den Tod verzückte" from *Wir sind*. As context for their discussion, they, like Klarmann, stress that poetry enabled Werfel to unleash his natural musical sense. They believe that it is through the musical quality of the verse that readers initially gain access to Werfel's poetry: the reader is impressed first by the form and the rhythm of a poem before grasping its content. Central to this poem, according to their interpretation, is Werfel's affirmation of piety and compassion. Since they argue that piety and compassion are specifically Christian concepts, the poem is an early indication for them of Werfel's lifelong concern with Christianity. Foltin and Heinen are particularly interested in the structure of the poem. It is a traditional sonnet, although, as they point out, Werfel enjoyed disregarding convention and loved to experiment. In this poem they see a dynamic tension created by juxtaposing mystical exultation and social awareness. They show that the poem's basic structural pattern is antithesis since Werfel contrasts the rapture of the poet's mystical love with the misery of humanity, the ecstasy of bliss and divine happiness with wasted lives and the meaninglessness of suffering. These antitheses, they argue, which make the poem oscillate between bleakness and happiness, give it its balance and tension (62-66). Like Wagner (1989), Foltin and Heinen suggest in their analysis of this poem that Werfel is far less careless with form than many have assumed. Their study is particularly valuable for the way it sheds light on Werfel's poetic technique, on how Werfel uses the structural pattern to reinforce his message, and on the underlying musical structure of his poetry.

In a recent analysis of an individual poem from this collection, Ives (1989) approaches Werfel's poetry from the consideration of making it accessible to students. Although her article accordingly addresses practical problems, it is also insightful since she points out reasons for the decline in interest in Werfel's poetry and also analyzes Werfel's technique in what she considers his more successful poems. Nowadays, she argues, many of Werfel's most famous poems are perceived as turgid and tasteless since they tend to be too rhetorical, declamatory, arcane, cryptic, bathetic, and ridiculous. Because of this, some of Werfel's early works, such as *Der Weltfreund* and *Wir sind*, are dismissed today as "outbursts of Expressionistic juvenilia that are more than a little embarrassing when reviewed in the cold light of the 1980s" (56). In her view, a poem such as "Eine alte Frau geht" from *Wir sind* can serve to stimulate interest in Werfel's poetry. On first reading, Ives observes, it seems to be a straightforward poem about an old woman, but this apparent simplicity is deceptive because, at a deeper level, the poem is concerned with the spiritual predicament as well as the spiritual potentiality of all people, including those on the fringes of society (57-58). In contrast to such poems as "An den Leser," in which, she believes, Werfel is at his most old-fashioned, "Eine alte Frau geht" is not marred by "programmatic posturings." This poem shows that "highflown rhetoric and complex imagery are not always the hallmarks of compelling poetry" (59). In this poem the reader can sense "the profound mystery of God and sacredness of His Creation that permeates all Werfel's works" (62).

Of Werfel's early collections of poems, *Einander* (1915) received the least amount of critical attention, and those critics who dealt with it emphasized different aspects of the work. Jacobson (1927), for example, notices a stronger religious tone and points out that the abstract titles of the poems reflect the poet's inner conflict (340). Schumann (1931) believes that because of Werfel's stress on mankind as strangers on this earth the mood of this collection is more hopeless than that of the previous ones. Of all the poems in the collection, Schumann especially admires "Jesus und der Äserweg" because in it Werfel expresses the possibility of redemption—ecstatic, self-overcoming love of all creation, even in its most repelling and nauseating form (38). Schumann calls it one of Werfel's supreme poems, an evaluation that differs radically from that of Wyatt (1983), who dismisses it as one of the most forced, inauthentic, and tasteless poems that Werfel ever wrote (268). For Schumann, the poems in *Einander* reflect Werfel's belief that redemption from mankind's estrangement and isolation lies in the ecstasy of love. He sees a clear development from the exuberant optimism of *Der Weltfreund* to the deep pessimism of this collection (40). Such recent critics as Wagener (1993) agree on this development. He points out that the basic tenor of Werfel's attitude has become much more gloomy in this collection (34-35).

In contrast, Puttkamer (1952) does not see the development from optimism to pessimism that Schumann, and later Wagener, perceived. Instead, she focuses on the similarities between the poems in the first three collections. She remarks that there are no rigid boundaries between Werfel's early collections—

some poems, in fact, could belong in each anthology. Common to all Werfel's early lyric poetry, in her view, is a hostility to the beautiful word and a longing for direct authentic expression. Despite the similarities between the early collections, she does acknowledge some development. As she points out, in this later poetry Werfel no longer uses the long line typical of his early verse; the melodic now replaces the rhythmic; and the musicality of the language is much clearer (8).

Some critics thought that the gloomy tone of the poems was shaped by the First World War. Siemsen (1945), for example, observes that *Einander* had the deepest impact of all Werfel's early works because the collection's accusations against the war, its call to the creative spirit to break out in revolution and renew the corrupted world, expressed their own bitter feelings (158). Grenzmann (1955) is struck by the influence of the war on these poems. In the midst of the slaughter, he writes, Werfel wanted to remind us that we are all people who belong together. Grenzmann believes, however, that Werfel criticizes people in this collection for withdrawing from love into loneliness and castigates the folly of violence and the coldness caused by a lack of love. Especially in such poems as "Veni Creator Spiritus" Grenzmann discerns a new religious tone, since the cry for brotherliness is no longer just a matter for Werfel of ethical conduct but is a cry for God (268).

It is surprising given his usual critical opinion of Werfel's poetry, that Thomke's (1972) assessment of *Einander* is among the most favorable ones. He believes that in these poems Werfel's world view has become clearer, and he perceives in them a development in Werfel's philosophy: his notion of salvation is now in the foreground, and his ethos of love for mankind has become firmer. Especially in the first part of the collection, Werfel succeeds, in his opinion, in creating some of his best poems, although there are also some that are unpalatable for us today. Thomke argues that the radical subjectivity of the poems is a decisive development since it led Werfel away from early expressionism to become the most important lyric poet of high expressionism. He defends Werfel by noting that even if Werfel's basic world view and his doctrine of salvation seem dubious to us now, the authentic, hymnic tone speaks for the personal belief of the poet. Like Puttkamer, Thomke also sees a development in the musicality of Werfel's language in this collection: unlike the poet's own imperfect and rigid language, music becomes a mystical language that can express the divine (265-77).

Wagner (1989) also views these poems positively; he believes that Werfel perfects and consolidates here the spiritual concerns and stylistic elements that he began to develop in *Der Weltfreund* and *Wir sind* (44). He calls *Einander* the "culmination and perfection of Werfel's Expressionist style and the most immediate statement of his belief in salvation through divine grace and through love and brotherhood amongst men" (46). For Wagner, Werfel's first three collections of lyric poetry are the most important, and he writes that it is not surprising that most of the poems that have received close attention and are still included in anthologies come from these collections (46).

In contrast to *Einander, Der Gerichtstag* (1919) aroused more lively critical attention. Many critics saw the collection as Werfel's reaction to the First World War. Specht (1926), for example, calls it a response to what for Werfel was the inferno of the war. In his view, *Der Gerichtstag* reflects the horrors of the age (138). Puttkamer (1952) disagrees, pointing out that hardly any of the poems center on events of the time. Although she concedes that the poems were shaped by the war, she believes that Werfel understood the war as the outer appearance of an inner decay. The trial was thus an inner trial, and the person judged was himself (13-14). Thomke (1972) observes that here, more clearly than in any other work, Werfel expresses how the war experiences shattered his previous philosophical security and made him question his belief in the subjective notion of redemption (292). Williams (1974) is struck by the turgid expressions of loathing and guilt and the nightmarish images of death and decay. He does not, however, see this collection as antiwar poetry in any conventional sense since, he believes, despite its accusatory title, it does not specifically indict either the war or those responsible for it (67). Wagener (1993) remarks that it is amazing that the poems Werfel wrote during the war and included in *Der Gerichtstag*, which he terms Werfel's most sprawling collection of poetry (41), are so abstract. He believes that the war is reflected in these poems only in their resigned and gloomy attitude and the brooding, heavy lines that have replaced the hymnic tone of *Einander* (39).

Other critics focused on a variety of different aspects of the work. Specht (1926) believes that *Der Gerichtstag* is Werfel's most personal and undistanced work. For Jacobson (1927), the despair, the disintegration and discordance, and the separation of people and the world are the main focus in the collection. These verses express for her the torment and oppression in the poet's soul. Despite this despair, she believes that the earlier ideals break through since the stammering seeker for God and humanity is still evident (342). Schumann (1931) remarks that although the collection does not express any new thoughts, the mood of the poems, which is characterized by hopeless brooding, is different (40). For him, these verses are a sharp protest against the dehumanization that Werfel perceived in his world. But although Werfel is sharply critical of society here, he is never a political poet, in Schumann's estimation, since his vision of the future of mankind derives rather from the tradition of Rousseau and Tolstoy (43). Grenzmann (1955) sees the collection as a summary of poetic concerns that Werfel had expressed earlier and calls it Werfel's lyric main work (269). Merlan (1961) argues that this is the last collection in which the poems show some originality of thought (35).

Although many reviewers received the work positively, later critics pointed out its deficiencies. Even the generally admiring Specht (1926) considers this collection to be Werfel's most problematic and undisciplined one. He sees it as

Werfel's cry of conscience and his settling of accounts with himself and the world—the reason, in his opinion, for its discordant intensity. Specht praises this intensity and regards the volume as a testament of Werfel's times, but he finds the work aesthetically displeasing. He deplores the abstractness of many of the poems and Werfel's tendency to lose himself in the metaphysical, and he is disturbed by the absence of Werfel's usual musicality. In this volume, Specht argues, Werfel is not at all concerned with language or form. For example, he mixes solemn dithyrambs with repulsive and grotesque images, moving confessions and beautiful and noble forms with verses that seem to be hurled down in a slovenly fashion. Specht explains these problems by noting that a person who strikes out is not concerned whether his hair or the creases in his pants remain tidy. Although a punch may be liberating, Specht observes, it is not a work of art. He writes that he would have loved to ignore the many weaknesses of the collection, but he finds the flaws of the book painful. He stresses that he wants to be honest in his criticism not only because it is important for the reader to get a true and complete picture but also because the poet himself must learn, and he suggests to Werfel that he revise the verses line by line (138-54).

Specht's sweeping criticism of the poems was taken up by others. Among them, Schumann (1931) complains that the language in its anguish sometimes deteriorates into obscene imagery to depict the perturbed emotional state of the poet (40). Because Werfel's doubts and struggles are so intense in this collection, the process of poetic transformation remains, in his view, incomplete (45). Although Puttkamer (1952) is, as usual, positive in her evaluation, she too notices Werfel's hatred of the poetic word in this collection (15). For Thomke (1972), the high expressionist style of *Einander* reaches its complete development here. Like Specht, he is critical of Werfel's use of language in the collection, in particular of what he terms a linguistic gluttony that makes a lot of the poems unpalatable, and he points to many examples in the poems of such linguistic degeneration. In his view, Werfel uses hyperbole so often that it loses its power of expression (291-92). Thomke believes that the disorderliness of the style reflects the inner contradictions and the philosophical unclarity of the content. He finds the poems in this collection illuminating only as testimony of personal development and of *Geistesgeschichte*. As a work of art, he emphatically states, they can scarcely be taken seriously.

In his recent article, Wagner (1989) rearticulates this criticism and broadens it to show problems inherent in expressionism as a whole. He argues that some of the tendencies that marred the content and style of Werfel's previous poetry become even more prevalent in *Der Gerichtstag* and indicate not only a turning point in Werfel's own poetic development but also the crisis and decline of expressionism in general (46). Wagner sees in many poems a tendency to preach rather than to create, and he complains about Werfel's increasing use of abstract "theological" speculations. From the beginning, he remarks, many of Werfel's verses were characterized by their unusual and daring images, but in this collection these images become extreme and occasionally indicate a lack of taste. Wagner's article is perceptive in showing that the problems evident in *Der Gerichtstag* suggest two main reasons for the demise of expressionism as a whole and of Werfel's expressionist writing in particular. First, the ethical appeal is vague and indeterminate; second, it is impossible to sustain hymnic and ecstatic poetic expression for a long period. These problems lead to ideological stagnation and to linguistic and stylistic degeneration (47).

Much of the critical debate about Werfel's early lyric poetry centered around his contribution to expressionism. As reviews at the time demonstrated, Werfel's contemporaries regarded him as the leading voice of German expressionist poetry, and most later critics took the same position. Virtually alone among critics, Specht (1926) emphatically denies that Werfel was part of the movement, a reflection of his concern with always showing Werfel's originality and genius and his distaste for the expressionist movement. In a lengthy section of his book, he sharply attacks expressionism and seeks to rescue Werfel from the expressionist label. Those who saw Werfel's connections to expressionism misunderstood him, he declares firmly. This mistaken impression stems, in his view, from two main causes. Both Werfel and the expressionists reacted against impressionism and stressed inwardness; and the expressionist style favored exaggeration, caricature, simplification, and distortion, elements that some noticed in Werfel's style. Specht asserts emphatically—and wrongly—that Werfel never used this stylistic method in the same way, except in the defiant experiments of some of the poems in *Der Gerichtstag*—the reason Specht disliked this collection so intensely (155-57).

Virtually all other critics disagreed with Specht. Sokel (1959), for example, includes Werfel among the naive expressionists and argues that he was one of the most eloquent and persistent spokesmen of the expressionist cult of "man" and "mankind" (124). Klarmann (1969) also emphasizes Werfel's important contributions to expressionism. According to him, Werfel's dithyrambic poems, filled with warmth and love, his focus on childhood memories, his sympathy with the lowly and oppressed, and his humble words to God gave early expressionism a new tone (414). Klarmann also discusses Werfel's later rejection of expressionism. The first signs of this beginning alienation, he believes, are evident in the essay "Die christliche Sendung" (1917), in which Werfel rejects activism and professes a Christian mission (415), views that shaped his later works and his religious and political thinking. Yet because Werfel was from the beginning a religious person, Klarmann argues, in this sense he remained an expressionist even though he distanced himself from the movement (423).

Another characteristic of Werfel's early poetry that aroused some critical interest was the poet's struggle with language. Keller (1958) notices Werfel's distrust of the language because of its inability to express both the divine and the innermost person (40-41). In an article devoted entirely to this struggle, Wood (1961) analyzes the evolution of Werfel's poetic language and focuses on the problem of *Wortschuld*. He argues that in his growth as a poet Werfel was confronted with the tragic implications of *Wortschuld*, especially in *Der Gerichtstag*. In nearly all Werfel's early poetry, he notes, he was sensitive to the treachery of the poetic word, a problem that preoccupied many writers of his generation. According to Wood, Werfel was aware of the tension between the banal communication of everyday speech and the truly poetic idiom of inner communion with experience, and he viewed the prefabricated language of everyday as a sign language rather than as a poetic medium (40-43).

Critics have neglected the poems that Werfel wrote after *Der Gerichtstag*, in contrast to his early lyric poetry, even though he published more collections of poetry in his later years than he had in the first decades of his life. The few critics who mentioned these collections often dismissed them as mediocre. Wagner (1989) finds this situation unfair and asks whether it is justifiable to concentrate almost exclusively on Werfel's early poems and neglect the later ones (37). Such recent critics as Klinger (1991) and Weissenberger (1992) have taken up this challenge.

Specht (1926) was one of the few early critics to discuss *Beschwörungen* (1923), and, as could be predicted, he is positive in his evaluation even though he acknowledges that the collection would not reach a large group of readers. In his view, this is not because the poems are of a lesser quality than the earlier ones. Specht thinks, in fact, that in many cases they are superior in their use of imagery and in the expression of intense experience. But he believes that, in contrast to the poems in the earlier collections, which Werfel wrote for everyone, these are aimed at a narrower audience. In them Specht senses a darkening of a soul that has given up trying to have an impact on others since it has to come to terms first of all with itself (249-50). According to Specht, the poems in the middle part of the collection are the strongest since they are most compelling in their vision. For Jacobson (1927), the poems in this collection clearly indicate that Werfel has matured as a poet. Here the ecstasy, the distortion, and the bleakness of some of the earlier poetry have disappeared. In her view, Werfel's old faith has reasserted itself, and his expressions of piety have become more sincere. Jacobson admires the rich images and metaphors, the music, and the rhythm of the verse, and she notes that Werfel manages to avoid the linguistic flaws that often plagued the earlier verse (343). In contrast, Schumann (1931) dismisses these poems as the outcome of some heavy erotic experience (46). In this collection, he observes, Werfel's spiritual crisis reaches its climax. According to Puttkamer (1952), Werfel's poetic expression has become richer and more relaxed, and many of the poems in this volume attain a lyrical perfection (27). Neumann (1974) thinks the collection belongs to Werfel's early poetry, which he greatly admires (242). Wagener (1993) observes that the feeling of resignation that was evident in *Der Gerichtstag* is intensified in this collection. Despite this resignation, Wagener believes that the basic outlook for man that is expressed in the poems is still a hopeful one (41-42).

Werfel's later collections of poems, *Gedichte* (1927), *Neue Gedichte* (1928), *Schlaf und Erwachen* (1935), *Gedichte aus dreißig Jahren* (1939), and *Gedichte aus den Jahren 1908-1945* (1946) aroused little critical interest. In a discussion of *Neue Gedichte*, Schumann (1931) notices that the old motifs of individuation and estrangement reappear, and he senses a mood of resignation (50-51). Puttkamer (1952) remarks that illness, dying, death, and the dead are the predominant themes of the later poems (171), and Stöcklein (1954) sees in them a close connection to the baroque. Klarmann (1961) believes that *Schlaf und Erwachen* reveals Werfel to be a more mature poet, one who has become more conscious of form. In his opinion, the angry thunder and optimistic joy of the early poems have disappeared, and the poems now express a new humility and a growing openness to God as well as a premonition of death (30). Merlan (1961), however, contends that the poems of Werfel's middle age do not tell us anything essential about the poet. In her opinion, there is nothing in these later poems to distinguish Werfel from any other sensitive writer (35-36). Neumann (1974) is similarly negative. Werfel's later poetry, he argues, displays a disturbing unevenness and a literary bravado that were evident even in his earlier poetry but become even more obvious in the later verse. He concludes that Werfel's later verse does little to enhance his standing in this literary genre (242).

More recently, Wagner (1989) argues for a reassessment of Werfel's later volumes of verse, although he acknowledges that they lack the formal and spiritual boldness of the early ones (47). He points out that in these poems Werfel transforms individual experiences into parables about mankind. Wagner calls attention to the change in Werfel's language and imagery in his later verse. In his view, these poems are less artificial and more accessible than his earlier ones, although, in comparison with his expressionist verse, they also show a loss of intensity and a mood of resignation. A poem such as "Ich staune," for example, which is written in a conventional style, displays, according to Wagner, an attitude of pious contemplation that appears inadequate at a time when the world was being torn apart by war (48-49). Wagner regards this attempt to recall the beautiful yesterday and disguise the present as a typical consequence of exile.

The sparse amount of work that has been devoted to Werfel's later verse was often sparked by an interest in the poems as reflections of Werfel's exile. Foltin and Spalek (1976) note that the poems of Werfel's last years are filled with thoughts of the fate of exiles and of unavoidable death. Many were written from his sick bed and reveal his sense of threatened existence (658). Unlike other critics, however, Foltin and Spalek believe that Werfel's later poems are among the best he ever wrote (663). In a discussion of *Gedichte aus den Jahren 1908-1945*, Ash (1982) remarks that the poetic themes of exile grow out of Werfel's own illness in his last years. She argues that the exile, separated from his or her own culture, is left to contemplate, as Werfel does here, his decaying body and fettered spirit. Werfel's focus on illness, she believes, is without equal in exile poetry (11-12).

In one of the most thorough discussions of Werfel's later poems, Klinger (1991) also explores Werfel's later poetry within the context of his exile, and he notices a variety of differences between the concerns of Werfel's exile poems and those of other German and Austrian exile poets. Unlike many exile writers, Werfel does not deal with such problems as adapting to a new country. Klinger disagrees with Wagner (1989) that Werfel attempts to recall the beautiful yesterday in his exile poetry. He argues that Werfel does not depict the past as idyllic, and avoids the elegies of homesickness that characterize much exile writing (29). As Klinger points out, Werfel was strongly opposed to the Hitler regime, but, unlike other exiles, he did not write militant poetry against the Nazis (30). Yet although Werfel's poems deal only occasionally with events of the time, Klinger argues that they are the spiritual expression of this time and reflect Werfel's unheroic and therefore honest courage in bearing this earthly purgatory. Klinger also senses Werfel's feeling in these poems that he does not have much time left. Above all, the critic is struck by the trust that Werfel has in language, a radical change from the suspicion of language that Wood (1961) notes in his early verse. Klinger believes that this trust in language is the result of the exile experience; language was in many cases all that the exiled writers had left, and they loved and defended it. Klinger also remarks that Werfel transforms the pain and suffering of exile into man's judgment of himself (31).

Weissenberger (1992) argues that Werfel's exile poetry, and in fact all of Werfel's exile works, must be understood within the context of his aphorism collection, *Theologumena*. For Weissenberger, this is a key text for understanding the aesthetic and philosophical foundation of all Werfel's exile production, and he shows the close parallels between the philosophical and aesthetic views that Werfel expresses in his aphorisms and his exile poetry. Weissenberger decries the lack of critical interest in this poetry and argues for a reevaluation. In his opinion, there are two main reasons why Werfel's exile poetry has been neglected. First, Werfel's growing reputation as a dramatist and novelist in the 1920s and 1930s led critics to focus on these genres and forget his poetry. The more important reason for the critical neglect, however, is, in his view, Werfel's lack of political and ideological engagement. Weissenberger finds this critical neglect regrettable since, in his estimation, the exile poetry represents a real improvement over Werfel's expressionist poetry (67).

Although most critics acknowledge the pioneering impact of Werfel's early poetry, there is a great deal of disagreement about its lasting quality, as the range of responses from enthusiasm to rejection indicates. The more enthusiastic evaluations tend to be the earlier ones, with more critical voices being raised later. Buber (1917-18) calls Werfel's poems compelling poetic truth and notes that his sphere is not life but experience (110). Naumann (1923) admires the ethical basis of Werfel's art, which he sees as a complaint about the brutality of the age; a cry of longing; and a call for goodness, purity, and salvation (360). Deutsch (1924), who with her husband, Avrahm Yarmolinsky, translated a few of Werfel's poems for their anthology *Contemporary German Poetry* (1923), considers Werfel to be the foremost German poet of his generation. Her article is significant because it is one of the first written in English about Werfel's poetry, and it shows the same kind of admiration that German-language critics at the time shared. She admires Werfel's striving for spiritual renewal and the piety in his works. She considers the outstanding characteristic of Werfel's work its expression of his compassion for all created things and his belief that the rejected should be cherished. She also admires his lack of sophistication, his direct language, and his passionate simplicity (158-60). Specht (1926) is loud in his praise of Werfel's poetry, with the exception of *Der Gerichtstag*, and stresses time and again that he is a genius. Drake (1928) praises what he sees as the deeply ethical quality of Werfel's early lyric poetry since in all his early verse Werfel expresses his vision of the eventual perfectibility of the universe and his disgust with its present shortcomings. In Drake's view, Werfel had attained moral greatness and had repeatedly approached artistic greatness (42). In a review of Werfel's *Gedichte aus den Jahren 1908-45*, Kahler (1948) calls Werfel a bad author but a great poet (186), a view that other reviewers at the time shared. In Werfel's poems, Kahler argues, the suffering individual is alone with himself, and this, in his estimation, is the precondition for all true poetry (188). Keller (1958) praises Werfel's poetry for its spontaneity of expression and its directness (51).

Much of the later critical response to Werfel's early poetry echoes these positive evaluations. Merlan (1961), however, inserts a critical note. She argues that the poems that have literary and human value belong to Werfel's expressionist stage; but even here, especially in *Der Gerichtstag*, she thinks that Werfel indulges too often in abstractions. Merlan concludes that when Werfel expresses genuine feeling, his poetry is usually simple and beautiful, but when he begins to preach, as he does increasingly in his later poetry, his language becomes forced. She believes that in Werfel's early poems feelings predominate but that as he grew older Werfel turned into the preacher and the poet of reason (36-38), and this spoiled his lyric poetry.

Klarmann (1969), as always, staunchly defends Werfel, particularly against those who accused him of lack of form. In his article he stresses that Werfel's poetry should be experienced acoustically because the sound of the word, the rhythm of the lines, and the music of the rhyme dictate the logic of the whole poem (412). Above all, Klarmann values the lyric poetry for its expression of

Werfel's religious thinking, for his Gnostic search for the reason for guilt, evil, and sin (417). Neumann (1974) argues that Werfel's early lyric poetry has, in addition to its historical and literary importance, an artistic integrity and strength. At his best, Werfel is, in his opinion, a poet of major stature, an artist who combines fantasy, a remarkable thematic originality, and a hymnic verve and melodiousness with a powerful verbal inventiveness and an unflagging religious and ethical purpose. He acknowledges that there are flaws, such as occasional emotionalism, facileness, and bathos; but these flaws, he notes, are endemic to expressionism, and he points out that Werfel was breaking new literary ground and was only a young man in his twenties when he wrote the works under discussion (243). In his recent article Wagner (1989) takes issue with Thomke (1972) for relegating Werfel to the archives. Like Klarmann, Wagner believes that the roots of Werfel's poetry are religious and are based on reverence for the world and its creator. Wagener (1993) agrees that Werfel is fundamentally a religious poet and points out that from his earliest poetry Werfel struggled with the relationship of man to God. He also notes that it is in his poetry, more than in any other genre, that Werfel expresses his inwardness (44).

Although critics such as Wagner and Wagener today still think highly of Werfel's early poetry despite the flaws they see, other voices are more negative. Muschg (1963), for example, calls Werfel's piety suspicious. He considers Werfel the classic representative of the salon socialism of his generation. Although Werfel's poems, in his view, are the best that pacifist expressionism produced, he concludes that, with their "divine kitsch," they are, like much of expressionism, considered insipid and unpalatable today (38, 370). Thomke's (1972) is also a critical voice. With the exception of a few poems, he considers Werfel's expressionist work to have only historical value now. He criticizes Werfel for his overconcern with philosophical problems which he believes made him neglect the actual task of the poet to create art. (Thomke's comment here points out also the problems with much of Werfel criticism, which similarly has tended to neglect the artistic aspects of his work.) Nevertheless, for the literary historian, Thomke argues, Werfel is one of the most interesting figures of the twentieth century (302-3). Wyatt (1983) also assesses Werfel's poetry negatively, especially because of his overuse of exalted language and his sentimentality. Werfel, he asserts, was never concerned with rigorous thought and strictness of form, despite his later inclination to mystical religious thinking (256-57).

As this discussion of the critical responses to Werfel's poetry indicates, there is still controversy about how to assess the lyric poetry. There is no consensus about whether, as Thomke (1972) and Wyatt (1983) claim, it is of historical value only, or whether some of it has literary merit, a view that Wagner (1989) and Ives (1989), for example, hold. Generally, most critics of Werfel today believe that he wrote his most original poems in his early years

(Wagener 1993, 28). Consideration of Werfel's later poems is only, however, in its beginning stages, although the articles by Wagner (1989), Klinger (1991), and Weissenberger (1992) may encourage more critical interest in the half of Werfel's poetic output that has been neglected. Because of this neglect, we do not have today a comprehensive understanding of Werfel's development as a poet. The critical literature offers only a few brief insights into how Werfel's imagery and use of language evolved over his lifetime. In the case of Werfel, this is a particularly serious neglect since he considered himself primarily a poet and viewed poetry as the most significant genre.

# 3: Franz Werfel's Dramas

OF THE THREE major genres in which Werfel wrote, his dramatic works received for many years the least amount of critical attention, although there are signs today that this situation is changing. Until recently, most critics of Werfel's dramas, like Klarmann (1945, 1959, 1962), Puttkamer (1952), and Wimmer (1973), for example, tended to be chiefly concerned with the philosophical, political, and metaphysical ideas that they expressed, to the neglect of their aesthetic qualities and dramatic techniques. In more recent criticism, such as Huber's article on *Spiegelmensch* (1989b) and Warren's essay on Werfel's three history plays (1989), critics have become interested in Werfel's theatrical techniques and the role of his dramas within the theatrical context of his time.

Werfel was highly respected as a dramatist in Germany and Austria, especially in the 1920s, and his plays were performed on leading stages in these countries. He became well known in theater circles in the United States after the successful productions of *Goat Song* and *Juarez and Maximilian* by the Theater Guild in New York in 1926. Werfel's reputation as an important dramatist was later reinforced in the United States through *The Eternal Road*, the English title of *Der Weg der Verheißung*, which was directed by Max Reinhardt in New York in January 1937, and, during his exile, through the highly successful production of *Jacobowsky and the Colonel* on Broadway in 1944. *Jacobowsky and the Colonel* was to become Werfel's most famous play and his only play that is well known today outside of academic circles. Because of this, it is the play that has aroused the most critical interest.

Most of the critical literature dealing with Werfel's dramas has focused on the plays he wrote in the 1920s and later, beginning with *Spiegelmensch* (1920), the plays for which he was most recognized as a dramatist. In contrast, his early expressionist dramas and dramatic sketches aroused little critical interest. From virtually the beginning of his literary career, Werfel was drawn to the drama, and his early dramatic sketches, dramas, and fragments, while by no means great aesthetic achievements, nevertheless provide insights into the development of his philosophy and his development as a dramatist, as Karlach (1968), Adams and Kuhlmann (1974), and Reffet (1992), for example, point out. The essay by Adams and Kuhlmann is their summary and interpretation of views expressed by Adolf Klarmann in a 1972 seminar on Werfel.

Werfel's earliest drama, *Der Besuch aus dem Elysium*, which he wrote in 1910, was first performed in June 1918 at the Deutsches Theater in Berlin, directed by Max Reinhardt. For several critics, what the play revealed about Werfel's life was most significant. Klarmann (1962), Foltin (1972), and Jungk

(1987) all see Werfel's love for Marianne Glaser as the stimulus for the drama. Klarmann (1962, xii) and Adams and Kuhlmann (1974, 197) argue further that Werfel's banishment to Hamburg in 1910 gave the drama its metaphysical basis because in his loneliness he thought of his time in Hamburg as a banishment from life. Thus, for Klarmann, the play is significant as an early example of the central theme of exile in Werfel's works, a theme that, as he argues in later articles, Werfel always understood metaphysically as an exile from God.

Critics also pointed out the close thematic and stylistic links between this early drama and Werfel's lyric poetry of the time, although they did not analyze these connections in any depth. Luther (1922), who mostly summarizes the plot, stresses that Werfel's hymnic longing for union with the universe in the play is characteristic of his early poems (14). Karlach (1968) calls the play poetic rather than dramatic (94), a quality that typifies all Werfel's early dramas. Wimmer (1973), who, like Luther, gives lengthy plot summaries and uses hymnic language to describe Werfel's dramas, summarizes the theme of the drama as the poetic expression of Werfel's conviction that death should be seen not as the end but as the possibility of a heightened existence (47). Adams and Kuhlmann (1974), who recognize the play's lyrical and romantic aspects, are most interested in its expressionist elements. The themes of love for all creation, the miracle of existence as a divine calling, and the exalted language, they argue, are all typical of expressionism and characteristic of much of Werfel's early lyric poetry. They see the play as an example of Austrian expressionism, which, they observe, did not demonstrate the excesses of its German counterpart (197).

Werfel's early one-act play "Das Opfer," which appeared in *Wir sind* in 1913, was virtually ignored. The usually laudatory Specht (1926) rejects it sharply for what he scathingly terms its gluttony of thought and feeling (116). Klarmann (1939, 1945), however, sees this work as an early important key to Werfel's religious thinking and his notion of salvation, despite the lack of taste he thinks the play shows (1939, 195). The work's stress on redemptive love, sacrifice, divine grace, and salvation, together with its allegorical structure, are concerns that he considers central to all Werfel's works. Klarmann argues that the play expresses symbolically the role of Israel in God's plan of salvation. According to his thesis, by rejecting the Messiah, Israel had assumed the role of "agnus," an Old Testament scapegoat, the role played, in his opinion, by the dog in this work (1939, 195). Klarmann thus dates Werfel's notion of Israel's role in the divine plan, a concept that plays an increasingly important role in Werfel's later works, to this early piece.

The sparse criticism of Werfel's dramatic dialogue *Die Versuchung: Ein Gespräch des Dichters mit dem Erzengel und Luzifer* (1913) focused on what it reveals about Werfel's sense of mission and the insights it gives into his metaphysical and religious thinking at this early stage in his development. Puttkamer (1952) points to the poet's strong sense of mission that at times, in

her view, verges on spiritual arrogance. In this work, she observes, the poet
clearly sees himself as chosen, and being chosen means having a responsibility
to serve God (47). Keller (1958), also interested in this piece as an example of
Werfel's notion of his mission, argues that the poet here takes on a priestlike
role. He defines the difference between the poet and Satan in the play as that
between contemplation, the realm that is not of this world, and action, the
realm of this world (43). As Lea (1968) points out, the poet in *Die Versuchung*
chooses the role of mediator between creation and God, a mission that, in his
opinion, reflects Werfel's concept of his own role as a writer (319). Lea argues
that this work, which is modeled on the temptation of Christ—a parallel that
Ritchie (1976) and others also noticed—is significant because it shows
Werfel's ideological position at this early stage and introduces the struggle
between good and evil for the individual soul, a theme of major importance in
Werfel's later work (319). Adams and Kuhlmann (1974), who like Lea were
students of Klarmann, see the poet as a kind of Christ figure and as a vessel of
God. They argue that the theme of suffering and sacrifice derives from
Werfel's closeness to Catholic tradition (197-98). The work is, for them, an
early indication of Werfel's attraction to Catholicism.

Some critics were interested in *Die Versuchung* because they viewed it as a
key work in the development of Werfel's political thinking. They stressed what
they saw as Werfel's rejection of political activism in the piece, something that
other critics dated from his 1917 essay "Die christliche Sendung." In his
insightful treatment of *Die Versuchung*, Lea (1968) argues that Werfel's rejection of activist politics is already strongly evident here. According to Lea, when
the poet rejects Satan's temptation of power, fame, and immortality, he rejects
political power as vanity and recognizes that political institutions do not satisfy
mankind's deeper needs. Lea concludes that in this piece, which resembles *Der
Weltfreund* in its poetic fervor, hymnic style, and expression of longing for
universal brotherhood, Werfel equates the satanic elements with the desire for
secular power and the longing to change society and the world (319). As Lea
perceptively observes, this notion of political power as satanic appears in many
of Werfel's later works.

Werfel's adaptation of Euripides' *Die Troerinnen*, which was written in
1913 but not published until 1915, was his first dramatic work to be a popular
success. The play, which had over fifty performances at the Lessing Theater in
Berlin in April 1916, was an important theatrical event at the time. Much of
the initial response as well as later criticism centered on the play's topicality
and Werfel's strong antiwar stance. In his introduction to the play, Werfel
pointed out that the fall of Troy could be seen as a metaphor for his age since
in both times the world was suffering a period of upheaval and a crisis in values
(Jungk 1987, 36). As Ritchie (1976) remarks, audiences quickly saw the play as
antimilitarist. In his view, its theme was explosive, and Werfel's treatment of
the material emphasized its relevance and modernity (145).

Many at the time interpreted the play as prophecy and antiwar protest. Although Werfel finished his adaptation before the war broke out, it was widely assumed that it was written in response to the war. Luther (1922) describes how audiences at the time found *Die Troerinnen* gripping. Its effect was so powerful and moving that it seemed as if the two-thousand-year-old play had been written in their day (19). Specht (1926) calls it prophetic in its interpretation of what was to come (132-33). For Jacobson (1927), Werfel's powerful language underscores the horrors of war (346). Like Specht, Puttkamer (1952) stresses the prophetic nature of the play. Despite the horrors of war that it depicts, she detects in it an underlying optimism since, in her view, Hecuba's last words are not lament but express her determination to keep on living even in defiance and despair (10). Braselmann (1960) is another critic who was impressed by Werfel's powerful treatment of the horror of war (21).

Not all critics, however, saw criticism of war as the main thrust of the play. Wimmer (1973), for example, argues that Werfel was most interested in the universal human problems raised by Euripides, such as why the innocent suffer and why justice turns into injustice (42-43). Klarmann (1961) finds in this play the first important avowal in Werfel's works of his faith in Christianity (13). Like Klarmann, Williams (1974) stresses the religious aspect of the play. Although he points out that many saw the play as antiwar protest, he disagrees that it is the work of a politically conscious writer since by this time Werfel was contemptuous of politics. He writes that, although Werfel clearly felt compassion for the victims of war, expressing this feeling was not his real purpose in the play. Rather, he wanted it to depict the cruelty, irrationality, and absurdity of life in general and to portray Hecuba's moral victory over the calamity as a first step in the awakening of religious faith (60-61). Unlike Klarmann, Williams is not prepared to call this religious faith Christianity. Both Klarmann and Williams thus see the play as an important stage in the development of Werfel's religious views, which were to take an increasingly central part in his works and their reception.

Several critics stressed that the play was no mere adaptation but contained a lot of originality; they detected this in its powerful language. Luther (1922) remarks that, although Werfel is faithful to the original in plot and motivation, his language is his own (19). Specht (1926) refuses to accept that it is an adaptation and claims that it is a new work (133). Like Jacobson (1927), Specht praises Werfel's powerful language. Ivernel (1971), however, stresses that Werfel's adaptation is much closer to Euripides' original than to Opitz's earlier translation because Opitz's version is marked by Christian melancholy while Werfel's is energetic (85).

Like Werfel's first three plays, his next play, *Die Mittagsgöttin* (1919), which was originally part of *Der Gerichtstag*, received little attention. Specht (1926), who dislikes the poems in the collection, finds the play, which he terms wonderful magic theater, impressive for its music and the rich images

that Werfel expresses in a language of star-like glow (205). Drake (1928) calls
it a fairy romance in verse (35). Puttkamer (1952) focuses on Werfel's depiction of Mara, who represents, for her, the motherly woman in her perfection
who finds completion and fulfillment in love and motherhood. She also
stresses the importance in the play of love as a means to self-realization and
salvation (32). Like Puttkamer, Wimmer (1973) sees Mara as the embodiment
of the eternal feminine, a symbol of fertility (58); and Adams and Kuhlmann
(1974) view her as a heathen, mythical figure (202). These brief comments
were all positive but were not developed in any depth.

In the only article devoted entirely to the play, Loram (1961) tries to rectify
this neglect. He is particularly interested in the play's religious aspects and in
the way it diverges from expressionism. He argues that, in contrast to plays by
such expressionist dramatists as Toller, Kaiser, and Hasenclever, Werfel's play
is more obviously religious. In his view, the play differs also from other
expressionist dramas in that its mood is more lyrical and it is more symbolically
obscure. For Loram, the nucleus of the play is man's longing and need to find
his way back to the origins of life, a theme expressed in Laurentin's journey,
which leads him to reject his old, false life and be reborn in his pure form. He
observes that throughout the play the religious element—for example, the
search for the divine and absolute—is unmistakable. Like Loram, Wimmer
(1973) stresses the religious and cosmic aspects of the play and views Laurentin's wanderings as an allegory of his search for God. This image of wandering
signifies for him a longing for transformation (58).

Loram does not, however, ignore the many dramatic weaknesses in the
play. Although he admires the dynamic quality of Werfel's writing, the sincerity of his style in his play, its lyrical mood, and its rhapsodic and hymnic
elements—qualities that characterize Werfel's early poetry—he points out that
the errors of inexperience and the urge to say all are too evident. Loram is
critical not only of the language of the play but also of its content, imagery,
and characters. For example, he argues that the funeral scene in the second act
does not contribute to the plot in any significant way. He finds the compli-
cated symbolic pattern irritating, and he criticizes Werfel for his depiction of
Laurentin: his attempt to portray the character as both creator and created
fails, Loram believes, largely because of Werfel's naive and awkward handling
of the sexual implications (67). But despite its faults, Loram concludes, the
play is an important stage in Werfel's development both as a dramatist and as a
thinker since in this "dream world of the absolute" Werfel tried to work out
problems that haunted him and that he felt haunted the world (57-68).

Werfel's first play to arouse lively critical attention was *Spiegelmensch:
Magische Trilogie* (1920), which premiered in Leipzig in October 1921.
Immediate critical reaction ranged from enthusiasm to sharp rejection. Many
pointed out the play's close reliance on other works of literature, an aspect of it
that some found problematic, although others saw it more positively. Most

critics from the beginning were struck by the play's similarity to the Faust theme. Luther (1922), for example, calls it Werfel's *Faust* (26). Not only such early critics as Naumann (1923), Jacobson (1927), and Block (1939) but also later critics such as Braselmann (1960), Zahn (1966), and Wimmer (1973) emphasize this parallel. In contrast, Specht (1926), always a strong advocate for Werfel's originality as a poet, plays down this influence when he argues that there is scarcely anything of the Faust figure in Thamal; rather, Thamal is Werfel's own creation (209).

In a recent article on the play, Huber (1989b) notes even more literary sources. In this "dramatic kaleidoscope" (65), he writes, the reader can detect influences of *Faust*, the Romantics, *Peer Gynt*, Raimund, Dostoyevsky, and Strindberg as well as more recent contemporaries and even operas by Offenbach and Wagner. Looking at the play as a dramatic kaleidoscope was also common with earlier critics. Luther (1922) mentions such literary models as Grillparzer's *Der Traum ein Leben*, Ibsen's *Peer Gynt*, and Strindberg's *Dream Sonata*. Even Specht (1926) has to confess reluctantly that Werfel relied on other works of literature. For him, it is disturbing to sense that in creating the play Werfel was remembering something he had read; in Specht's estimation, a poet of Werfel's inner power and richness of fantasy should not need to rely on other literary models (207). Other critics noticed affinities with Ibsen's *Peer Gynt* (Zahn 1966, Wimmer 1973); Raimund and Nestroy (Fox 1964, Zahn 1966, Bauer 1971b); Strindberg, especially his play *To Damascus* (Zahn 1966, Bauer 1971b, Wimmer 1973); and Calderón (Wimmer 1973).

Although these similarities were often mentioned, they were not explored in any depth. An exception is Brynhildsvoll's (1981) investigation of the play's close thematic connections to Ibsen's *Peer Gynt*. He concludes that Werfel's play is strongly dependent on Ibsen's, not only in its theme and content but also in its motifs and formal structure. Despite this conclusion, he rejects the accusation, voiced by some critics, that Werfel's borrowing verges on plagiarism. Rather, he argues, Werfel's use of Ibsen is thoroughly legitimate since he took aspects of Ibsen's play and shaped them dramatically to make them conform to his own conception (333). In his view, the play's creative and linguistic variety saves Werfel from the charge of plagiarism.

Critics were interested not only in the literary models for the play but also in its philosophical underpinnings. Several, including Naumann (1923) and Jacobson (1927), point out that the philosophical content of the play derives in part from Indian-Buddhist philosophy, and Wimmer (1973) emphasizes that Werfel was conversant with Indian concepts and religion (79). Sokel (1959) also notes the debt to Buddhist mysticism at the end of the trilogy, but he observes that Werfel's interest in Buddhist philosophy was only an extreme and passing stage (217).

Although there was wide agreement about the literary models that Werfel used, critics disagreed about what he intended to say in the play. Naumann

(1923), for example, believes its focus is the renewal of the spiritual, ethical person (128). For Specht (1926), the play depicts the resurrection out of the sleep of the self (206). It is Werfel's accounting with himself, he feels, a view that such later critics as Fox (1964) and Zahn (1966) share. Fox writes, in fact, that the play served Werfel as a form of personal exorcism (112). For Jacobson (1927), Thamal's attempt to find refuge, humanity, and perfection links the theme of the play to Werfel's early poetry (346). Drake (1928) sees the main focus of the play as man's search for perfection (35). As Block (1939) reads it, Werfel's faith in the affirmative spirit of man forms the center of the play. According to her, Werfel expresses his belief that negation of life means decadence and death and that only in affirmation based on spiritual strength can there be life and the struggle for human advancement and freedom (137). For Grenzmann (1955), the main theme of the play is the disintegration of the ego into two (270). Werfel, he believes, wanted in *Spiegelmensch* to show his contemporaries a caricature of themselves (271).

Several critics saw Werfel's rejection of political activism and his avowal of religion as the heart of the play. Klarmann (1959), who thinks the work has been unjustly neglected, calls it Werfel's great mystery play: in his view it is filled with philosophical and religious ideas. Klarmann thinks critics have erred in comparing *Spiegelmensch* with Goethe's *Faust* and calls attention to the dangers of self-satisfied salvationism (98). Lea (1968) stresses Werfel's message in the play that political activism is an expression of egomania disguised as messianism (320), a view that Wimmer (1973) also develops when he remarks that Werfel shows that utopian voluntarism leads to self-deification and the superman and that only the conscious rediscovery of the self and devotion can lead to spiritual rebirth. Wimmer perceives Thamal's arrogance and the Mirror Man's raging egoism as the guilt around which the play revolves, and these concerns are, in his estimation, central to Werfel's works as a whole (81). Adams and Kuhlmann (1974) similarly point out Werfel's criticism and rejection of self-appointed salvationism, but they also stress his depiction of the role of woman as man's redeemer through love and motherhood (203).

Although most critics were interested in the philosophical ideas of the play, there was, for Werfel criticism, an unusually lively interest in and appreciation of Werfel's theatrical and aesthetic achievements in it. For Luther (1922) the structure and the ideas of the play are clear and transparent (27), a rather remarkable statement given the confusion with which most reviewers greeted the play at the time. Specht (1926) particularly admires the intensity and the music of the language that he found so impressive in Werfel's early poetry. *Spiegelmensch*, for him, is an opera in words (214). Fox (1964) focuses on the theatricality of the play. Werfel's use of spectacle and his intermingling of operatic effects and pantomime are characteristic, in his view, not only of this play but of all Werfel's dramatic works. Together with the plot and the characters, he argues, these elements show Werfel's closeness to the Austrian tradition of Raimund and Grillparzer (113).

Ritchie (1976), who calls the dramatic heart of the play the Faustian motif of two souls within one breast, focuses on the play's structure and on how Werfel intended it to be staged. He praises Werfel's fusion of the worlds of dream and reality, subject and object, appearance and essence. As he points out, the play has the structure of a review in the tradition of Goethe's *Faust II* and Ibsen's *Peer Gynt*, a structure that enables Werfel to confront his protagonist with the many temptations of life. Ritchie shows how Werfel creates the atmosphere of a magically remote, unreal world through his use of constantly changing scenery and lighting. He perceptively demonstrates that the choreographic element is fundamental to the structure of the play. Through constant movement, he believes, as in the example of the Spiegelmensch, Werfel expresses the superficiality of the real world. In contrast to this constant motion, truth and purity are motionless, as the unchanging ritual and static poses of the monks in the monastery demonstrate. Ritchie shows that this combination of the static and the dynamic, of stillness and movement, is typical of expressionism as a whole, but he argues that Werfel gives the technique an allegorical dimension that is underscored by the two main characters, who are allegorical figures rather than individuals or types. According to his argument, the movement in the play reflects the path of man through a false reality to the stillness of truth and purity. Like Specht, Ritchie also points out the rich, musical quality of the language; although occasionally, he writes, the lines become empty jingles more typical of operatic libretti than serious drama. In fact, the whole play, in his view, has an operatic theatricality. The scenic and acoustic riches are not, however, there for their own sake but are intended, he suggests, to overwhelm the audience with the magic of the stage, to make the theater a magic place. The play, he concludes, is a quasi-dionysian theatrical cult-ceremony (148-50). Ritchie's discussion is particularly valuable for his analysis of Werfel's use of theatrical techniques, staging, and lighting, characteristics of his dramas that have generally been ignored.

In one of the most perceptive analyses of the play, Huber (1989b) discusses its complex structure and notes how Werfel holds its many elements together with an amazing dramatic energy. He argues that there are four distinct layers in the play: a mythological and archetypal layer that contains a wealth of mystical ideas; expressionist elements indebted to Nietzsche; a critical attitude to expressionism that includes a satirical treatment of his own literary past, his contemporaries, and contemporary movements in literature; and romantic irony. In his view, Werfel skillfully combines all these various layers into a complex and rich structure that he holds together by verse capable of pathos as well as puns. Huber's article is particularly valuable for its discussion of the mythological and archetypal elements in the play, especially for the mirror-*Doppelgänger* motif. The act of looking into a mirror, as he points out, is an ancient motif that signifies the process of self-realization, as J. G. Frazer's *The Golden Bough* and Jacques Lacan's "Le Stade du miroir" (1936) make clear. He also points out that primitive superstition attributes an independent existence to the mirror image (66). Huber concludes that the play fluctuates between myth and *Zeitdrama*, between messianic ecstasy, coolly distancing irony, and biting satire (77). In addition to the valuable insights it provides into the mythological and archetypal elements, Huber's analysis sheds light on how Werfel weaves his complex structure together.

How the play relates to expressionism was a topic of critical interest, as Huber's article demonstrates. Several critics such as Luther (1922) saw the play as an example of expressionism, while others, like Sokel (1959), viewed it as a sharp critique of expressionism. Sokel argues that, in *Spiegelmensch*, Werfel shows that vitalism and activism, which Sokel calls the two main strands of expressionism, are stages in man's self-deification. According to his thesis, Werfel believed that expressionism's fatal hypocrisy was its deification of mankind, a disguise for the deification of the self that Werfel considered blasphemous. He argues that Werfel's sharp rejection of vitalism and activism is particularly obvious in the figures of Thamal in this play and Gebhart in *Barbara oder die Frömmigkeit*. For Werfel, Gebhart's and Thamal's guilt lies in their relationship to the future that is symbolized by their children: both want to renew the world, but, when they have this opportunity for renewal with their children, they fail. Sokel concludes that the play's message that the world can be saved by being preserved and continued from father to son, this notion of the sacred continuity of the generations, repudiates the activist, expressionist goal of the kingdom of the spirit or the paradise on earth (214-17). Lea (1968), however, calls the play Werfel's only expressionist *Ich-drama*, a subjective drama that expresses the author's own struggles (320). For Bauer (1971b), the play is a typical product of late expressionism. Such themes as patricide, the desire to be one with the universe and with a new mankind, and the notion of transformation, as well as the language, are typical of expressionism (323). He thinks that although the play embodies, in many respects, a continuation of expressionist traditions, it is also the beginning of its critical overcoming (325). Huber (1989b) acknowledges the expressionist level of the play, which, in his opinion, consists of elements indebted to Nietzsche and centers around such key expressionist concepts as liberation, redemption, transformation, renewal, rebirth, ecstasy, vision, ultimate perfection, authenticity, sense of mission, and an all-pervading messianic pathos (66). But he argues that central also is Werfel's critique of expressionism in the play. He considers it an example of a late expressionist play, a work about expressionism, and a critique of the author's own past (73).

In their overall assessment of the play, critics varied considerably, as the following early responses indicate. In a review in 1922, Polgar calls the play "too much." He writes that its spring is overwound, its mechanism overcomplicated (240). Luther (1922), however, believes the play is dramatically effective. The will to form and the struggle for the last clarity, he says, are what give Werfel's magic trilogy its value (27). Specht (1926) finds the play problematic and feels more distant from it than from other of Werfel's works. Although he argues that the conception is brilliant, he faults the play for taking too much from other literature. Despite its power and intensity, he views it as a conglomerate work that is not on a par with Werfel's other writing (206). Yet he believes that this is Werfel's first real attempt to master the drama. (*Die Mittagsgöttin* is in his estimation less a drama and more a poem in dialogue.) In his opinion, this religious and at the same time parodistic play is conceived and thought out magnificently and includes scenes of incredible power. In fact, it contains so much knife-sharp irony, so much visionary power, so much humor and spiritual prophecy, that he regrets that imperfections in verse and rhyme disturb the beauty and greatness of some parts (213). He calls the play a satire and a merciless self-knowledge, a fascinating opera in words (214). Block (1939) terms the play a symbolic drama that is so vast in scope and so rich in philosophical content that it is no more a work for the theater than its classical prototype, *Faust* (134).

Later critics also did not agree about the quality of the play. Puttkamer (1952) sees the drama as one of the most important steps in Werfel's development, showing the transition from the time of his youth to maturity and an accounting with himself. For this reason, she thinks it unsatisfactory as a poetic work since Werfel could not find a unified style but fell from high pathos into the sloppy and the banal, from the tragic to journalistic digressions and allusions (37). Sokel (1959) and Ritchie (1976), however, view the play positively. Sokel finds it powerful (213), and Ritchie calls it the play in which Werfel came closest during his expressionist period to creating a masterpiece. Ritchie asks why the play, which was successful when it was first performed, was no lasting success. In his view, its many parallels with other masterpieces of literature were too obvious and led to it being dismissed as derivative. In addition, it was difficult to stage because of the many scene changes. Another problem was that Werfel's use of contemporary references offended both Nationalists and the followers of Karl Kraus. Ritchie raises the question of whether Werfel created a masterpiece full of religious wisdom and prophetic insights into the dangers of the Führer mentality or whether he was, as Karl Kraus suggested, merely a benevolent windbag with a talent for letting off metaphysical steam. Ritchie concludes that time has worked against Werfel. Since the play's production, its magic has gradually faded, and its mixture of Babylonian myth, Indian mysticism, Buddhist faith, and Christian renunciation does not appeal to modern literary tastes (148-51).

More recently, Abels (1990) views the play as a significant caesura in Werfel's life and works (54). Wagener (1993) agrees. He writes that the drama constitutes a kind of self-reckoning and thus marks a transition from Werfel's youthful exuberance to his later self-critical maturity (47). Like others, he points out its many debts to other literary works, but he notes that this is important only for academics. What is more important, in his estimation, is how Werfel manages to fuse all these disparate influences into a very personal expressionist *Wandlungsdrama* (48).

Several critics used the play, because of its sharp attacks on Karl Kraus, as a starting point from which to discuss the notorious feud between Werfel and Kraus, and they agreed that neither author enhanced his reputation through the fight. Some critics looked closely at the relationship between the two men—a biographical focus that tended to show the pettiness on both sides—while others concentrated on the vastly different aesthetic values of the two writers.

In one of the early detailed discussions of this quarrel, Reichert (1957) calls the long-lasting feud one of the most interesting literary feuds of recent times (146). He outlines the early relationship between Werfel and Kraus. For a while they were good friends—Kraus had, for example, published some of Werfel's poems in *Die Fackel* in 1911—but this initial liking and respect changed into complete estrangement and embitterment. Reichert documents the growing fight, which Werfel's attack in *Spiegelmensch* on the editorial policy of *Die Fackel* intensified. He discusses Kraus's response to *Spiegelmensch*, the parody *Literatur oder Man wird doch da sehen: Magische Operette in 2 Teilen* (1921), which ridicules not only Werfel but also other expressionist writers such as Stefan Zweig, Heinrich Mann, Fritz von Unruh, and Hermann Bahr. In his satirical parody, Reichert observes, Kraus attacks three aspects of Werfel's play: his pseudoidealism, his dependence on Goethe's *Faust*, and his tasteless and affected use of language. Reichert sees in Werfel's play *Paulus unter den Juden* (1926) a continuation of this feud. In his view, the Rabbi Beschwörer, who rules through heartless logic, is a thinly disguised portrait of Kraus. Reichert regrets the literary outcome of the feud. In his view, Kraus's satirical parody, despite its stylistic virtuosity, is petty, and Werfel's vulgar attack on Kraus in *Spiegelmensch* detracts from the charm and unity of the play (146-49).

Other critics followed Reichert's argument closely. Foltin and Spalek (1969) and (Bauer 1971b) argue that the feud began with Kraus's criticism of Werfel's poetry, but it soon became bitterly personal. Kraus accused Werfel of artistic or political opportunism and censored him as a representative of the Prague group for imitating instead of creating. Kraus admired Werfel's poems at first but then he began to suspect that Werfel's experience of childhood was inauthentic. In a 1978 article, Bauer stresses the reason for the origin of the feud: treated contemptuously in Rilke's presence by Sidonie Nádherny, Werfel revenged himself by asserting that there was a close relationship between her and Rilke. Kraus was deeply hurt and abandoned Werfel and refused to accept his apologies (178-79). Steiman (1985) argues that the break came because of the two men's radically different attitudes to language, art, and the responsibility of the artist. Whereas Kraus believed that language should "clarify reality," Werfel "tended increasingly to transcend the limitations of language and experience in the mystic transport of words" (19).

Critics found Werfel's next play and his first play in prose, *Bocksgesang* (1921), bewildering when it was first performed at the Raimund Theater in Vienna and in Frankfurt am Main on 10 March 1922. Although the public and the critics at the time found the play confusing, many appreciated its lyrical intensity and the poetic beauty of the language. Several later critics valued the play's dramatic power, its mythical background, its grotesque elements, and its prophetic quality (Ritchie 1976, 147). The play, which opened in New York at the Theater Guild on 25 January 1926, and ran for fifty-eight performances, made Werfel known as a dramatist in the United States. Although the reviews were mixed, many praised the play's poetic and symbolic qualities and its multiple layers of meaning.

Both contemporary and later critics could not agree about what the play meant. They tended to focus on either its religious or its political aspects. Specht (1926), who thought that of all Werfel's works he had read *Bocksgesang* was one of the two unsuccessful ones (the other was *Beschwörungen*), believed that people misunderstood the drama when they focused on its social and human aspects and overlooked the mystical elements, which he found most significant (236). In his view, the play had a Shakespearean power. He writes that he loves this drama passionately because of its wild, elemental music; its orgiastic, religious, and almost animalistic impetuosity; and finally because of its social moral (241). Specht's enthusiastic language testifies to his intensely personal reaction to the play and warns us not to expect a carefully measured critical response in his book. Chandler (1931) thought the drama was marked by poetic sweep of action and a picturesque clash of forces, but he also notes that critics at the time found it bewildering (433-34).

Several critics were particularly interested in the significance of the beast in the play. For Drake (1928), the beast represents evil or destruction. He argues that humanity in the play is reduced to the elemental and cleansed by fire. Man's brutal and passionate energies are released and given free rein until they exhaust themselves so that the spark of divinity, which is concealed in each person until such a crisis occurs, can manifest itself (36-38). Puttkamer (1952) sees the creature as a symbol of all that is terrible and incomprehensible in people (38). For Klarmann (1961) and Adams and Kuhlmann (1974), the basis of the play is metaphysical since the beast represents the principle of evil that continues to reproduce (Klarmann, 21-22; Adams and Kuhlmann, 204). Wimmer (1973) stresses the ambiguity of the figure. In his view, the goat is a symbol not only of the depraved but also of the Orphic-Dionysian and the fruitful. As he points out, Dionysus was thought to appear in the form of a goat (89). But beyond that, he argues, the beast represents to Werfel all that is unholy and impure. It is a symbol of people's destructive instincts that can be temporarily repressed but can break through at any time (92-93).

For other critics, the social and political implications of the play were of the greatest significance. Grenzmann (1955), for example, views the work as an image of revolution and observes that it contains a social plot against the background of myth (271). For Scharbach (1960), the play is a prefiguration of Nazi madness (416). Lea (1968), who notes many expressionist elements in the play, argues that it is part of Werfel's continuing critique of political messianism. Lea calls Juvan a false prophet, a dedicated anarchist, and a professional rebel whose desire for blood is more convincing than his final regeneration because he is motivated by resentment and frustration (327). Wimmer (1973) sees in the play two major concerns, the mystical nature of becoming human and the conflict between the franchised and the disenfranchised (89). According to Jungk (1987), the Pan figure, which he calls Werfel's Golem, is a personification of revolution, a symbolic idol of the disenfranchised and the weak. He shows that Juvan, the self-appointed leader of the disenfranchised, is a composite of anarchist Red Guards and Russian propagandists whom Werfel had met during the revolution in Vienna (86).

In an article that draws on his 1954 dissertation, "Mythological and Supernatural Elements in Four Early Plays of Franz Werfel," Lambasa (1961) discusses the play's mythical elements, its ambiguity, its richness, and its theatrical effectiveness. He begins his discussion by pointing out that most critics have dismissed the play as a strange mixture of revolutionary and social drama, myth, and folklore. In this article, Lambasa investigates whether the play has any merits and whether it has anything relevant to say today. He clearly believes that the neglect of the play, which he calls one of Werfel's major works, is unwarranted (69). Lambasa argues that in this play Werfel states more ambiguously than in his other works the philosophy that is central to all his writing. In his view, this is, to some extent, to the play's disadvantage since it leads to confusion, but it is also to its advantage because a certain amount of ambiguity allows a variety of different and contradictory interpretations. In no other work by Werfel, he believes, are there so many contradictory interpretations. From the outset, the title already suggests this ambiguity and breadth of meaning since it refers both to the Greek word for tragedy and also to the goatlike creature. For Lambasa, the dramatic plot is fascinating because Werfel combines traditional myths such as the myth of Pan, folk tales, social and human passions, and class war and rebellion with individual tragedies of love, hate, and anguish. Lambasa sees *Goat Song* as human drama in which people hate, love, and destroy one another and in which crowds swirl in anger, murder carelessly, and give themselves over to a riot of abandoned drunkenness and lust. He argues that the characters in the play are particularly effective because they have tremendous vitality and transcend the mere types that often make expressionist drama lifeless. Although he concedes that some of the symbolism is vague, the play represents for him one of Werfel's highest dramatic achievements because of its power, suggestiveness, and high moral and spiritual appeal. Lambasa also praises Werfel for being prophetic in his central idea that the beast, this ghastly nightmare of humanity, is ever present—although, he remarks, Werfel's audience in the 1920s may not have believed that such mass hysteria and destruction could exist except in some semibarbarous country beyond the Danube. After the experience of the Second World War, Lambasa observes, it is not impossible for us to imagine a beast, worshipped with outstretched hands and frenzied cries, demanding its innumerable human victims and laying waste an entire continent (69-82). The play is thus for him a prefiguration of the Nazi years.

Although many critics such as Polgar (1922b) were critical of the play for its lack of unity, its weak symbolic power, and its uninteresting characters, others shared Lambasa's view that it was dramatically effective. Grenzmann (1955) admires the way Werfel interwove the various plots into a unity through relating them to the central figure of Pan (272). Scharbach (1960), who considers it one of Werfel's most typical expressionist plays and complains that it was neglected, is interested in the irony of the play, which he believes stems from Werfel's skillful deception or dissimulation. Werfel begins with dramatic situations that at first appear simple and innocent but soon take unexpected turns. Such dissimulation and reversal, in Scharbach's opinion, give *Bocksgesang* its great tensile strength and dynamism. He argues that the play's power and impact grow out of its basic ironic perceptions and representations (410-11) and that Werfel's startling stage effects and typical expressionist devices do not detract from its ironic structure (416).

Recently, Wagener (1993) points out that the confusion about the play stems from its number of different themes. He sees the play partly as a reflection of Werfel's own revolutionary period at the end of the First World War, but, in addition to its sociopolitical elements, he stresses that the mythical element is strong. He argues that Werfel suggests that the beast (which, like other critics, he sees as the incorporation of evil, demonic powers) is always present. The goat thus represents the irrational, unconscious evil inside everyone. In his view, the play is about the omnipresence of this mythical evil. Such an interpretation, he observes, lends a kind of prophetic quality to the play, which "seems to prophesy the adoration of the evil of the Third Reich under the leadership of the social outcast Adolf Hitler" (51).

Werfel's next play, the tragedy *Schweiger* (1922), was his last expressionist one. Kafka disliked it intensely, and it had a mixed critical reception. When it was produced in 1922, it took stages in the German-speaking countries by storm: 83 decided to include it in their program, and in Berlin it had 100 consecutive performances. It was not, however, popular among the critics, and this led to its oblivion, according to Lenz (1936, 168). Polgar (1923), for example, sharply criticizes the play because Werfel crowds into it too many themes, including the relationship between men and women, between mother and child, between the world and the individual, between God and man, and between desire and responsibility in addition to thoughts about religion, science, politics, faith, this world, and the world after death (288). When the play was produced in 1926 at the Fifth Avenue Playhouse in New York critical response was largely negative, primarily because the work was felt to be too morbid (Frey 1946, 124).

For several critics, the play's religious and existential aspects were most significant. Specht (1926) views Schweiger as having a kind of pure, savior nature (242-43). Around this pure, wrestling soul, which wants only to devote itself to love, he observes, fight the powers of the world, politics, church, and superstition (245). Drake (1928) notes that in the tragic figure of Schweiger one can detect the divine flame that Werfel believed burned in the sordidness of every human heart. For Drake, the play expresses the most bitter kind of tragedy because it is unnecessary tragedy, the tragedy of waste (39). Chandler (1931) praises Werfel's insight into the power of hypnotic suggestion and insanity and argues that central to the play is Werfel's view of man as the battleground of two warring forces (433). For Lenz (1936), who produced the play with the Deutscher Verein of University Heights, New York University, in April 1935, Werfel's central theme is the vain search of the reformed criminal for heroic unselfishness in his world (169). He argues that Werfel states his philosophy clearly in the play. He proclaims a new faith in life, man, and God and urges a new spirit of communality and brotherhood, a message that, in Lenz's view, has true universal validity. The lack of these spiritual forces in his world makes life impossible for Schweiger (171). Lenz stresses that these themes still have relevance at the time he is writing. Wimmer (1973) argues that in the theological and cosmic sense *Schweiger* is one of Werfel's strongest dramas. Schweiger's suicide, in his opinion, is an act of moral self-assertion: by offering himself as a sacrifice, he is brought close to the divine. Although he fails in the material real world, through his expiation he attains a new innocence (102).

Other critics were interested in the politics of the play. Lenz (1936), for example, argues that Viereck is a true National Socialist, and he praises Werfel for being prophetic (171). According to Puttkamer (1952), Werfel uses the figure of Schweiger to confront such intellectual trends of the time as spiritualism, psychoanalysis, and socialism (39). Klarmann (1961) and Lea (1968) also see in the figure of Viereck the fanaticism of National Socialism, which, in their view, Werfel already sensed in 1922. Ritchie (1976) focuses on Werfel's critique of socialism and his depiction of the lust for power and the psychotic drives that tear at Schweiger's soul (147).

Evaluations of the play were mixed. Polgar (1923) and Specht (1926) both think it suffers from an overabundance of themes. Specht dislikes Werfel's focus on problems of the time but believes that the play's stage effects are among Werfel's strongest (242). Jacobson (1927) praises the play for its symbolism and visionary power (348). Drake (1928) admires its theatrical effectiveness but argues that it is the lyrical quality rather than the dramatic situation that is more powerfully felt. In the play, which he likens to a Christian miracle play, he concludes that Werfel as dramatist and prophet achieved his noblest and most satisfying utterance (39-40). Lenz (1936) believes that the superabundance of forces and motifs that Specht had noticed in the play are woven together into a neat pattern, and the characters appear real, alive, and consistent (169-70). In Lenz's opinion, Werfel is effective both in his technique of suspense and in developing concerns that have universal validity. Ritchie (1976) points to the problems with the reception. Such complex motivation did not make for clarity of plot or intention, and the play was condemned for its mixture of politics, psychiatry, and mysticism (147).

In a recent evaluation of the play, Wagener (1993) argues that the often unfavorable evaluations of the play by critics at the time it was first produced stemmed from their perception of the plot as a hodgepodge of motifs and events that were reminiscent of nineteenth-century melodrama. Wagener thinks, however, that in spite of its melodramatic plot, all the characters and their motivation are quite believable (52). He agrees with such earlier critics as Drake (1928) and Wimmer (1973) when he terms Schweiger's suicide a true self-sacrifice: in his death, he becomes a "true Expressionist hero of humanity and a near saint" (53).

*Juarez und Maximilian* (1924), Werfel's first attempt to write a historical play, was well received in Germany, Austria, and the United States. This was, in fact, Werfel's first real theatrical success, and he was awarded the Grillparzer prize for it in January 1926. It premiered in Magdeburg in April 1925 and was subsequently performed in Vienna in May of the same year at the Theater in der Josefstadt, directed by Max Reinhardt, who also directed it at the Deutsches Theater in Berlin in 1926. When it was performed by the Theater Guild in New York in 1926, it was also favorably received. Although some critics found the structure of the play weak, many praised it for its handsome, historical subject and for its dramatic power. In 1939, John Huston adapted it for Hollywood as the film *Juarez*, a further indication of its favorable reception in the United States.

Much of the critical interest centered around the figure of Maximilian, particularly his nobility, his sense of mission, and his illusions, and most critics viewed him positively. Specht (1926) sees the play as the tragedy of the pure and beautiful person who enthusiastically dedicates himself to a great idea but who is misused and made into his own opposite by the baseness against which he is defenseless. As Specht remarks, without wanting to and at first without realizing it, Maximilian defiles the noble idea that he wants to serve (299-300). In Specht's opinion, Maximilian becomes through his death the great, almost holy, trusting person that he could not be in life (301). According to

Puttkamer (1952), Werfel shows that Maximilian must be defeated because, unlike his opponent, Juarez, he is a human being. His humanity makes him weak and vulnerable. Because Maximilian wants to do good but instead does wrong, she argues, he becomes trapped in tragic guilt. She sees Maximilian not only as a human and thus weak person but also as a regal figure whose death reveals his noble nature. Although he has the opportunity to save his life, he refuses to do so, for if he saved himself, he would lose his nobility (82-83). Grenzmann (1955) also considers the downfall of Maximilian, whom he calls a pure and beautiful person, to be the center of the play. In his opinion, this downfall occurs because Maximilian is forced to come out of the realm of the noble and pure idea into the realm of concrete political power with all its unavoidable baseness. Like Puttkamer, Grenzmann stresses the nobility of Maximilian's death. Through his death, this critic believes, Maximilian becomes free. At the end, he sees through all lies and recognizes that his guilt demands expiation (273). For Wimmer (1973), Maximilian is the beautiful, the *musische* person, who believes in his calling and acts out of noble senti-ments. He respects the talents of the Indians and does not think of them as inferior (112). More recently, Wagener (1993) argues that Maximilian is not only a representative of the Hapsburg dynasty but also a ruler who is willing to give up power and politics to try to bring happiness to the people. For Wagener, the play is the tragedy of a well-meaning "beautiful person," a ruler who wants to do good but fails because history has surpassed him and his beliefs (56).

Other critics, however, pointed out the more problematic aspects of Maximilian's nature. Chandler (1931) calls Maximilian an incompetent idealist who is doomed to failure by his own character (435). Lea (1968) observes that Maximilian's behavior in the play is characterized by a pervasive unrealism, a combination of political innocence and self-righteousness, and a misplaced idealism. He points out that the mirror theme of self-worship, a frequent one in those works in which Werfel criticizes political figures, underscores Maxi-milian's concern with his image (321-22). Despite these character flaws, Lea believes that Maximilian vindicates himself and acquires tragic stature as an idealist whom history has passed by when he takes responsibility for the illegal acts committed in his name and with his consent and accepts death as expia-tion for his guilt (322). Lea agrees with other critics that Werfel portrays Maximilian as noble—a result, in his view, of Werfel's Austrian perspective, which made him romanticize Maximilian (323). Rieder (1968) views Maximil-ian more negatively. He argues that Maximilian sees only himself. Throughout the play, he *observes* his role and works on this role in order to form himself according to his ideal. He thus experiences himself consciously. According to Rieder, Maximilian is fascinated with his mirror image, which reflects what he would like to be, namely the noble Hapsburg ruler known for good, noble deeds and open to the greatness of his task, and he is able to see only this ideal image of himself. Rieder sees Werfel's Maximilian as a typical monomaniacal hero of modern Austrian literature (88-89). Schalk (1988) calls Maximilian an unsocial utopian who passively reacts but fails to act (82-84).

Maximilian's opponent, Juarez, and his conflict with Maximilian aroused a great deal of critical interest. Polgar (1925) sees Juarez as pure, practical reason, cool and sober, and he calls him a pedantic fanatic of mission (383). Specht (1926), who points out that the play's theme of love of one's enemy links it to Werfel's novel *Verdi*, believes that Juarez, not Maximilian, is the main figure in the play, which Werfel skillfully suggests by having Juarez remain invisible, a technique that, in his view, mythically elevates Juarez's greatness (304). Like Specht, Puttkamer (1952) notices in the play the thematic parallels to *Verdi*, and she observes that, although Juarez does not appear, his shadow lies over the play. She perceives Juarez as being historically, legally, and politically right. In her view, Werfel portrays him as amoral, as a person for whom good and evil do not exist but who always does the right thing (81-82). Lea (1968) notes that Juarez always acts carefully. Everything he does is calculated and executed with the precision of chess moves. Like Puttkamer, he argues that Juarez is legally, politically, and morally right. Yet although the future belongs to Juarez, Lea shows how Werfel depicts him as a professional politician who is ruthlessly efficient, legalistic, cold-blooded, and radically secular. Thus, despite his legitimate position, Werfel criticizes him as a modern dictator who introduces nationalism and mob rule (323). Rieder (1968) argues also for Juarez's legal legitimacy (92). Like Lea, Wimmer (1973) notes that, in contrast to the humane Maximilian, Juarez represents ice cold, abstract, and unfeeling reason. He comments that Juarez is the pragmatist of power (114). From his Marxist perspective, Metzler (1988) views Juarez positively because he believes that he represents the power and will of his people (329). Schalk (1988) calls Juarez the hidden director of the historical stage spectacle, the personification of abstract, rationalizing power, a symbol for Werfel of the automatism of history (83). In contrast to Juarez, he observes, the emperor is only a marionette.

For many critics, the political and historical aspects and what these indicated about Werfel's own views of politics and history were the key elements of the play. Jacobson (1927), for example, thinks the conflict between Maximilian and Juarez represents the conflict between two political worlds, the monarchistic and the democratic-republican (348). Puttkamer (1952) sees in the play a strong anticolonialist message because, with all his idealism, Maximilian is the victim of the already hollow claim of European rule over peoples of color (82). Braselmann (1960) notes that the play had been defined as a political play against politics (40). In one of the most insightful treatments of this topic, Lea (1968) argues that the play shows that Maximilian's misguided attempt to establish a utopian society leads to tragic ends. The play is thus another of many examples of Werfel's critique of political activism. Lea writes that if

Werfel wanted to demonstrate the pitfalls of political activism, he could hardly have chosen a better example than Maximilian, who sincerely wanted to do good but was misguided by others (320). Rieder (1968) is most interested in what the play suggests about Werfel's notion of history. He argues that Werfel depicts history in this play as the drama of a soul. In Rieder's view, Werfel was convinced that the history of people is made by individuals. But Werfel lived in the twentieth century, a time of class struggle and ideology, when the collective assumed greater importance. Because of this, according to Rieder's argument, Werfel feared that history was no longer the history of people, of souls, and of personalities but had become inhuman, faceless, and soulless. Werfel's story of Mexico was thus intended as a warning. In Rieder's view, Maximilian's tragedy is the tragedy of a human soul and the humanistic belief in mission, and it thus expresses Werfel's hope for a history of mankind that still has human features (95-96). For Wimmer (1973), the play was a Hapsburg drama, the drama of a dynasty and its members. In his view, however, Maximilian not only is a Hapsburg but also personifies a ruler who no longer equates himself with the state but wants to serve the state. He is another example in Werfel's works of the *musische* person who wants to create a kingdom of love on earth (113). Wimmer defends Maximilian's claim to power as legitimate because of his ethical and moral attitude. His tragedy stems from the destruction of his great idea of a kingdom of love on earth by the cold, calculating reason of the practical politician. Like Rieder, Wimmer stresses that the drama shows Werfel's growing recognition that the time of great individuals has been replaced by the rule of anonymous power. Werfel's realization that the faceless mass now rules is expressed dramatically by the absence of Juarez on the stage (115). From his Marxist perspective, Metzler (1988) interprets the play as the final stage of the suppression of Mexico through foreign rule. In his view, Werfel depicts the people's ability to change society but he does not show them as humane. Instead, Werfel shows morality to be on the side of Maximilian, a view of which Metzler is highly critical; he implies that Werfel's thinking here is reactionary. In this play, Metzler criticizes Werfel for allowing his ethical idealism to gain supremacy (329). Schalk (1988), who is interested in how Werfel's philosophy of history is developed in the play, sees here an example of Werfel's belief that people are entrapped and seduced by substitute religions of various political ideologies (81). Although some critics, such as Magris (1966, 266), saw in the idealization of Maximilian Werfel's longing for the Hapsburg past, Schalk denies that there is any idealization of Hapsburg history in the play. For Werfel, the person who acts historically is an automaton, tossed by historical forces. The play thus demonstrates Werfel's pessimism about history, his belief in the hopelessness of effecting any social change, and his suspicions of politics (83-85).

Polgar (1925), who acknowledges the intensity of the play but complains that the characters are like wax figures (385), is one of a minority of critics who viewed it negatively. Most, however, found it impressive. Specht (1926) admires above all its intensity and its subtle characterizations; he considers it the first example of Werfel's full maturity as a dramatist (304). Drake (1928), however, disagrees. He sees it as nothing more than a first-rate historical play (41). Grenzmann (1955) praises the play for its suspense (273), and Foltin (1961b) calls Werfel's portrayal of the Hapsburg emperor of Mexico splendid (4).

Most critics focused on the ideas or the characters of the play and paid little attention to its dramatic techniques except for pointing out how Werfel's decision to keep Juarez off the stage contributes to the suspense of the play and the heightening of Juarez into a mythical figure. Schalk (1988), however, addresses Werfel's theatrical technique briefly when he argues that Werfel's figures are characterized not only through the dramatic dialogue but also through the epic commentary. In this way, they are doubly objectivized, he believes, since the epic commentary creates a realistic milieu and the historical material shows the figure acting in a causality (79-80).

Recently, Wagener (1993) points out how Werfel's dramatic style here has changed from the mythical style that characterized his expressionist dramas to the realistic style of New Objectivity. Wagener perceptively notes that Werfel is not interested primarily in recreating history in this play but rather in giving expression once again to his spiritual ideals. For example, Juarez, the modern, abstract man, and Maximilian, the introspective man favored by the muses, prefigure the two types Werfel discusses in his later essay "Realismus und Innerlichkeit" (1931). Wagener comments that Werfel wanted to present the story as a series of historical pictures, as a dramatized history rather than a play, and he emphasizes that these pictures should be seen not just as expressionist stations but rather as historical tableaux (54).

In contrast to the success of *Juarez und Maximilian*, Werfel's next play, *Paulus unter den Juden* (1926), received little critical attention. When it was first performed in Breslau, Bonn, Düsseldorf, Cologne, and Munich in October 1926, it was not favorably received (Foltin 1972, 64). Although it was not nearly so successful as *Juarez und Maximilian*, the fact that so many theaters chose to perform it is testimony to Werfel's stature as a dramatist at that time.

Critics who dealt with the play stressed its philosophical and religious content and neglected it as a work for the stage. Overwhelmingly they saw the play as an example of Werfel's beginning preoccupation with Jewish themes and his confrontation with Jewish and Christian beliefs. The play was for them less a work of art and more a theological debate. They saw it as a metaphysical drama that had at its heart the struggle between Christianity and Judaism and as an example of Werfel's own struggle to come to terms with these religions and his own beliefs (Puttkamer 1952, Grenzmann 1955, Braselmann 1960, Klarmann 1959 and 1961, Arnim 1961, Kühner 1965, Wimmer 1973, Grimm 1985). Wagener (1993) points out that Werfel incorporates in the characters in the play the types of people he later discusses in his essays. For example, Chanan is the political activist who, because of his activism, must fail, and the members of the Sanhedrin represent the abstract ideologists. In Wagener's opinion, Paul and the others who believe in Christ are the only ones who act from within. They have the inwardness that Werfel later advocates in "Realismus und Innerlichkeit" (58).

Very few critics went beyond a discussion of the religious theme. Specht (1926), however, states that the tragedy has a Shakespearean grasp. He stresses the strong spiritual aspects of the play, which, according to him, indicate how "masculine" Werfel is in his spirituality (308). Jacobson (1927) is reminded by the figure of Gamaliel of Nathan der Weise, Lessing's hymn of tolerance (349). Chandler (1931) also sees Werfel's idealism in the play but criticizes it for being sober, solid, and somewhat dull. He complains that although it is rich in philosophy, it lacks a love interest, any strong dramatic appeal, and any evidence of the originality that marked its author's earlier work (435-36).

Werfel's next play, *Das Reich Gottes in Böhmen* (1930), was not well received when it was first performed in 1930 at the Burgtheater in Vienna, and it aroused little critical attention until recently. In his discussion of the play, Kunisch (1968) focuses on what he sees in it as Werfel's resignation. In his opinion, although Werfel's focus is still on justice and power, the play demonstrates that those who seek justice are conquered by those who are violent (75). Kunisch compares the play unfavorably to other Austrian dramas, especially those by Grillparzer and Hofmannsthal. He views it as a last echo of the old Austrian *Staatsdrama*. In its dramaturgical, dramatic, thematic, and scenic variety, he believes that the play is richer than the plays of Grillparzer and Hofmannsthal, but in its ideas it seems to him considerably weaker. He concludes that the drama shows signs of having been written by a latecomer whose geographic and religious origins prevented him from being the heir to this tradition (83), an author who lacked a spiritual, religious, and national home. Kunisch accounts for the neglect of the play by commenting that its religious aspects discouraged its later production (75).

Lea (1968) is interested in the play as a further example of Werfel's critique of political activism since in it Werfel depicts another misguided and tragic attempt to establish a utopian society on earth. He argues that, although the play's protagonist, the Hussite leader Prokop, is convinced of the need for social and ecclesiastic reform, his movement fails because of his messianic presumptions, moral corruptness, and personal vulnerability. Like Maximilian, Prokop has to face a similar disparity between ideal and actuality. According to Lea, he is thus another example of a figure with a strong sense of mission who fails when he becomes an activist. In Lea's opinion, Werfel shows that the Hussite movement fails for three reasons: the weakness of its leadership, the injection of nationalism into an essentially religious cause, and the utopian attempt to establish a Kingdom of God on earth (323-25).

In contrast, Wimmer (1973) is fascinated by Prokop, whose character he analyzes at length. In this tragedy of the leader, he argues, Prokop, who preaches nonviolence, is forced to turn to violence. According to his thesis, by turning to violence he becomes another person, his opposite, his mirror man. Like Maximilian, Prokop wants to do good. He is horrified by baseness and wants to destroy the corrupted world. But he cannot create order within himself. Prokop sacrifices thoughtlessly not only his own happiness but that of his relatives, and he fails as son, husband, and brother. His great idea is to liberate mankind, but, instead of liberating people, his kingdom enslaves and persecutes them because he overlooks the fact that the realization of this goal presupposes the liberation of each individual. His messianic fervor thus leads him to become a dictator with a will to power who intends to attain his goal at all costs, even with inhumane means. Although his intentions are pure, he gets increasingly involved in guilt. Prokop becomes his opposite: he turns into an insensible and dogmatic despot. Wimmer concludes that this work, together with such plays as Grillparzer's *Bruderzwist in Habsburg* and Hofmannsthal's *Der Turm*, belongs to the most significant works not only of Austrian but also of European drama (124-26). Klarmann (1961) and Adams and Kuhlmann (1974) also argue that the play reveals Werfel's conviction that the kingdom of God can neither exist on earth nor be created by people, even those with great idealism. They point out that Prokop cannot stay pure. Werfel shows Prokop's idealism to be a lie, his cosmos a chaos. In their view, he is one of Werfel's Lucifer figures.

Recently, Reffet (1989c) discusses Werfel's development from *Das Reich Gottes* to his later plays and argues for a reevaluation. He considers *Das Reich Gottes* to be the high point of Werfel's dramatic writings of the 1920s (94) and the apex of historical tragedy (102). He believes that what separates Werfel's dramas from his lyric poetry is their political content. In his estimation, *Das Reich Gottes* compares favorably with the best works of Grillparzer and Hofmannsthal. Reffet is, however, critical of Werfel for relying too closely on his historical sources: for audiences who are not familiar with this period of history, he remarks, the lack of explanations of the various relationships in the play can be confusing.

Wagener (1993) argues that, as in the case of Maximilian, Prokop's good intentions ultimately have the opposite effect. Like Wimmer, he sees him as an idealist who has been turned into a distorted image of his former self and who has contempt for human beings. He agrees with Lea that the play is a further critique of political activism because it reflects Werfel's judgment on all kinds of political, utopian thinking that ignores man for an abstract ideal. As such, it is a critique of twentieth-century attempts to establish a utopian state (59-60).

Warren's recent article (1989), in which he discusses the three history plays, *Juarez und Maximilian, Paulus unter den Juden,* and *Das Reich Gottes in*

*Böhmen*, is valuable for setting Werfel and his plays within the Austrian and German dramatic traditions and the historical context of his times. Warren, who considers Werfel to be a protean figure at home in all genres, argues that the range of his drama ensures him a firm place among Austrian dramatists. He believes that Werfel's turn to historical drama took him into the mainstream of the German classical tradition. These three plays demonstrate Werfel's dependence on and knowledge of the German dramatic tradition, particularly the Austrian *Staatsdrama*. Werfel's choice of themes clearly suggests his receptiveness to the German dramatic tradition. For example, Warren indicates that the problem of the intellectual who incurs guilt through action or force, a central problem that Maximilian experiences, is one that haunts German heroes from Faust to Brecht. Their distaste for the realities of political power also puts Werfel's protagonists firmly into the tradition of German intellectual tragedy. In addition to thematic connections, Warren argues that in his exemplary use of stage properties and costumes Werfel follows in the tradition of Grillparzer. In these plays, Warren also notices echoes of other dramatists such as Goethe, Schiller, Büchner, Kaiser, and especially Grillparzer, but he finds these echoes problematic since the audience tends to compare such scenes in Werfel's plays with their originals. This works to Werfel's disadvantage; the borrowing distracts the audience's attention from the effects that he was trying to create and adversely shapes the critics' assessment of his dramatic skills (157-62).

Warren also analyzes Werfel's history plays within the context of the theatrical tradition of his time. He points out that in Vienna in the 1920s historical dramas dominated the repertoires of nearly all theaters. Most of them were set either in a mythological past or at some time before the First World War. Werfel's three history plays clearly fall into this tradition. *Juarez und Maximilian* was also part of what Magris (1966) called the Hapsburg myth, which flourished at this time in Vienna. Warren argues, however, that Werfel's historical plays are of less interest as examples of this generally escapist genre and more as demonstrations of Werfel's attempts to apply contemporary developments in the theater (162-64).

A particularly valuable part of Warren's article shows how Werfel's notion of theatricality was shaped, an aspect of Werfel's dramatic production that has generally been neglected. Warren demonstrates how Werfel's view of the theater was inspired significantly by the work of Max Reinhardt, whose call for the reintroduction of color, music, dance, and mime into the theater decisively changed theatrical production of the time. All three of Werfel's history plays, for example, are rich in the chiaroscuro that Reinhardt favored. Although this chiaroscuro was in part inspired by Reinhardt, it was also a technique used widely in expressionist art and film, which Warren does not mention. Warren believes that Reinhardt's influence extended to virtually all aspects of Werfel's history plays. It can be seen in the staging and the acoustic effects in which music is used to underscore the action, create atmosphere, and provide an ironic counterpoint. Werfel's use of crowd scenes in which the mob triumphs over the individual also shows a debt to Reinhardt. In addition to the clear influence of Reinhardt on Werfel's dramatic techniques, Warren argues that these plays were shaped by Werfel's passionate love of opera, which provides the basic structure of some of his works, as Adolf Klarmann frequently argues. Warren points out that Werfel worked on *Das Reich Gottes*, which he considers his most "operatic" work, while he was writing the libretti for *Die Macht des Schicksals* (1926) and *Simone Boccanegra* (1929), although Warren believes that the strongest operatic influence on the play was not Verdi but Pfitzner's *Palestrina* (164-68).

Another important focus of Warren's article is how Werfel deals in these plays with issues of the time. Although the plays reveal Werfel's baroque Christian mysticism, Warren shows that in different ways they all address concerns of the age. A pressing concern in Central Europe at the time, he argues, was the problem of leadership, in particular that of the idealistic leader set against the growing power of the masses. Other concerns included the question of political behavior and skill, the role of the church, and the problem of anti-Semitism. Werfel addresses the pressing problem of anti-Semitism only in *Paulus unter den Juden*. When Murullus, for example, argues that the temple should be destroyed, Warren observes that this is a spine-chilling prophecy of the *Kristallnacht*. According to his argument, *Das Reich Gottes* was written as an allegory of the present. Reviews at the time it premiered, for example, stressed the analogy to the Russian revolution of 1917, but Warren shows that there was an analogous situation closer to home, namely the attempt by the socialist leadership of Vienna to create a workers' paradise with decent housing, welfare services, and a fairer system of education. Thus, Warren argues, although Werfel's plays are set in a distant past, they transcend the escapist historical plays of the time and address the serious issues that preoccupied people in the 1920s (168-72).

Werfel's next play, *Der Weg der Verheißung: Ein Bibelspiel* (1935), was performed in English as *The Eternal Road* on 7 January 1937 under the direction of Max Reinhardt, with music by Kurt Weill and settings by Norman Bel Geddes. From the start, the production experienced countless problems that delayed the premiere, an aspect that several critics discussed. Arlt (1951) points out Werfel's reaction to these problems. Werfel and Alma Mahler-Werfel arrived in New York on 12 November 1935 at the invitation of Max Reinhardt to help with the rehearsals of *The Eternal Road*. Their time was filled, however, with endless bickering with managers, producers, actors, and musicians. Half a million dollars was squandered on the production before the first rehearsal. In February 1936, Werfel returned to Europe disappointed, disgusted, and sick without having seen the opening of his play (2). When it was finally performed, it was well received by critics, who were impressed with it as a biblical pageant. Most reviewers thought that the spectacle was genuinely magnificent and admired the power and beauty of Werfel's text. Although it played to full houses, however, it had to close after five months: because of the extravagance of the production and the large cast of actors, dancers, and singers, the production costs were enormous, and it was a financial failure. A vivid firsthand account of the many problems that the production faced is given by Harry Horner (1973), who was involved in the stage design and other aspects of the production. Brown (1989) also discusses in detail the many problems that beset the production.

Several critics saw the play as an exile work. Wächter (1973) remarks that much of the interest at the time was less in the content of the play and more in its analysis of the exile experience, and many reviewers interpreted it as a work of emigration. Wächter believes that it was one of the artistic high points of exile. Werfel's drama and the whole production had its origins in the persecution of the Jews, to which it pointed warningly. Because of this, he considers the play and its production to belong in the context of antifascist dramas (157-59). Brown (1982) argues, however, that, strictly speaking, the play is not an exile drama since Werfel was not at that time in exile, although some leading exiles were involved in the production (70).

Until the 1980s, the play aroused little critical interest except for fairly brief and passing mentions in the context of Werfel's religious themes. Steiman (1985) looks at the play as a reflection of Werfel's attitude to Judaism, and two recent articles by Brown (1989) and Clark (1989) discuss the play in the context of Werfel's collaboration with Meyer Weisgal, the producer, and Max Reinhardt, the director, although the play itself is still neglected.

Steiman (1985) is interested in what the play tells us about Werfel's attitude to Judaism. Although many at the time were impressed with what they perceived as a genuine depiction of current and historical Jewish concerns, Steiman argues that the Jewish characters in the play are all "either rogues or simpletons" (170). The characters in the play who are sympathetic are either not Jewish or Jews who are unaware that they are Jewish. Steiman is disturbed that Werfel chose for his play "the same material used by anti-Semites and skeptics down through the ages" (171). He believes that Werfel portrays such stereotyped examples of "Jewish" behavior to encourage Jewish spiritual regeneration, although he does not think Werfel is successful in this (172). For him, the play is thus a further example of Werfel's uneasy ties to his Jewish heritage.

Brown (1989) focuses on Werfel's working relationship with Meyer Weisgal. He argues that in the play the Jewish people are seen from a Jewish point of view without any reference to Christian beliefs and that this differs sharply from many of Werfel's previous works in which Jews are seen from a Christian perspective. There are two reasons, he believes, for this difference. Meyer Weisgal wanted a play that would arouse American Jews' ethnic and religious pride in their heritage, and he also wanted to arouse the solidarity of

Christians for the persecuted Jews of Europe. To realize these goals, he needed a play that emphasized the value of Jewish tradition. *The Eternal Road* should not only justify the continuing existence of the Jews but also show the importance of Judaism to the development of the world. Weisgal's views led inevitably to conflicts with Werfel because Werfel believed that the significance of Judaism lay in its relationship to Christianity. They also differed in their understanding of anti-Semitism. Whereas Weisgal saw it as a real and immediate threat, Werfel saw it as a metaphysical phenomenon. Weisgal rejected the first version of the play because it seemed to him too Catholic (1595-96). According to Brown's argument, Werfel was forced to shape his views to conform to those of Weisgal, a problem inherent in a work that is commissioned.

Clark (1989) also discusses Werfel's collaboration in this play, but her focus is the problems that Werfel faced in his collaboration with the play's director, Max Reinhardt. To set the context for her discussion, Clark analyzes Werfel's interest in new developments in the theater of his time, in particular those of Reinhardt, an aspect that Warren (1989) also explores. These treatments are examples of a new and much needed trend in Werfel criticism. Clark points out that in 1913, for example, Werfel visited the experimental theater of Adolphe Appia and Jean-Jacques Dalcroze at Hellerau, where the proscenium arch was removed and the audience drawn closer to the stage. Werfel was attracted to this attempt to involve the audience rather than keep the viewers at a distance. His essay "Die Bühne von Hellerau" (1913), collected in *Zwischen Oben und Unten* (1975), expresses his concern that traditional theater architecture and techniques of staging distort theatrical events. From this visit, Werfel realized that theatrical production requires the collaboration of several figures and a number of factors of which the dramatic text is just one. Clark argues that *The Eternal Road*, technically the most exacting of Werfel's plays, provides fascinating insights into the way in which Werfel incorporates from the outset an awareness of the staging of his plays into their dramatic conception. It also illustrates, in her view, the dangers Werfel faced in subscribing too readily to the notion that his role as dramatist was no more significant than the roles of other members of the team of artists and craftsmen (211-13).

Werfel's collaboration with Max Reinhardt forms the main focus of the article. Clark argues that what began as a collaboration soon became dominated by Reinhardt's desire to use Werfel's text as a vehicle for his own ideas. Reinhardt devised a number of scenes for the production. When it finally reached the stage, it was, in Clark's estimation, as much a product of his creative imagination as it was of its nominal author, Werfel. For example, the fourth act was not a success, and after the premiere Reinhardt cut almost the entire act for the remainder of its run. The production New York audiences saw was thus a revised and much abridged version of *Der Weg der Verheißung* of which Reinhardt rather than Werfel was the author. Reinhardt wanted to collaborate with Werfel again later, but Werfel was not interested. Clark concludes that the experiment of harnessing his talents and tailoring his writing to produce a performance rather than a work of literature was not one he was prepared to repeat (219-21).

Recently, Wagener (1993) takes a fresh look at the play. He points out that its value lies in its skillful interweaving of Old Testament events with events in the synagogue to express the concerns and fears of Jews about their persecution in modern times. In his view, the characters are timeless incorporations of typical ways that Jews have reacted to persecution through the ages. Although Weill, Reinhardt, and Weisgal all intended to draw attention to the plight of the Jews in Hitler's Germany, Wagener argues that it is to Werfel's credit that he resisted setting the action in Nazi Germany and instead set it in an unnamed kingdom that represents modern times in general. Through this choice, the elements of history and timelessness became part of the representative frame. Wagener also remarks that, with its epically presented Old Testament material, the play belongs in the series of large-scale film productions of biblical themes of the 1930s and 1940s rather than on the stage (61).

*In einer Nacht* (1937), Werfel's next play, premiered at the Theater in der Josefstadt in Vienna on 5 October 1937 and was the last work to be directed by Reinhardt before his exile. It aroused very little critical interest. Willibrand (1945a) discusses it from a religious point of view. Lea (1968) sees in the play a continuation of Werfel's analysis of the failure of political activism, and Wimmer (1973), who mostly summarizes the plot, believes that the play deals with a vision of limitless love (176). For Wagener (1993), the core of the play is the concept of predestination. Like Wimmer, he stresses the power of love with its ability to conquer even death. In his opinion, Werfel depicts death in the play as "a secret, mystical fulfillment—the zenith of life" (62).

Werfel's next and last play, *Jacobowsky und der Oberst* (1944), did not suffer from the critical neglect that was the fate of *In einer Nacht*. The English version, *Jacobowsky and the Colonel*, premiered on 14 March 1944, at the Martin Beck Theater in New York. After the war, it was regularly performed in Germany and Austria and was popular at the Vienna Festival of 1983 (Steiman 1989, 310). Of all Werfel's plays, this one aroused the most critical interest, partly because of its successful dramatic qualities and its humor—the latter was appreciated all the more because of its rarity in the German dramatic tradition—and partly because of the growing critical interest in German exile literature.

The success of the play in S. N. Behrman's adaptation, a version with which Werfel was highly dissatisfied, is well documented. It was the most successful exile play and received the New York Drama Critics Award for the best foreign play of the 1943-44 season. Through this production, which had 417 performances (111 of them on Broadway alone), Werfel gained the reputation of being the most successful German exile dramatist (Brown 1989, 1601). It was the only play by an exile dramatist to be given respectful and full professional treatment (Ritchie 1989, 200). A film version, *Me and the Colonel*, was produced in 1958, starring Danny Kaye as Jacobowsky and Curt Jürgens as the Colonel. Ritchie points out the many transformations that the play went through. It appeared, for example, as an opera by Giselher Klebe, which was a sensation in 1965; and a Broadway musical, *The Grand Tour*, was based on the play. Ritchie writes that it went from farce to fairy tale, comedy to tragedy; from Behrman's Broadway hit to a film, a book based on the film, an opera, and a musical (203).

This success was all the more remarkable since it was extremely difficult for exile writers to have their plays performed, as several critics pointed out, and they explored the reasons for Werfel's popular success. In a 1951 article Werfel's translator, Gustave O. Arlt, suggests that, although the subject of the play was European, there was evidence that it was written with an eye to the American stage. For example, he notes, the sentence structure in the original was so simple, so un-German, that it practically translated itself (4). In articles in 1982 and 1989, Brown points out the immense difficulties that exile writers confronted in having their plays performed. European dramatists, for instance, lacked knowledge of American theatrical conventions and the different audience. Brown investigates why Werfel managed to be successful. One important reason, in his view, was that the stimulus for the play came from others who were familiar with the theatrical possibilities of the material for the American public and who also knew the American audience and its expectations. As he points out, most exile dramas were imported from Europe and did not appeal either thematically or stylistically to American taste. In response to advice on this issue, Werfel made his play accessible to a wider audience. Brown argues that Werfel intended to write a comedy for Broadway, and with the plot and characters he was successful (1982, 71). Another factor in the play's success, in his opinion, was Werfel's cosmic view of history and the role of the individual, which gave his drama a universality that transcended the topicality of most exile plays that limited their interest for an American audience. Werfel's religious views gave his work universality, and its optimism appealed to the American spirit of the times (1982, 72). Brown argues too that Werfel knew from Austrian theater the importance of the stress on magic, and his use of magic and magical effects tied in well to American show business. Unlike most exile writers, Werfel also had the advantage of being a well-known writer in the United States. *Jacobowsky* was performed because Werfel had already attracted the public's attention as a novelist and a dramatist (Brown 1989, 1603-4). Although, like Brown, Ritchie (1989) stresses that Werfel wrote with an eye to the Broadway stage, he denies emphatically that Werfel was doing something cheap for box-office success (197).

Another aspect of the play that aroused lively critical attention was S. N. Behrman's adaptation. The original adapter was Clifford Odets, but the Theater Guild thought the play needed more reworking and chose Behrman for this task. As several critics point out, Werfel was extremely disturbed by Behrman's adaptation. He protested that Behrman's changes had distorted the meaning of his play and was afraid they would damage its chance of success (Brown 1989, 1600). Many critics bitterly complained that Behrman had ruined the play. Wächter (1973) criticizes the Behrman adaptation for damaging its deeper layers by stressing coarse and melodramatic high points. He argues that Behrman eliminated much of the serious and tragic nature of the play and emphasized instead its comic and burlesque aspects at the expense of the symbolic figures and the allegorical elements (185). Krispyn (1982) remarks that Werfel was particularly upset that the scene between the Eternal Jew and St. Francis was cut, because, as Klarmann (1945) had argued, it contains the main message of the drama (225). Krispyn shows how throughout the play Behrman cut surrealistic elements, realizing that the American public would not appreciate them. More recent critics such as Ritchie (1989), however, credit Behrman with making the play a success. Ritchie defends Behrman as the best in the business, a recognized master of polished stage comedy, and an expert on treating serious matters with gentle humor. He was an ideal choice to adapt the play; he turned Werfel's European comedy into an American hit. Ritchie claims that Behrman did not falsify, simplify, and sentimentalize a German masterpiece and argues that nearly everything Werfel wanted to say, except for the scene with St. Francis and the Wandering Jew, is retained in Behrman's adaptation (198). Brown (1982, 1989) notes that Behrman tried to adapt the play for American public taste, which demanded a quickly unfolding and easily understandable sequence of scenes. To do this, he simplified the psychological and symbolic nuances and cut or revised several minor figures and scenes in order to eliminate references that would be incomprehensible to an American audience and to make the plot tighter (Brown 1989, 1599-1600). Recently, Nehring (1992) concludes that in some respects Behrman improved the play, but in others he made it worse. His main improvement was to make the plot more plausible, but in several ways he damaged the original. Nehring argues that Behrman made the play one-dimensional and deleted its symbolic and miraculous aspect. In addition, Nehring believes, he coarsened Werfel's subtle love story into a sentimental-rational hybrid. Another aspect of the play that Behrman weakened, according to Nehring, was Werfel's sharp criticism of the indifference of other countries to the plight of the Jews and the danger of the Nazis (116-18).

Most critics agreed in their assessment of the figure of Jacobowsky. Willibrand (1945a) calls him a superior character and an aristocrat of the spirit whose resourcefulness, unfailing sense of humor, and clearness of perception are the life of the play. He sees Jacobowsky as an optimist who has a will to live because he believes in God and in the values that spring from this belief. Willibrand remarks that, because Jacobowsky has no bourgeois attachment to personal belongings, his heart and mind are free for spiritual activity (156-57). Fox (1964) calls Jacobowsky the truly tragicomic figure of the piece (114). Reich-Ranicki (1965) sees in Jacobowsky's futile search and longing for peace, and in his lack of belonging, a portrait of Werfel himself (233-34). Wagener (1985-86) views Jacobowsky as a modern picaro. Like the Spanish picaro, he points out, Jacobowsky is concerned not with social position or wealth but only with survival in a hostile world. Wagener does not argue that Werfel consciously drew on the picaresque tradition, although these elements are evident, particularly in the way in which Jacobowsky is forced to rely on his resourcefulness and his natural wits (73-75). In his 1993 monograph, Wagener again points out that the relationship between Stjerbinsky, with his hollow concept of honor, and Jacobowsky, who travels on his wits and who is an expert in surviving against the odds, may have been influenced by the relationship of Don Quixote and Sancho Panza. In various dangerous situations Jacobowsky succeeds time and again, and, like the picaro, he never gives up (63-64).

As usual, the religious aspects of the play aroused a great deal of interest, particularly among the earlier critics. Klarmann (1945) believes that in this play Werfel's basic philosophy and eschatology have not changed fundamentally from his earlier works but merely deepened. Although the surface of the play deals with the fall of France, Klarmann argues that the play is allegorical since in all his works Werfel tried to state a metaphysical truth (201). In this article, Klarmann traces the play's allegorical elements through the symbolism of names that, in his view, sheds light on the hidden allegorical meaning. Klarmann observes that the name Jacobowsky suggests the son of Jacob, the son of Israel, whose eschatological mission is to act as the agnus. One aspect of the Colonel's name associates him with the first Christian King of Poland, who propagated Christianity. Marianne has several meanings: she is the Eternal France; she is Mara from *Die Mittagsgöttin*, the person who is instinctively close to God and the conceptive vessel of the divine spirit; she is Mary, the mother of Christ; and finally she is Anna, the mother of Mary, who symbolizes earthly, motherly love and the church (206-8). These names reinforce for Klarmann his interpretation of the play as a drama of salvation. He also stresses the importance of the scene with the Wandering Jew and St. Francis, one major significance of which, he argues, is the symbolic presentation of the two-thousand-year-old passion of redemption (208). According to his thesis, the metaphysical plot of the play depicts the road that leads to the final suspension of antagonism between Israel and other nations, without which, in Werfel's view, there can be no return to God (203). In a later article Klarmann (1959) calls *Jacobowsky* the most successful mystery play of the present, in which the cosmic tragedy of the mission of the Christian and the Jew is revealed (101). Willibrand (1945a) also stresses the religious aspects of the play. In his view, life becomes meaningful to the Colonel and Marianne only when they begin to practice the Christian virtues taken for granted by Jacobowsky. Although he concedes that scant space is devoted to religion in this work and thus it could be read as sociology or secular morality, Willibrand argues that Werfel scorned the idea of morality without metaphysical meaning (157). Siemsen (1945) emphasizes the Jewish element in the play and argues that Werfel finds himself here back to his old Jewish world after a long wandering and says yes to his Jewishness, his Jewish fate, and the future of his people (162). Brown (1982, 1989) notes that Werfel wanted to write a religious allegory of divine salvation that only by chance played in the present (1982, 71). Steiman (1989) also points out that the play is an allegory on the Last Judgment and Werfel's vision of the Jews as witnesses for Christ. In his opinion, Werfel's belief in the interdependence of Judaism and Christianity is illustrated by the Jewish businessman and the Polish aristocrat who contribute to each other's salvation, not by forswearing their respective Jewishness and anti-Semitism, but by being themselves (310).

Some critics protested, however, that the religious dimension had been overstressed (Reffet 1989c, 110). Davidheiser (1982), for example, notes that although Klarmann saw the play as a religious quest, its national and cultural elements are even stronger. In his view, Jacobowsky's amazing openness to new horizons and new lands and his acceptance of his fate as a refugee are far removed from the characteristics of nationalism that Davidheiser sees in *Verdi*. He argues that Jacobowsky is the culmination of the process of transcending national ties that had begun in *Musa Dagh*. Jacobowsky is a whimsical cosmopolitan who is forced to seek identity independent of national boundaries. Davidheiser believes that Jacobowsky's cosmopolitanism is Werfel's solution to the painful search in his works for cultural and national identity (63-65).

Another central theme, that of exile, aroused attention from the start. Early on, Willibrand (1945a) observes that the play is filled with Werfel's own reactions to the fall of France. In his view, Werfel suggests the causes of the nation's downfall and stresses the need for spiritual values that can bring about renewal. Willibrand sees in the play Werfel's belief that intellectualism is one of the causes of the decay and tragedy (154). Wimmer (1973) remarks that *Jacobowsky* is in part a topical drama but points out that Werfel believed Hitler was only another word for the evil of the world. In the play, both Jacobowsky and the Colonel become symbolic figures of European culture fleeing from the Nazis, the machine people (171).

Krispyn's (1978) main interest is in how the style of the play is representative of that of exile writers as a whole. He shows that the play wavers stylistically between tragedy and broad farce, between the obvious and the grotesque, between stark realism and dreamlike vision. According to him, this sudden alternation of realism and strong surrealistic elements is almost a structural characteristic of exile writing, and he attributes it to the impact of the exile experience on the writer's mind. According to his thesis, the exiled authors' personal feelings were so deeply involved that they lacked sufficient distance from their subject matter to impose a consistent artistic form on it. Their memories were so vivid and painful that the realism of the scenes they described overwhelmed their powers of literary composition (140-42). In a later article, Krispyn (1982) develops this argument. Werfel's overwhelming painful memories of his flight through France, in such striking contrast to the middle-class life he had lived before, lamed his powers of composition and led to the resulting mixture of realism and surrealism in the play (228). Krispyn believes, however, that this mixed style is already evident in Werfel's work prior to his exile, although his exile experience intensified it (229).

Koopmann (1983) approaches the play from a similar interest in the exile experience. He calls the play a victory of the intellect over a hopeless situation. If we laugh about the tragic, he argues, then we can raise ourselves above it. It is a small triumph of the spirit, an act of liberation. Werfel's drama demonstrates that a tragedy can be changed into a comedy. Koopmann points out that Werfel was criticized for making light of the Nazi regime and overestimating the ease of outwitting it. He denies that Werfel downplays the threat of the Nazis since, although the play is a comedy, the humor of the scenes decreases as the horror and the hopelessness of escape increase. In his view, Werfel vividly describes the fear of the refugees and its impact on the characters. The Colonel, for example, the boastful *miles gloriosus*, changes into a fearful refugee. The drama shows among other things how a military hero becomes a failed defeatist, a demoralized and nervous antihero. Koopmann perceptively argues that the essence of the comedy is the overcoming of fear and all dangers not through fortune or violence but through speaking. He stresses that this comedy of a tragedy is above all a comedy of language, for, although Werfel shows the growing powerlessness of physical resistance, he also shows the power of the word—particularly in the case of Jacobowsky, through whom this victory of language is expressed most strongly. Words win over force, the improvised speech over the organized manhunt. Koopmann observes that the play demonstrates not only the victory of reason and language but also the triumph of the emigrant over the persecuting powers, or rather the emigrant's wish-dream of such a victory. Which emigrant would not have enjoyed the victory of his words over brutality, Koopmann remarks, since the language was all that the exile now possessed (260-67).

Although most critics were interested in the ideas of the play, some briefly commented on its aesthetic qualities. Klarmann (1945) notes that Werfel could be relied upon to tell a story well and with a natural sense of drama (201). In a 1959 article Klarmann praises the play for its suprarealistic and allegorical qualities (101). Guthke (1961) thinks it is comparable in its tragicomic qualities to Chekhov's *Cherry Orchard* (372). Fox (1964) particularly admires the comic elements (114), and Reich-Ranicki (1965) believes that

Werfel created a work with wit, humor, charm, jokes, and cheerful bons mots (233). Wimmer (1973) finds the play appealing because it reveals that Werfel, himself in bitter pain, has not forgotten how to smile. He considers the play important because it shows how conflicts caused by origin and education disappear in the face of danger (171). Davidheiser (1982) concludes that Werfel's injection of humor into the potentially tragic plot is a real achievement (64). Reffet (1989c), who points out that Jacobowsky is the only figure in Werfel's plays who is intrinsically comic (100), argues that the comedy in the play is created through naiveté—for example, through the untragic figures who obstinately ignore the danger of their situation (104).

In a recent article, Nehring (1992) argues for a fuller appreciation of the play. He points out that literary critics often complain that there are few comedies in the German language. In Nehring's opinion, the canon of German comedies needs to be revised. He believes that if this is done *Jacobowsky* will appear as an important part of the comic canon. In the first part of his discussion, Nehring deals with frequent objections that critics raised about the play. Some accused Werfel of being frivolous because they thought the fall of France and the flight of the persecuted were not appropriate topics for a comedy. Nehring argues that the audience's enjoyment comes not from the fall of France but instead from sympathy with the refugees. He points out that Werfel does not laugh away the Nazi terror but rather shows that it is always present as a terrible threat. The play is tragic, but the figures add a comic dimension. Nehring believes, in fact, that Werfel's notion of comedy here resembles that of Dürrenmatt. Critics also accused Werfel of misrepresenting history and downplaying the Nazi reality, and they asked how a Jew and a Pole could triumph over this terror. Nehring points out that Werfel himself managed to escape from France. In his view, Werfel was not prepared to give immorality limitless power over the individual. For this reason, the spirit of the play is optimistic; Werfel stresses the courage of the individual. The central values of the play, in his estimation, are humanity, even in inhumane circumstances, and optimism in despairing situations. Nehring argues strongly that Werfel did not minimize the historical situation.

After he discusses the genesis of the play and the problems with the adaptation, Nehring turns his attention to an analysis of the characters, particularly Jacobowsky. In his view, Jacobowsky is not only an individual but also a representative of the Jew who is forever looking for a home and friends and who is forced to flee. Nehring addresses the criticism voiced by some that Jacobowsky's personality conforms to anti-Semitic stereotypes. He argues that since Werfel wanted to create a sympathetic picture of a Jew, he could not have chosen a figure that differed from widely held stereotypes of Jews; such a figure would be easy to ignore as an exception. Nehring believes that it was more effective to give Jacobowsky "typical" characteristics and then show them from a positive side. The fact that some of Jacobowsky's traits correspond to anti-

Semitic views, he remarks, speaks not against Jacobowsky or his traits but against anti-Semitic prejudices (111-26).

Although interest in Werfel's dramas has become more lively in recent years, and there has been a greater appreciation not only of his religious and philosophical ideas and his views of history but also of his theatrical techniques, not many critics have attempted either to assess Werfel's dramas as a whole or to evaluate his contribution to European dramatic literature. Klarmann (1959) believes that Werfel's drama is theological drama like that of the Spanish dramatists of the Golden century whom he so much admired. For him, Werfel belongs to the tradition of such dramatists as Grillparzer and Hofmannsthal. Like the characters created by these dramatists, Werfel's undergo a probationary period of testing under the omnipresent eye of God. Klarmann's articles are especially helpful in pointing out Werfel's closeness to his theatrical tradition. Like the Spaniards, and like Grillparzer and Raimund, Werfel knew that the lifeblood of the theater is entertainment and spectacle (99). Klarmann discusses Werfel's baroque-Austrian joy of theater, and he points out the magic, enchantment, tricks, illusions, overpowering thrills, and excitement that characterize all of his dramas. He stresses that music permeates the innermost structure of Werfel's plays (102). Klarmann also believes that although Werfel differed from Brecht, he nevertheless anticipated the realism of the epic theater without, however, its paralyzing ideology (100). In many of Werfel's plays, Klarmann notices a suprarealism that he defines as a kind of realism in which reality is crystalline. From early on, he remarks, Werfel was concerned in his plays with needling his audience out of their emotional sluggishness and complacency—another parallel, in his view, to the epic theater of Brecht (98).

Like Klarmann, Fox (1964) stresses Werfel's baroque heritage and his close connection to the Austrian theatrical tradition, demonstrated by his use of spectacle, his notion of entertainment in its broadest theatrical sense, and his intermingling of operatic and pantomime effects. In contrast to expressionist plays, Fox writes, Werfel is concerned with the inner conflict of his protagonists, not so much with the tragic outward clash of society and the individual who claims to be its judge or savior. Werfel continually presents realistically conceived plots and characters in a framework designed to reveal their metaphysical import (113). Fox thus closely follows Klarmann's views. In the preface to Wimmer (1973), Kurt Becsi, the editor of *Profile*, a biographical series about Austrian dramatists, calls Werfel one of the most visionary, most prophetic representatives of Austrian poets and dramatists (7). He chose Werfel to open the series, an indication of the high regard he held for him. Wimmer himself stresses the religious and metaphysical aspects of the dramas, as his title, *Franz Werfels dramatische Sendung*, suggests.

Reffet (1989c) notes that Werfel's significant and coherent dramatic production of the 1920s is largely unknown today. This neglect, he believes, is surprising since in this period Werfel anticipated several political areas that later became central to the well-known French theater. For example, many comments from Werfel's plays about the problematic nature of state power, even when this power is the outcome of a revolution, are, according to Reffet, equal to the insights of Anouilh, Camus, Malraux, Montherlant, or Sartre (93). Warren (1989) believes that Werfel's three historical plays are important contributions to mainstream Austrian drama of the twentieth century. In his view, *Juarez und Maximilian* occupies a more than honorable place among those plays that chronicle the fortunes of the Austrian imperial family, and he notes with approval that it lacks the sentimentality and the flag-waving associated with many productions of this genre. He groups *Paulus unter den Juden* among plays on Jewish themes by Beer-Hofmann, Stefan Zweig, and Rudolf Henz. *Das Reich Gottes in Böhmen* continues, in his view, in the tradition of the Austrian *Staatsdrama* but succumbs to the pessimism of the 1930s. He argues that these three dramas reflect the theatricality of the interwar years, when there was a revival of the theater that owed much to Reinhardt, and as such they deserve to be reread or even staged. For those whose interest lies in an understanding of the spiritual as well as the political concerns of the interwar years, he observes, they are key documents because they reflect the fascination with the problems of political leadership, the Christian response to revolution and violence, and a prophetic awareness of the depths to which mankind would sink. Above all, he concludes, they are striking testimony of Werfel's multifaceted genius and of an idealism that was never entirely destroyed by a hostile world (172).

Recently, Abels (1992) and Reffet (1992) look at Werfel's dramatic oeuvre as a whole. In an expanded version of the sections on drama in his Werfel biography (1990), Abels surveys the history and the main themes of Werfel's plays. Reffet rearticulates and develops the arguments he expressed in his earlier article (1989c). He is critical of previous research on Werfel's dramas since, in his view, it has consisted mostly of analyses of individual plays and has not tried to show the unity of his dramatic production. If connections were made, they were made for the most part between the content of the plays and that of Werfel's other genres. Reffet argues that love and politics, themes that are not central in his estimation to Werfel's poetry and prose, are central in the plays. In the early plays, love predominates, but the six plays that Werfel wrote in the 1920s are closely unified by their perceptive analysis of politics. Reffet believes that with some scenic and theatrical revision these plays would become real tragedies of the modern period because Werfel demonstrates in them in a modern and brilliant way the connection between tragedy and politics. In his view, Werfel's dramas are the equals of his poetry and novels (19-37).

Although some critics believed that Werfel's plays were a significant contribution to dramatic literature, others were more negative. Steiman (1985), for example, argues that what weakens the impact of Werfel's dramas is an almost pathetic awareness that there can be no compromise between religious hope and political reality, and he complains that Werfel's weak heroes topple too easily. Recently, Nehring (1992) observes aptly that some of Werfel's dramas are justifiably forgotten. Especially in his early dramas, he points out, Werfel did not analyze the themes sufficiently or give the problems clear form (111).

Although criticism of Werfel's dramas has been useful in throwing light on Werfel the thinker, only recently has Werfel the dramatist aroused attention. With the exception of Wimmer (1973), there has been no attempt to give a comprehensive and thorough analysis of Werfel's development as a dramatist from his neglected early dramas and dramatic sketches to his last play, *Jacobowsky und der Oberst*. Wimmer's study is outdated, and much of it relies on plot summary and contains a lot of discussion of Werfel's life. There is need for a new and comprehensive study of Werfel's dramas, which should include Werfel's entire dramatic oeuvre as well as his theoretical statements about drama in his essays. Such a study should investigate more thoroughly the dramatic tradition that shaped Werfel's writing and should attempt to answer the question, raised by Foltin and Klarmann, of his anticipation of epic theater. Above all, it should seek a balance between Werfel's philosophical, political, and aesthetic concerns. Most earlier studies were simply too one-sided in their focus on Werfel's ideas. A new study of Werfel's dramas could address what until recently has been an unjustly neglected area of Werfel's literary production. Huber's collection (1989a), with four out of the thirteen articles devoted to an analysis of Werfel's dramas, and recent articles by Abels (1992) and Reffet (1992) are perhaps an indication that critical interest in Werfel's dramas and his contribution to the German-language dramatic tradition will grow.

# 4: Franz Werfel's Prose

WERFEL WAS NOT only a respected novelist but also a very successful and popular one in German-speaking countries, in other European countries, and especially in the United States. Of all the genres in which he wrote, his novels aroused the most popular and critical interest. During his lifetime, they were widely reviewed, but interest in them waned after his death. More recently there has been renewed critical appreciation of his novels. Steiman (1985), for example, focuses primarily on them, and in the 1992 collection of essays that Wolfgang Nehring and Hans Wagener edited, four of the eleven articles are devoted to his novels. As with Werfel's dramas and lyric poetry, many critics have been most interested in the philosophical and religious views that they discern in the novels and less concerned with them as creative works. Little attention has been given to such literary concerns as Werfel's narrative techniques and his storytelling skills or to the structure and imagery in his novels.

The sketches and other short prose pieces that Werfel wrote early in his career aroused little critical attention, even though they can provide valuable insights into the development of Werfel's prose style, as a recent article by Beck (1992) points out. Brunner (1955) remarks that these early prose pieces give little indication that Werfel would become a famous novelist (9), but he notes that they are valuable because of their freshness and directness (10). An exception to this general neglect is "Cabrinowitsch" (1915), collected in *Das Franz Werfel Buch* (1986). Werfel wrote this piece shortly after he had seen Cabrinovic, one of the assassins of Sarajevo, briefly at the garrison hospital in Prague in November 1915. Politzer (1949) finds this work significant because he detects in it Werfel's intellectual debt to Austrian journalism as well as many characteristics of Werfel's later prose style. From the tradition of Austrian journalism, Politzer argues, Werfel adopted such aspects as the brilliant inspiration, the bon mot, and the fusion of psychology and musicality. But he also took such weaknesses as a flatness of perspective and a tendency to digress, to want to make the point for the sake of the point, and to be prolix. This sketch indicates, Politzer believes, Werfel's lack of interest in order and discipline, a complaint that critics frequently voiced about many of his works. Politzer points out that this early sketch already shows Werfel's sharp realism, his love and sympathy, his pathos, and his stylistic bravura. Also evident here is the sudden plunge from reality into the depths of mystery that is characteristic of Werfel's prose technique in his later works (284-85). Later critics were most interested in Werfel's portrayal of the assassin. Although they differed in their interpretations, they agreed that Werfel portrays him positively. According to

Politzer (1974), Werfel makes the assassin into a Russian Christ figure (26). Reffet (1986) argues that Werfel's depiction of the assassin as a martyr reflects his political conviction at the time that the monarchy and the aristocracy should be overthrown (353), while Jungk (1987) stresses that, rather than depicting Cabrinovic as a fiendish murderer, Werfel makes him a dignified hero, an instrument of God (44).

Werfel's first major prose work, *Nicht der Mörder, der Ermordete ist schuldig* (1920), did not arouse much critical attention, and the attention it did receive was mixed. Several of the early reviewers tended either to see the work as autobiography or, like Storfer (1931), to focus on what they saw as its psycho-analytical aspects, especially its close reliance on Freud. Specht (1926) and Jacobson (1927) typify some of the early critical responses to the work. Specht, who argues that the strength of the work lies in its vivid portrayal of characters and Werfel's ability to lay bare the dark areas of the soul (234), disagrees strongly with those reviewers who thought that the work was autobiographical. According to him, it reflects neither Werfel's nor his father's experience. Specht is concerned, as always, with stressing the originality of Werfel's works; this is why he strongly denies any autobiographical element. In contrast, Jacobson notices a close affinity to Russian writers, a characteristic that later critics also observe, and she stresses how the conflict between the generations, a theme evident in Werfel's early poetry, is further developed here. In her estimation, however, the work is not very valuable (344).

Later critics tended to focus on the way Werfel depicts the father-son relationship in the work. Puttkamer (1952) thinks the father-son conflict is central to it. Like Jacobson, she points out that this theme is also important in much of Werfel's early lyric poetry, but she believes that it was strengthened by his getting to know during the First World War the patriarchal principle of power in its crassest form, namely that of political, military authority. In the general in the novella, she observes, there is a merging of physical fatherhood and military and political authority. Puttkamer does not, however, argue that the work is only a critique of patriarchal authority. She also points out the meta-physical nature of the father-son relationship. According to her, Karl both fears and loves his father like a god. Because of this, Karl's hatred, although it is psychologically understandable, is sacrilege, the reason for his morbid sense of guilt. She also suggests that, when Werfel conceived the novella, he may have been thinking of the murder in Sarajevo, in which the bullet reached its mark but did not bring about freedom (17-18). Bach (1957) argues that the novella focuses on the problems of bourgeois society before the First World War, especially its military nature. Like Puttkamer, she sees in the conflict between father and son a metaphysical tension, but she also believes that the conflict represents the struggle between the spiritually fine person and the brutal demands of a mechanistic and therefore soulless state (191). Brunner (1955) also stresses the father-son problem, but, in his view, Werfel does not present it as a generational problem as in expressionism. According to his thesis, the father in the novella is, above all, a symbol of brutality, irrationality, and lack of love. He believes that the hostility to the father suggests Werfel's strong skepticism about the male in general. This hostility could, he suggests, have influenced Werfel's turn from Judaism to Catholicism. Brunner also argues that the novella contains a sharp critique of militarism as well as auto-biographical elements. The identity between the author and his hero, he remarks, is obvious (19-20).

Fox (1957) was the first to devote an entire article to this work, and he, too, focuses on the father-son conflict. Although many works written at the same time as Werfel's deal with this conflict, he argues, Werfel's work differs from them in the ambiguity with which he approaches the problem. For Fox, the work exemplifies the violent hatred that results from the clash of different generations (25). Fox is critical of Werfel for his choice of the first-person narrative because it makes the work too one-sided and subjective. According to him, this restriction to one point of view prevents a clear understanding of both sides. Unlike most critics, who viewed Karl Duschek as a sympathetic figure, Fox is highly critical of him. In his letter to the public prosecutor, Karl accuses his father of egoism and megalomania; this charge, Fox writes, could apply equally well to the son himself. Here it is not the father but the son who seeks power (30). Fox believes that Werfel intended to stress the son's guilt. The epilogue, for example, leads the reader to interpret the text not only as a case for the son, as most critics argued, but also as a case history of festering self-pity in which there is grotesque exaggeration and distortion (32). Fox thus differs from other critics at the time in his far more sympathetic analysis of the role of the father and his far more negative interpretation of the son.

After this brief renewal of interest in the novella in the 1950s, little atten-tion was paid to it except for such basic plot summaries as are characteristic of the work of Zahn (1966) and others. In an important article in 1965, however, Lea draws attention to the work for the light it sheds on Werfel's political thinking, and he points out that it reveals Werfel's sharp rejection of his earlier political activism. In this work, he argues, the prodigal son theme, one that appears in several of Werfel's works, is central. According to Lea, the prodigal sons in Werfel's works suffer, like Karl, from a kind of messianic complex; they want to remake the world in their own image. Werfel shows here that, although the revolutionary appears to act out of good motives, these disguise vanity and self-aggrandizement. The revolutionary, in fact, merely wants to replace one tyranny with another (42). This is a negative assessment of revolu-tionary activity that Werfel underscores in his novella through his depictions of the inferno-like atmosphere of the anarchists' meetings. Lea argues that Karl joins the anarchists to protest against the world of the fathers, who represent the autocratic power and hierarchic order of the army with its glorification of military discipline for its own sake and its disregard of the individual. Yet, although Karl's revolutionary activity is directed against the authority of his father, it also shows, according to Lea, his alienation from himself. Despite Karl's honorable intentions in joining the anarchists, Lea argues, it is his ego rather than mankind that benefits. Only when he liberates himself from anarchy can Karl put the sickness of his youth behind and begin a new life (44).

After Lea's article, little attention was paid to the novella. Two critics in the 1970s approached it from different perspectives. Derré (1974) analyzes both the father-son problem and Werfel's depiction of military education. Her article is useful for the close parallels she points out between Werfel's novella and Joseph Roth's *Radetzkymarsch*, but it is even more valuable for its discussion of Werfel's narrative technique and his use of caricature, an aspect of Werfel criticism that is usually neglected. Derré believes the poetic originality of the work lies in Werfel's ability to intensify daily events and turn them into unforgettable experiences, a technique that owes much to his use of caricature (60-61). Like some of the earlier reviewers, Reffet (1977), who considers this work the high point of Werfel's early narrative, takes a psychoanalytic approach to the novella, one that is not very common in Werfel criticism. He focuses on the work as an example of the Oedipus complex and argues that the reason for Karl's revolt is the inherent antagonism between father and son. According to Reffet, Freud's influence is so obvious that it is clear that Werfel read *Totem und Taboo* before he wrote the work (81).

Later critics mentioned the work only in passing. Jungk (1987), however, calls attention to its philosophical underpinnings. He argues that Werfel derives some of his views from the anarchist Otto Gross, whose attacks on the patriarchal world are combined here with Werfel's own experiences with his father. Jungk also sees in the work traces of Buber's critique of militarism and Werfel's former sympathy for the Czech irredentist movement. Unlike Lea, he fails to see that Werfel portrays the politics of the anarchists not positively but negatively. Like Jacobson earlier, Jungk notices the Slavic influence on the work, particularly that of Dostoyevsky's *The Brothers Karamazov* and Turgenev's *Father and Sons*, proof for him that Werfel was still very insecure as a stylist and still greatly dependent on literary models (77). The Marxist critic Metzler (1988) calls it a key work. In his view, it is Werfel's first significant prose work and an important stylistic turning point because it is here that Werfel begins to mix the expressionistic style of pathos with analytical realism. From his Marxist perspective, Metzler is particularly interested in the analysis of pre-First World War society, which he terms a dehumanized military one that the father represents (326).

Recently, Abels (1990) remarks, echoing some of the earlier reviewers, that in its narrative concentration the novella can be considered the first real high point of Werfel's prose (57). Wagener (1993) points out that the father-son theme links the novella to the expressionist theme of the conflict between the generations and to the problem of authority in general. Like Lea, Wagener is interested in what the novella reveals about Werfel's politics at the time the piece was written, and he argues that Werfel's depiction of the anarchists makes clear that he does not subscribe to their way of thinking. In fact, Werfel warns against such revolutionary activity. Wagener points out other close thematic and stylistic ties to expressionism. One such example is the expressionist vision of the new man that concludes the novella, the idea that human salvation and atonement can come only from a return to a simple way of life. Wagener stresses also that Werfel's later ideas of inwardness versus nihilism or realism are already evident in this work, but in expressionist guise (75-77).

Much to his surprise, Werfel's first major novel, *Verdi, Roman der Oper* (1924), became a best-seller. The first printing of 20,000 copies sold out quickly, and the second edition followed immediately. As Jungk (1987) points out, the novel was a turning point in Werfel's career since, despite its unevenness and its "purple prose," it was the first clear demonstration of his talent as a novelist (99). Werfel had long been an enthusiastic admirer of Verdi and his music. In addition to his novel, for which he carefully researched Verdi's life, he revised, translated, and adapted three of Verdi's operas (*La Forza del destino*, *Simone Boccanegra*, and *Don Carlos*) and edited a volume of Verdi's letters for which he wrote the introduction. Some credit Werfel, in fact, with sparking the renewal of interest in Verdi in German-speaking countries in the 1920s and 1930s (Klarmann 1961, Polzer 1961).

Like the response to Werfel's other works, critical reaction to *Verdi* differed enormously. Specht (1926), as usual, is enthusiastic about the novel. He agrees with others that the apparent theme is the torment of the artist in an unproductive period of his life, but he argues that the main theme is really music. For him, the music here is baroque art; it is ambiguity, earthly and divine message, sensual joy, and religious anchorage (262). Specht was one of the first to point out the significance of music both in Werfel's life and as the structure and content of his works. Another aspect that Specht considers important is the theme of Franz Werfel himself. He believes that Werfel was, in many respects, similar to Verdi, particularly in his romantic joy in the senses, his delight in arias, and his love of exaggeration (263). In Specht's view, Werfel depicts Verdi in the novel as a mirror image and a confession. Specht also admires Werfel's vivid portrayal of Venice. In another early response, Jacobson (1927) praises the excellence of the novel, which, she argues, shows a development in Werfel's epic art. She focuses on how Werfel depicts the cultural clash between the North and the South, and she also points out that such themes in the novel as guilt, repentance, and salvation through love show a continuity between Werfel's early lyric poetry, his dramas, and his novels (345). Like Specht, Kohn-Bramstedt (1934) praises Werfel's depiction of Venice, which he compares to Thomas Mann's *Tod in Venedig*, as do several other critics, but he observes that Mann's North German temperament and style differ from Werfel's more southern and exuberant character. For him, the central idea in the novel is the tragedy of the aged artist whose inspiration has failed, and he believes that Werfel recreates the inner struggle of an artistic genius with the sympathetic intuition of a fellow artist. Unlike Specht, however, Kohn-Bramstedt is not enthusiastic about Werfel's focus on music. He complains that Werfel's excessive preoccupation with music theory and an irrelevant love affair detracts from the unity of composition (71-72).

With hindsight, several critics in the 1950s saw the novel as prophetic, as Werfel's warning about the rise of fascism. Like other critics, Puttkamer (1952) argues that in the antithesis between Wagner and Verdi Werfel lays bare the roots of fascism, and she points out the close connection between Hitler and the house of Wagner. Like earlier critics, Puttkamer praises Werfel's depiction of the spirit of the age in Venice. For her, the novel is significant for what it reveals about Werfel's development. Werfel's epic style now shows, in her view, evidence of the powerful realism that characterizes his later novels (68-74).

Brunner (1955) makes several perceptive comments about the novel. He argues that Werfel was attracted to Verdi not only because of his music but also because of the parallels between Verdi and himself. Like Verdi, Brunner points out, Werfel was something of an anachronism, despite his avant-garde early lyric poetry. In his narrative works, Werfel was old-fashioned, and his emotionalism and inwardness contrasted with the intellectuality and the nihilism of his age. Thus Werfel's preoccupation with Verdi was, according to Brunner, a coming to terms with himself (23). Unlike many of the early critics, Brunner was interested in the structure of the novel. In his view, it is not a novel but rather a novelistic story since Werfel compresses the crisis into a period of a few weeks (25). Brunner perceives the main plot as basically a long monologue broken by a baroque abundance of subplots. He argues, however, that most of the large number of characters have some connection to Verdi since they either serve as a foil or as a mirror (28). Brunner considers the work to have three major themes: Verdi, opera, and Venice. He also points out that Werfel's depiction of Verdi agrees generally with Verdi scholarship, but, in his view, Werfel's Verdi has a directness and vitality that are lacking in biographies of the composer (33).

Sokel (1959) was interested in the novel for its expressionist aspects and Werfel's depiction of the artist in crisis. In a perceptive analysis, he argues that *Verdi* is the great epic of Werfel's expressionist period but that it is also its critique and that it marks the end of his expressionist phase. According to his argument, Werfel analyzes and sums up here many of the fundamental problems of expressionism, particularly that of creativity, a problem that Werfel approaches by exploring its failure. In the novel, Werfel depicts the artist's agony when he senses his creative impotence. In his despair, Werfel's Verdi considers himself a fool who has exchanged his god-given life for baubles, for

vanity (134-35). During the course of the novel, Sokel argues, Verdi changes
from a machine of creativity into a simple human being. As this happens,
Verdi's creative powers are reawakened and his music becomes even greater
than before (151).

Except for descriptive plot summaries that are typical of Braselmann's
(1960) and Zahn's (1966) monographs, there was little critical interest in *Verdi*
in the 1960s. In the late 1970s, however, Gresch (1979) devoted an article to a
discussion of its themes and structure. In this article, he defends Werfel from
the criticism voiced by reviewers when the novel was translated into English
that Werfel had not depicted Verdi's life accurately and that the plot was
diffuse. Gresch argues that the structure of the work is tightly unified, and, like
Brunner, he shows that Werfel's depiction of Verdi corresponds to the portrait
of him by his biographers (30). He explores the reasons for Werfel's interest in
Verdi, some of the more superficial of which, he notes, include Werfel's
tendency to set novels in places he had visited and places he loved. Another
reason was Werfel's strong opposition to the growing fascist movement in
Italy. Gresch believes that Werfel saw Verdi, because of his political activities
on behalf of Italian national independence, as a strong advocate for freedom.
He argues, however, that the main reason Werfel was attracted to Verdi as a
biographical subject was that he saw in Verdi's character and in his political life
themes that were characteristic of German expressionism. Gresch sees the
theme of the artist in the novel as a variation on the expressionist theme of
brotherhood because only after his own spiritual regeneration can the artist
achieve a spiritual relationship with other people. Like Sokel, Gresch believes
that the main plot illustrates the artist's transformation. Unlike Sokel, however, Gresch does not view the novel as a critique of expressionism. Rather, he
argues that Werfel's Verdi embodies the expressionist ideal of the spiritually
regenerated person and his integration into the brotherhood of mankind.
Particularly useful in Gresch's article is his argument that the plot is tightly
unified. Although several critics have thought the subplots irrelevant to the
main plot, Gresch points out that the main theme of the regenerated individual is central not only to the main plot but also to the subplots, and he agrees
with Brunner that most of the characters in the subplots function as the
antithesis of the main theme and thereby serve to set the ideal character of
Verdi into bold relief (30-38).

Some interest in the novel revived in the 1980s. Davidheiser (1982) focuses
on an aspect of the novel that critics had not previously discussed. For him, the
search for cultural identity is central to the novel. He argues that it is understandable that Werfel created protagonists who struggle to attain a cultural
identity amidst opposing national forces since Werfel himself faced a similar
problem and was an émigré for part of his life (58). The novel also reflects the
growing nationalism in central Europe at that time (61). Davidheiser shows
that in the novel the composer Fischböck espouses a new objective form of

music that transcends nationalism, while Verdi is unable to go beyond a nationalistic approach. By having Verdi refer to Wagner as the German and himself as the Italian, Werfel further colors Verdi's inner struggle with national and cultural overtones (59).

Following a Marxist analysis, Metzler (1988) focuses on the relationship in the novel between the artist and the people. In contrast to the unity of art and the people that Verdi represents, Metzler stresses that in their elitism and snobbism Wagner and his disciples are totally divorced from the people (330). Although Metzler approves of the close connection he sees between Verdi and the Italian people, he criticizes Werfel for depicting a socially determined historical movement in moral and religious terms (330-31).

Recently, Furness (1989) looks at the role that Fischböck plays in the novel, a topic that has been neglected. Unlike Davidheiser, who thought Werfel viewed Fischböck positively because his music transcended nationalism, Furness argues convincingly that Fischböck represents for Werfel certain trends in twentieth-century culture, including aspects of expressionism, which he came to criticize and reject. At the outset, Furness analyzes Werfel's depiction of Wagner in the novel. He shows that Werfel saw Wagner as a paradigm of modernism and a representative of tendencies he found deplorable. For Werfel, Wagner represented the triumph of the ego. He saw him as a ruthless genius who imposed his will without compromise, regard, or consideration. In contrast, Werfel saw Verdi as a musician who never lost touch with common people, an argument that is similar to that of Metzler, without, however, Metzler's ideological thrust. Furness argues that, for Werfel, Verdi embodied sanity, humane normality, and genuine popularity. In contrast, he viewed Wagner as a twisted genius who, as heir to romantic subjectivity, created a self-centered oeuvre that exerted a narcotic influence. As Furness points out, Werfel deplored the self-deification of such artists as Wagner. Furness then turns to an analysis of Fischböck. In contrast to the narcotic effects of Wagner's music, Fischböck's compositions reflect the purity of polyphony, the rigors of fugal patterns, and the clean spare lines of Bach and Buxtehude, demonstrating a theory of music that reminds Furness of Thomas Mann's Adrian Leverkühn. Furness notes that Werfel rejects Fischböck's music of pure expression since only the composer can understand it. Through the figure of Fischböck, Furness believes, Werfel criticizes certain developments of his time, especially the excesses of abstract expressionism and its arrogant disregard for communication and comprehensibility, which he despised. Furness suggests that not only does Werfel reject the kind of art that Wagner and Fischböck represent, but he also questions the nature of art in general. As Furness sees it, Verdi's soul-searching implies that, for Werfel, all art contains a fatal flaw, namely the stigma of personal self-gratification (143-48).

Like Furness, Wagener (1993) is also interested in the kind of art that
Werfel advocates in the novel. Wagener agrees with earlier critics that Verdi is
a man of the people, a popular artist in the best sense whose music, in Werfel's
interpretation, is the pure expression of the spirit of the people (81-82). He
points out that Werfel was one of the few German writers at the time who was
able to resist the influence of Wagner's music. In the novel, German art as
personified by Wagner is not an art of the people but that of an individual who
creates in isolation (82). In Werfel's view, Wagner's music furthered the
development toward greater abstraction in art. Like Furness, Wagener argues
that Fischböck represents modern music that is based on abstract theory rather
than aesthetic pleasure. He is the modern artist who does not write for an
audience or for posterity but only for himself. Wagener perceptively observes
that Werfel's sharp rejection of modernity in *Verdi* anticipates themes he later
developed in his essays of the 1930s (83).

Among Werfel's short stories, only *Der Tod des Kleinbürgers* (1927) elicited
a significant amount of critical attention, although recently Wagener (1993)
gives a thorough introduction to the most important stories. Most critics who
discussed *Der Tod des Kleinbürgers* agreed that the work had strong literary
merits. Brunner (1955), for example, thinks that it is Werfel's most perfect
novella and one of the best works Werfel ever wrote. He praises Werfel for
observing here an unusual discipline and artistic self-control (45-46). Klarmann (1961) calls it perhaps Werfel's best novella and views it as depicting the
moving passion of a father who sacrifices himself for his mentally retarded son
(24-25). For Jungk (1987), it is a remarkable work of prose that will stand the
test of time for its compellingly candid portrait of a truncated Austria in the
post-First World War period (114), and Bahr (1991) believes that it should be
counted as part of the canon of modern prose. There, however, the agreement
ends.

Most of the early critics saw the protagonist, Fiala, as a heroic figure.
Brunnner (1955) stresses his heroic nature when he notes that Fiala's death
represents a victory of the spirit over the body (46). Bach (1957) thinks that
the noble motives of the dying man indicate the holiness of the human heart
(192); and Braselmann (1960), who calls Fiala's battle against death apocalyp-
tic, observes that Werfel has made a heroic poem out of the death of the petit
bourgeois (46). This theme of heroism forms Tober's (1965) central argument.
In this novella, according to him, Werfel protests strongly against a world
whose materialism and nihilism endanger people's freedom, a world that leaves
little room for religious faith. For him, Werfel's detailed and analytical depiction of Fiala's milieu is intended not to create a picture of misery but rather to
show the religious fulfillment of the new man (67). Because Werfel wants to
make art and literature instruments of religious faith, he creates persecuted and
suffering people who raise themselves out of pain and collapse (68). In Tober's
view, Werfel turns the story of a proletarian death, set in impoverished post-

First World War Vienna, into a story of salvation that suggests the martyrdom of man. Through a close analysis of Werfel's imagery in the novella, Tober argues that Werfel underscores his theme of salvation by interweaving motifs of darkness, light, and illness and through repetition and heightening.

Dolch (1972), however, strongly disputes this view of Fiala's heroic death and salvation. In fact, he is critical of Tober for his overemphasis on the religious and metaphysical concerns of the work and of Bach for her stress on the heroism of Fiala's struggle with death. Dolch argues instead that when Werfel wrote the novella he thought of Fiala as a typical representative of the petit bourgeois form of life that he detested (135). Werfel's original attitude to the story, he believes, was pleasure in the ironic brilliance with which he grotesquely depicts the petite bourgeoisie (140). Dolch traces how, in his view, the original meaning of the story became distorted through its English translation. One English title, *Death of a Poor Man*, suggests a sentimental tone that is lacking in the German title and downplays Werfel's critique of the philistine petit bourgeois world. Another English title, *The Man who Conquered Death*, emphasizes the heroism of the protagonist even more, a reading that is further underscored by deleting references to the oppressive petit bourgeois world in the translations. Dolch argues that the reinterpretation of the story was not just caused by the bad translations but that Werfel himself took an active role in its reinterpretation. When the novella was included in *Twilight of a World* (1937), Werfel stressed in his notes to the collection that Fiala was a hero and his death a superhuman deed. In Dolch's view, Werfel changed the strong critique of Austrian society in the original story to conform to the rosier picture of Austria that he paints in "An Essay upon the Meaning of Imperial Austria," which introduces the collection. Werfel's attempt to change the originally sharp social criticism of his stories in the collection to conform to his now idealized view of imperial Austria was something that reviewers at the time also noticed and criticized.

Recently, Bahr (1991) distances himself from virtually all the previous interpretations of the work. He disagrees with Jungk's (1987) view that the story can be adequately explained as a vivid portrait of a truncated Austria and with Dolch's reading that Werfel disliked the life of the petit bourgeois and argues that Werfel wanted to create an unsentimental rather than a critical portrait of this class. Bahr believes that it is a mistake to see Fiala, as Tober does, as a suffering savior. His approach is to place the work within the tradition of the theme of marriage in German literature. He acknowledges that the work reveals an antibourgeois tendency, but he believes that the Fialas' membership in the petite bourgeoisie softens Werfel's critical stance: as a petit bourgeois Fiala belongs to the lower classes which Werfel had portrayed sympathetically in his earlier works. Bahr is especially interested in the connection between money and love in the novella. As a member of the petite bourgeoisie, he argues, Fiala can express his interest in money but not his feelings. His inability to express his feelings does not mean, however, that he is incapable of love. In fact, Bahr argues that just the opposite is true, because without love Fiala's fight would be senseless (43-44).

Although Abels (1990) continues in the tradition of viewing Fiala as a heroic figure who attains tragic greatness (78), Wagener (1993) picks up and develops Dolch's argument. In his view, attempts to interpret the novella as the heroic death of a poor man miss the ironic, often sarcastic undertone (85). According to Wagener's thesis, Werfel makes it clear by referring to Fiala not by name but by his social standing that he is talking not about an individual but about a typical petit bourgeois. Wagener comments that it is Werfel's contention that the petit bourgeois longs for permanence and security, even beyond death, and that this security mania leads him to insure everything (86). Wagener stresses that in his seemingly heroic refusal to die, to beat death by a few days to make some money for his family, Fiala is not heroic. Instead Werfel ridicules him. In his view, Werfel intended the novella to be a social criticism of the philistine mentality of the petite bourgeoisie. Wagener agrees with Dolch that Werfel subsequently tried to take out the biting sarcasm to make the story conform better to his later idealized memories of the Hapsburg empire (89). Thus the novella shows how Werfel moved from sarcastic criticism of the Hapsburg empire's class structure to a melancholy longing for a mythic golden age (90). Wagener also points out how the style of the story reinforces this reading. The irony and the sarcasm that pervade it prevent any feeling of social pity, and they increase as the story unfolds (87).

Werfel's next prose work, *Der Abituriententag* (1928), aroused little critical interest except for short mentions in studies of Werfel's life and works. Recently, Binder (1992b) and Wagener (1993) have taken a fresh look at the work. In his lengthy article, Binder argues that the novel is autobiographical, and he shows how Werfel draws closely on events and people from his Prague years in the work. Wagener believes that Werfel tells the story with an extraordinary vividness and mastery of the language. In particular, he thinks the satire of the classroom events and the language of the teachers, reproduced by Schulhof during the class reunion, is masterful. He also shows that Werfel depicts Sebastian in a convincing manner. Since the narrative perspective is Sebastian's, however, Adler's character is less convincing and more abstract and theoretical (96). Drawing on Werfel's own interpretation of the work, Wagener sees the story as an example of Werfel's attitude to the role of Jews in the world. As Wagener points out, the guilty man, Sebastian, is a high official, and the victim, Adler, a Jew. The story thus demonstrates Werfel's belief that the role of the Jew is to bring about sin, which in turn necessitates redemption, and it is this struggle for survival between Judaism and Christianity that Werfel allegorically describes in the novel and from which Adler emerges as the moral victor (97).

In contrast, Werfel's next major novel, *Barbara oder die Frömmigkeit*, (1929) has been the subject of lively critical commentary and was the work that, despite some negative criticism, established Werfel's reputation as a serious novelist. Some critical attention centered on the major characters, Ferdinand, Alfred Engländer, and Barbara. Of special interest to several critics were the religious and philosophical ideas in the novel. Others saw the novel as a documentary of the period and an important key to Werfel's political views. As is typical in much of Werfel criticism, there was little concern with the literary and aesthetic qualities of the work. The focus has been virtually solely on Werfel's ideas.

From the beginning, the central role of Ferdinand in the novel aroused a lot of critical debate. Kohn-Bramstedt (1934) notices Ferdinand's resemblance to Goethe's Wilhelm Meister or Thomas Mann's Hans Castorp. Ferdinand, he argues, is a typical introvert, a noble and meditative figure who is not hostile to the world but lives aloof from it, supported by his awareness of his own dependence on God (67-69). Stamm (1939) sees similarities between Ferdinand's role in the novel and that of Alyosha in *The Brothers Karamazov*. Just as Alyosha possesses a harmony that Ivan and Dmitri (and Dostoyevsky) intensely desire, he argues, so Ferdinand has a steadiness that Engländer and Werfel envy. In Stamm's opinion, Ferdinand is an extreme individualist who comes to recognize the futility of political change and the illusory nature of all human relationships. As an essential part of his development, however, he has to contract the modern disease of intellectualism, which for a while leads him to social and political action. This step is important, Stamm argues, because it impresses upon him the animalism and vanity of man's life and his own unfitness to participate in the scramble for ambition and power. It confirms for him his unwordliness and spirituality. Ferdinand thus comes to accept his isolation as irrevocable. Because of his experiences, he can live within himself and devote his life to God (335-41). In the opinion of Klarmann (1946a), Ferdinand is another of Werfel's figures who attempt to redeem mankind. Unlike the others, however, Ferdinand is more the pushed than the pusher, more witness than actor. Klarmann observes that the faith Barbara gives Ferdinand serves as a safe anchor that allows him considerable freedom of movement but prevents a complete drifting out upon the waters of doubt (385).

Puttkamer (1952) believes Werfel uses Ferdinand to depict the rootlessness and disintegration of his age. She sees the execution scene in which Ferdinand struggles with his conscience and finally frees the three condemned soldiers as central to understanding him. Here, she argues, is a new concept of the hero as one who does not act out of some principle but out of the inner nobility of his nature, which prevents him from committing murder. For her, it is noteworthy that such a figure appeared at this time in Germany when a political principle was growing that rejected personal conscience (21). Like her remarks about

*Verdi*, Puttkamer's analysis here is shaped by the recent Nazi past. Brunner (1955) argues that, during the course of the novel, Ferdinand essentially does not change. Rather than a development, Werfel shows an unfolding and a maturing of Ferdinand's character (78).

More recently, critics have tended to view Ferdinand less positively. Williams (1970, 1974) is critical of his renunciation of the world in the last part of the novel, seeing this withdrawal as a pandering to the medical and social needs of the rich on whom Ferdinand depends for his material support. For him, Ferdinand's position at the end of the novel is defeat, not victory, and escape, not fulfillment (1970, 90-91). Steiman (1985) is also critical of Ferdinand and argues that his odyssey is not one of self-discovery and self-realization, as in the traditional *Bildungsroman*, but rather one of discovering the meaninglessness of the world and the futility of attempting to change it (49). Midgley (1989), who is less critical of Ferdinand, sees his role in the novel as the principal instrument through which Werfel depicts the disorientation of the contemporary world and the spiritual hunger within the psyche.

From early on, many critics were interested in the role that Barbara plays in the novel. Slochower (1934) notes that she embodies Werfel's ideal of a pure and rare individuality (105). Stamm (1939) views her as Ferdinand's religious teacher, not because of any conscious teaching, but simply through the power and example of her character. From her naive and complete faith in God, he argues, flow the calmness and peace that afford Ferdinand refuge and comfort. She is the magnet that guides him to the right path. Through her example, Ferdinand finds a truthfulness of character that forms the religious basis of his life (342-43). Bach (1957) also points out the important influence that Barbara exerts on Ferdinand. She argues that through her example Ferdinand gains inner equanimity. Like Barbara, he chooses a profession in which he can serve others and help those who are suffering. Bach observes that the feeling of community between these two people who have nothing of blood, class, or intellect in common gives the reader a sense of the affirmation of life that the novel conveys. In her view, the novel expresses Werfel's belief that a real community can arise only where love, shown in understanding, caring, and devotion, is strong. Bach remarks that a class-conscious poet would see in Barbara, the maid, an exploited figure. For Werfel, however, Barbara's behavior affirms a divine order, and she functions as the calm center of an otherwise chaotic existence (192-93).

Later critics generally agreed with the earlier critical views. Steiman (1985), for example, argues that Werfel's concept of piety is rooted in Barbara, who serves Ferdinand as a moral and experiential point of reference and whose invisible power guides him. Barbara is his connection to his past, to his family, and to the world that collapsed around him before he was grown (48-49). Midgley (1989) draws on Jung in his analysis of Barbara's role in the novel. On one level, he writes, the piety she represents is real, and she also functions as a mother substitute. Through her behavior, she refutes Engländer's contention that simple faith is impossible in the modern world. In the second half of the novel, however, it is not her physical presence that is important but rather the internalized ideal she represents for Ferdinand. Midgley argues that in Ferdinand's mind, she "has become invested with all the power of an imago that asserts itself ever more insistently, as a monitory symbol of spiritual devotion, the more his outward existence becomes devoid of spiritual content" (134).

Another figure in the novel that aroused critical interest was Alfred Engländer. Stamm (1939) sees Engländer as representative of the intellectual Jew who seeks faith. The figure of Engländer reminds him of the struggling, groping Werfel, familiar from his poetry. Like his creator, Stamm argues, Engländer is strongly attracted to Christianity but, despite his search for religion, is unable to overcome his uncertainty and restlessness. In Stamm's opinion, Werfel uses Engländer to attack what he viewed as the great disease of the modern world, namely the intellect that had fallen away from God, an intellect that analyzes and by so doing kills life. Like Werfel, Engländer accuses the godless intellect of trying to reduce people's sense of the wonder and mystery of life to rational and analytical formulae (334-35). Puttkamer (1952) also sees characteristics of Werfel in Engländer but argues that Engländer is a caricature of him (60), and such critics as Brunner (1955, 64), Braselmann (1960, 49), and Hautmann (1971) agree with her view of Engländer as a self-parody, although Wagener (1993) sees him not as a self-parody but as an ironic self-portrait (102). From his Marxist perspective, Metzler (1988) views Engländer as Werfel's spokesman in the novel. In Engländer's fate, Metzler argues, Werfel depicts symbolically his notion of the passion of modern Judaism, which no longer exists in a religious form but only in an intellectual one and which has adapted materially to capitalist conditions (332). Midgley (1989) again draws on Jung to explain the relationship between Ferdinand and Engländer. It is based, in his view, on complementarity since, in Jungian terms, Engländer's activities are plotted on the rational axis of the mind, on which thought and feeling are opposed, while Ferdinand's behavior occurs along the irrational axis (133). Although Midgley writes that it is uncertain whether Werfel's depiction of Ferdinand and Engländer was shaped by Jung, he argues that such a Jungian analysis is helpful in elucidating this relationship.

As is typical of much of Werfel criticism, many critics were interested in the novel for the insights it provides into Werfel's religious views at the time he wrote it. Stamm (1939) argues that, with its emphasis on the inner life of the individual, the novel is an affirmation of the Christian anarchism that Werfel had already expounded in "Die christliche Sendung." For Stamm, the novel plays a significant role in the history of Werfel's spiritual development; in his devotion to God, Ferdinand represents a shift in emphasis in Werfel's religious attitude from a social, humanitarian idealism to a greater concern with his own private contacts with God. It is thus the antithesis of the poems in *Der Weltfreund, Einander,* and *Der Gerichtstag,* in which Werfel hoped that man and his love would redeem the world. The turn to God in *Barbara* represents, in Stamm's view, Werfel's confession that the humanitarian idealism of his earlier poetry was inadequate (344). Bach (1957) considers the novel important because it marks Werfel's beginning confrontation with Judaism as a religious community and a community of fate, a theme which was to preoccupy him for many years (193).

In a lengthy and perceptive discussion, Steiman (1985) focuses on Werfel's attitude toward piety in the novel and remarks that the second part of its title (*oder die Frömmigkeit*) can be applied to almost all of Werfel's prose works. Steiman defines Werfel's notion of piety as a mystical state that enables one to grasp the truth and the value of worldly phenomena. Without this notion of piety, Steiman argues, Werfel's views of human relationships, war and revolution, and the individual and society, as well as his understanding of history, would be simply reactionary (48). But he is critical of Werfel for making mystical contentment and individual piety goals in themselves since Werfel suggests that self-realization can take place only within the self, not in society (55). Metzler (1988) reacts negatively to the religious aspects of the novel. The relationship between Barbara and Ferdinand reveals to him the deepening of Werfel's Christian-Catholic views. Metzler believes that Werfel's rejection of revolution in the novel enables the religious direction of his works to take over, and he regrets this development.

From the beginning, some critics appreciated the novel as a document of its time. Although he acknowledges that Ferdinand is central to the novel, Kohn-Bramstedt (1934) thinks the novel's significance stems from its comprehensive account of this period of Austrian history, and he praises Werfel for depicting clearly the mood of pessimism in Vienna at the end of the summer of 1918, a mood that, in his view, was characterized by a morbid voluptuousness of decline. Kohn-Bramstedt argues that Werfel analyzes the mood of the revolutionary soldiers and the disorders and psychoses of the time with great precision. According to him, Werfel's depiction of the revolutionary events is a valuable contribution to the study of the psychology of the masses (68-69). Paulsen (1938) also focuses on Werfel's depiction of the age and argues that in this novel Werfel confronts his time and the strengths and weaknesses of Austrian existence most intensively (421). Critics as recent as Jungk (1987) stress the documentary nature of the work. Jungk admires the gripping depictions of the atmosphere of collapse and self-inflicted dissolution of the Hapsburg monarchy and Werfel's compelling picture of Vienna in 1918, an aspect of the novel that Kraus (1992) also admires. In Jungk's opinion, Werfel's photographic eye and remarkable memory resurrected Vienna in the years after the First World War and cast a clear and harsh light on Austria's postwar despair (121).

For other critics, Werfel's depiction of the First World War in the novel was of special interest. Puttkamer (1952) argues that the war, which Werfel depicts with a realistic exactness that is almost like a higher form of reportage, is central to the novel. In her analysis, Werfel was especially interested here in the confrontation between the individual and authority, and he depicts the ordinary soldier as a helpless tool of an impersonal power that uses him without pity (19). Both Hautmann (1971) and Williams (1974) praise the novel for its masterly treatment of the horrors of the First World War, a theme that Williams develops at length. Williams argues that within a conventionally realistic framework Werfel attempts to depict the horror of war through the experiences of his hero on the eastern front. He cautions, however, that the novel tells us less about Werfel's reactions to the war as he experienced it at the time than about the way he intended his readers to view these reactions in retrospect. Williams praises Werfel for his powerful depiction of the corrosive distrust that undermined the morale of the Imperial Army after the desertion of a Czech regiment. Throughout the novel, Williams points out, Werfel does not glorify war. In fact, Ferdinand's encounter with the bath attendant (the former executioner) conveys to Williams a powerful sense of evil and perversity (67). Williams also focuses on Ferdinand's decision to free the condemned soldiers. By refusing to obey his orders, Ferdinand prevents yet another crime from being added to the catalogue of shame and misery. But, as Williams notes, Werfel also shows that his protagonist's action was an isolated decision that had little impact on the functioning of the military machine. Williams is, however, critical of Werfel for his lack of historical analysis in the novel. Werfel's account of front-line conditions is, in his view, generalized and superficial and gives little sense of the searing experiences portrayed by such writers as Jünger, Renn, and Latzko. He complains that Werfel uses the war only as a stage in Ferdinand's development.

Other critics focused on the way Werfel portrays the Austrian revolution and the group of anarchists with whom Ferdinand becomes associated. Sokel (1959) notes that the anarchist Gebhart embodies some of the basic ideas of the expressionist revolt. In his estimation, Werfel shows that Gebhart's self-sacrificing comradeliness, typical of the expressionist prophet, is in reality a subtle indication of a megalomaniacal will to power that is particularly vicious because of its deceptive similarity to Christlike love. Werfel shows that Gebhart's desire to save the world is merely a concealed form of self-aggrandizement (211). Like Sokel, Lea (1965) points out Werfel's strong criticism of the anarchists, whom he shows in the novel as extremists who thirst for power and believe in nothing except unrestrained sexual expression. Lea argues that they are driven more by their own frustration than by love for mankind (42), and he analyzes the technique that Werfel uses to shape the reader's perception of them. In order to show the anarchist episodes as a nightmare, Werfel has them meet in windowless rooms where no light penetrates. Williams (1970,

1974)) sees in the novel Werfel's most sustained critique of revolution. Like Lea, he emphasizes that the dilettante intellectuals are drawn to politics to gratify their vanity. Through their cliché-ridden harangues, Werfel shows that they lack any ideological conviction, and he develops the themes of hollowness and futility by highlighting the unreal, theatrical character of the revolution. Throughout the novel, Williams observes, Werfel criticizes the anarchists for their futility, vanity, insincerity, inconsistency, and ruthlessness, an indication of his own disenchantment with revolutionary politics (1970, 89).

The historian Hautmann (1971) approaches Werfel's depiction of the revolutionary period from a different perspective. He is above all interested in the novel as a roman à cléf, an aspect of it that also interests Kraus (1992, 5). In much of his article, Hautmann discusses how Werfel's fictional characters are based on people with whom the author associated during the revolutionary period in Vienna. For instance, Gebhart is based on Otto Gross, and Basil on Franz Blei. For Hautmann, the best part of the novel is Werfel's depiction of 12 November 1918, and he praises Werfel's understanding of mass psychology and his authentic descriptions of the events. Seldom, he remarks, has anyone described the atmosphere of the slowly dying Hapsburg monarchy in the last year of the war in such a fascinating way (477).

More recent critics such as Steiman (1985) also stress this sharp rejection of revolution that Werfel underscores by his emphasis on the anarchists' hypocrisy, duplicity, and inhumanity. Of all the anarchists and intellectuals, Steiman believes, Gebhart is the worst because he talks incessantly about love but treats his child brutally (51). Midgley (1989) argues that the novel presents politics as a self-deluding fiction (136). Following Williams (1974), he emphasizes that Werfel's presentation of these events should be seen not as a chronicle of what happened in 1918 but as a deliberate fictional construction (127). For Midgley, a striking feature of Werfel's treatment of the revolutionary period is how he presents political events and ideals in terms of sham theatricality and intoxicating rhetoric (128). Midgley believes that, although the work vividly reconstructs the Austrian experience of the First World War and its aftermath, it is really an important cultural document of the late 1920s since it contains a powerful statement of spiritual commitment that is inherently anti-political (135).

Many critics explored what the novel reveals about Werfel's philosophy of life and his view of politics and history as a whole. Slochower (1934), for example, argues that Werfel opposed revolution because he was primarily concerned with the problems of the individual rather than those of society. According to his argument, central to Werfel's view of life is his conviction that the inner transformation of the individual is more important than the re-organization of society. In Slochower's opinion, the novel refutes the belief that social movements or historic forces can be directed and controlled. Instead, Werfel shows that revolutions are the result of chance occurrences and that history is a kaleidoscope of accidental, haphazard events. Slochower terms this a skeptical philosophy of history in which there is no place for a social program because Werfel views the world in terms of disparate egos. He criticizes Werfel for his refusal to see that social situations exist and that they bring about social forces that condition and often determine the beliefs and acts of the individual (104-7). Stamm (1939) argues that, through Ferdinand, Werfel expresses his belief that political change is superficial and does not affect the essential character of man and the world. Stamm stresses what he sees as Werfel's gloomy view of people: no matter how many revolutions take place, man remains the same, basically a greedy creature whose life centers around the gratification of the senses (338-39). Unlike Slochower, who stresses Werfel's notion of history as accidental and haphazard, Williams (1970) believes that in the novel Werfel portrays history as a working out of providential design. He is, however, critical of Werfel's views of history and society. In his opinion, Werfel could conceive of only two alternatives, either unrestrained social conflict or the temporary restriction of social conflict through political tyranny. At this point Werfel could not envisage a workable, open, and just democratic system (89-90). Williams is disturbed by Ferdinand's fatalistic acquiescence since, in his view, it leads to apathy and an abstract caritas, divorced from social reality (91). Steiman (1985) complains that Werfel reduces social change to the egotism of those who would storm the control towers (51-52).

Wagener (1993) shows that the novel is not so much Werfel's attempt to describe the downfall of the Hapsburg empire but rather an expression of his own political opinion at the time he was writing. Like Lea, he argues that Werfel's negative depiction of the revolutionaries suggests his rejection of their political activities, which he views as meaningless and without inner truth. According to Werfel, their activities stem from distorted minds and lack any historical or spiritual basis (101). Thus the novel rejects social reform and political activism in favor of inwardness and religion. In contrast to Puttkamer (1952), Wagener views Ferdinand's release of the three condemned soldiers as an expression of the futility of revolutionary activity since, although he saves these lives, he inadvertently causes the death of fifteen other men when he is sent on a suicidal mission as punishment for his refusal to carry out the execution. Throughout the novel, Wagener points out that many of the ideas prefigure the views that Werfel expresses in his essays in the 1930s. This is particularly clear in Engländer's critique of the deification of the intellect and the radical realism of modern society with its resulting suppression of inwardness and the devaluation of the human spirit. Werfel expresses his view in the novel that the world can be spiritually healed only if it returns to Christianity (103). As Wagener observes, the novel is thus a strong criticism of Werfel's own time and "advocates absolute, religious values as embodied in a somewhat glorified past" (106). Because of its sharp rejection of modernity, the novel is philosophically very conservative (106). As these critical reactions demonstrate, Werfel's political views have from the beginning aroused a great deal of controversy and criticism, and, although there is agreement on what these views are, many critics continue to be disturbed by what they perceive as his reactionary, antidemocratic beliefs.

Another area of interest in the novel has been its autobiographical elements, which such critics as Braselmann (1960) stress. Puttkamer (1952) acknowledges these aspects of the novel, but she sees the part of it that deals with the revolutionary years as Werfel's attempt to come to terms with his anarchist phase and free himself from these tormenting memories (21). Both Hautmann (1971) and Schmitz (1987) believe that this is the most strongly autobiographical of all of Werfel's works. Midgley (1989), however, cautions that although it is important to recognize the strong autobiographical, exculpatory elements—and he believes the autobiographical elements give rise to some of the most vivid and emotionally intense scenes—this focus alone is not enough for an adequate interpretation (135).

Although there has been lively interest in the characters and the ideas of the novel, there has been little critical discussion about its success as a work of literature, and there is little consensus among those critics who have addressed this topic. A quality of the novel that several critics praised is Werfel's realistic technique in recreating the historical period. Puttkamer (1952), however, has reservations about the composition of the novel. Like several reviewers at the time, she believes that for the unity of composition it would have been better to end the novel with the war since Werfel's inclusion of the last part in Vienna weakens the artistic structure. She complains also that, in contrast to Werfel's usual characters, the characters here are too schematic (21-23). In her opinion, this is the weakest of Werfel's works, being too long-winded and too much a roman à cléf. Similarly, Brunner (1955) comments on the novel's lack of form. This is particularly evident, he observes, in the third section. Brunner remarks that Werfel is indifferent to purely artistic demands and often lacks formal discipline. In the third fragment, for example, there is, in his opinion, a kaleidoscope of scenes, episodes, and sketches that have little to do with the main theme, which he sees as the love between Ferdinand and Barbara (72). Unlike Puttkamer, Lea (1965) does not believe that Werfel should have ended the novel with the war but argues that its last part is an integral part of its structure since Ferdinand's confession of faith, which closes the story, represents a return to his spiritual heritage (44). Hautmann (1971) perceptively notes the irony with which Werfel portrays the revolutionary events and the anarchists. He considers the novel a treasure trove for literary historians, historians, political scientists, and psychologists (477).

More recently, Steiman (1985) complains that, although Werfel evokes the world powerfully, he does not evoke it analytically. In his view, Werfel does not depict family, school, war, and revolution as consisting of dynamic relationships and processes but simply as backdrops against which Ferdinand can move (49). He argues that the work is not a serious political or social novel. One reason for this, in his opinion, is that virtually all its characters come alive only to serve as the butt or vehicle for Werfel's polemicizing (a fault that reviewers at the time the book was published also noticed). The characters thus turn into caricatures or mouthpieces and lack credibility (55). Midgley (1989) gives a balanced view of the novel's strengths and weaknesses. He concludes that the novel is an uneven work in which elements of sentimentality and melodrama are combined with passages of vivid and sustained description (125).

The large amount of critical attention that *Barbara* received was not, however, accorded Werfel's next novel, *Die Geschwister von Neapel* (1931), a work that Werfel particularly liked. Most of the critical response centered on the figure of the father, Domenico. Hitschmann (1932), who praises the work, calls the father a masterpiece of the finest psychological characterization. He views him as a vain, self-confident autocrat who intimidates and breaks his children and destroys their talents; he argues that Domenico's paranoid attitude isolates the whole family. Yet underneath this hard exterior, in his opinion, one senses a lonely man who gradually sees his guilt and becomes softer. In this work, Hitschmann believes, Werfel wants to show fathers how they should not raise their children. According to him, the notion of education that Werfel expounds is in keeping with that of psychoanalysis (57-60). For Paulsen (1938), the father is an absolute dictator (421). Puttkamer (1952) also calls the father a tyrant but thinks that he behaves as he does out of love for his children (75).

Other critics viewed the father as an allegorical figure. Puttkamer (1952), for example, sees him as a representative of God (75). Brunner (1955) agrees, but he writes that Domenico is a reflection of the patriarch of all patriarchs, namely the old Jewish god Jehovah. In his view, Werfel's critique here of the father suggests his rejection of the god of the Old Testament in favor of the Christian god of love of the New Testament (82-83). Klarmann (1961) argues that the name Domenico signifies both God the Father and Christ. In his view, Werfel structures the family constellation in the novel according to the solar system in which the children (the planets) circle around the father (the sun). The sun, Klarmann remarks, is a symbol of God and Christ (27), an interpretation of the work with which Schmitz (1987, 345) agrees. Lea (1965) also views the father more positively. He acknowledges the children's wish for independence and the problems they suffer, but he likens Domenico to an Old Testament patriarch and argues that the novel supports Domenico structurally because it is his patriarchal authority that holds the family and the plot together. The chapter headings, he remarks, also give emphasis to the biblical cast of the story, although the theological framework, in his view, is not fully justified by the plot (46). Recently, Abels (1990, 89) and Wagener (1993, 111) point out that Werfel used the model of King Lear for his depiction of the dissolution of the family.

Another topic that interested several critics was Werfel's social criticism, in particular the way he portrays the growth of fascism. Puttkamer (1952), who notes that this is Werfel's only real love novel, sees as its center the crisis of the patriarchal family threatened from within by its own members but also from without by the totalitarian fascist state. She argues that the theme of fascism, which Werfel broached earlier in *Verdi*, is further developed here. The power of the father is broken by the power of the state since the fascist blow that hits Domenico hits the family as well, damaging not only the rights of the individual but also democracy, which cannot exist without the safety of the family and without human rights (76-78). Puttkamer thus believes that a central aspect of the novel is the hostility of the totalitarian state to the individual and the family. For her, the novel is both political and prophetic. More recently, Jungk (1987) sees the novel as a poetic metaphor for the crumbling of the patriarchal world order and male dominance (130). Wagener (1993) agrees with Puttkamer about the importance of the novel's political dimension. In this novel, he argues, Werfel criticizes the absolute state, which considers its own aggrandizement and power more important than the welfare of the individual (114-15).

On the whole, critics did not appreciate this novel. Reviewers at the time stressed again and again Werfel's strong narrative skills, but they also pointed out that his technique was old-fashioned (a reason for its later critical neglect). Puttkamer (1952) calls attention to the operatic structure of the novel. In her view, Werfel uses so many operatic effects that the work could almost be called a novel as opera or opera as a novel (76). Brunner (1955) criticizes the novel for being old-fashioned and underscores his view by noting that, while Musil was writing *Der Mann ohne Eigenschaften*, Werfel was writing an old-fashioned novel of a family (78). In Brunner's view, Werfel wrote this "epic anachronism," this southern, sentimental fairy tale, for his own relaxation after he had completed *Barbara* and before he started work on *Musa Dagh*. According to Brunner, the Italian material had an unfortunate effect on Werfel; it encouraged his inclination toward exaggeration and theatricality and freed him from the disagreeable obligations of control and moderation. He remarks that the plot reads like an operatic libretto: even the landscape looks like stage scenery, and the pictures of nature like stage properties (86). Günther (1965) points out the fairy-tale atmosphere but argues that in composition the novel is perhaps Werfel's most successful one (293). Wagener (1993) also picks up on its fairy-tale, operatic quality. He points out that, as in a fairy tale, all tribulations are resolved at the end. The tyrannical father, for example, changes into the loving old man. Like Puttkamer and Brunner, he notes that the characters are typical operatic ones. In his view, the novel has some serious flaws. For example, Domenico is an unlikely figure in the twentieth century, and even more improbable is the willingness of his children not only to tolerate such tyranny but to respect and love such a father. Wagener finds the happy ending aesthetically flawed. Although this can be explained by the operatic, fairy-tale character of the work, the novel, as he points out, is a realistic genre, and such happy endings do not normally occur in reality (115).

Werfel's modest but growing success as a novelist in the United States escalated radically with the publication in 1933 of *Die vierzig Tage des Musa Dagh*, which appeared in English translation in 1934. In Austria and Switzerland, the reading public received the novel with almost unanimous acclaim, but it was banned in Germany. In the United States, the response was enthusiastic. The reviews were overwhelmingly positive, and the novel quickly became a best-seller and a Book-of-the-Month-Club selection in 1934. Metro-Goldwyn-Mayer acquired the film rights, but the film was not produced because of Turkish opposition. The novel, however, made Werfel a hero to the Armenians. Today it is generally considered to be his most powerful novel and is still widely read. Pirumowa (1992), for example, points out its popularity in Rumania and Hungary (96-97).

Several of the early critics discussed the careful research that Werfel did for the novel and the authenticity with which he portrayed the historical events and Armenian life. They agreed that, although the novel rests on a firm historical foundation, it is not merely a documentary but blends together history, culture, and creative imagination. Schulz-Behrend (1951), for example, examines in detail the sources that Werfel used and concludes that, although the novel is close to its sources, both the main plot and the subplot are considerably amplified by imaginative invention (123). Puttkamer also notes the blend of historical authenticity, based on careful research, and creative imagination (86). Enright (1957) points out that the main incidents of the novel correspond to events mentioned in historical documents. For him, however, the special quality of the novel is Werfel's creative treatment of these documents (149). Recently Pirumowa (1992) and Wagener (1993) reaffirm Werfel's careful research of the historical sources (117).

Although most critics praised the authenticity of the novel and believed that Werfel presented the historical facts fairly, Lee (1986) attacks what she views as Werfel's slanted portrayal that favors the Armenians. Her article defends the Turkish side. She strongly denies that the brutality of the deportations was planned and asserts that the Armenian agony was not caused by human malice but was a result of chaotic conditions in a disintegrating empire that was waging war (62). In these views she is alone among Werfel critics.

Much of the critical debate centered on the figure of Bagradian. For Puttkamer (1952), the nucleus of the novel is the relationship between father and son, which in her opinion has religious implications, signifying the relationship between the individual and God (89-90). Brunner (1955) and Bach (1957) point out how Bagradian develops during the course of the novel:

through the desperate fight of the Armenians he comes to recognize the need to belong to a people and a religion (Bach, 194).

Lea (1965) argues that Bagradian is another example of the prodigal son in Werfel's works. In his opinion, Werfel shows Bagradian's return to Armenia as preordained since he is led back to the land and faith of his fathers to free his people from bondage. Lea points out that Bagradian does not completely identify himself as Armenian until he is persecuted for it. He finds it particularly ironic that Bagradian, who is a contemplative man at heart, takes on the role of the Western-oriented man of action and emerges as a dynamic leader. Through the Armenian crisis, however, he discovers abilities and inner resources that were dormant all his life, and he develops and grows as a human being. Lea argues that it is evident in the structure, theme, and wording of the novel that a man's life is being fulfilled in a cyclical form, from a sheltered childhood in Armenia to worldly sophistication in Paris and back to Armenia, where the cycle is completed in suffering, awareness, and self-transcendence (46-48).

In the 1980s, critical response to Bagradian varied. Davidheiser (1982) focuses on his search for national and cultural identity. In particular, he points out Bagradian's conflict between his French and Armenian identities and his slow development away from his French background to acceptance of his Armenian heritage (62-63). In his discussion of the novel, Steiman (1985) stresses its importance as a document of the life of its author, noting the similarities between Bagradian and Werfel as well as those between Juliette and Alma Mahler-Werfel (77). Steiman points out that Bagradian's experience of the persecution of his people forces him to reconsider who he really is, which reflects Werfel's own position at the time toward his own Jewish heritage. Metzler (1988) praises Bagradian as one of Werfel's great creative achievements because Werfel makes his protagonist perform a humane, social action, unlike his usual protagonists, who retreat into themselves. For this reason, Metzler views Bagradian as unique in Werfel's works (339). Abels (1990) sees the story as the homecoming of someone who is alienated and who finds his way back to himself. He points out that, for Werfel, the alienated person means always the person who is alienated from God. Like Moses, Abels remarks, Bagradian returns home but does not feel at home because he is not loved by his people. At the end, he is thus alienated from both the European and the Armenian worlds (96-97).

Many critics saw in the novel an analogy to the Nazi persecution of the Jews, an aspect that reviewers stressed at the time of the book's publication. Hyrslová (1958) argues that the threatened people Werfel had in mind were the Czechs: Werfel thought that they would be among the first victims of the destructive madness of the world. He wrote so passionately in his novel, Hyrslová believes, because he was fighting for his own people (735). Most other critics stressed the analogy to the Jews. Puttkamer (1952), for example, points out that in the fate of the Armenians Werfel recognized, as in a mirror, the fate that threatened the Jewish people (87). Critics such as Brunner (1955), Arnim (1961), Klarmann (1961), Zahn (1966), Wimmer (1973), and Nyssen (1974) all stress the topicality of the novel as well as its prophetic quality and argue that in his depiction of the murder of the Armenians Werfel prefigured the Holocaust and warned about Nazi policies. Metzler (1988) argues that the parallels to the Jews in fascist Germany are easy to perceive (337). As Jungk (1987) remarks, when the novel was published in Germany, even the most insensitive reader could not have missed the parallels between the ideologies of Young Turk Nationalism and the Nazis (144).

Steiman (1985), however, rejects this argument that Werfel had the coming persecution of the Jews in mind when he wrote the novel, believing instead that, since Werfel wrote it before the Nazi dictatorship was established, he could not have foreseen how the Nazis would treat his people. Steiman argues forcefully that Werfel's primary concern in the novel is depicting the world of the Armenians, not drawing parallels with the Jewish predicament in Europe, although he acknowledges that, in hindsight, the book seems an uncanny foreshadowing of the Holocaust. As he remarks, such aspects of the novel as the cold, bureaucratic nature of the Turkish operation, the refusal of the Armenians to face the truth, and the belief in the official lie that it was a resettlement program make the work eerie reading in the light of what happened to the Jews (75-76).

Davidheiser (1991a), however, disagrees strongly with Steiman and presents evidence that Werfel did, in fact, intend to confront National Socialism in his novel. In his view, the novel marks the beginning of just such a literary confrontation that ended with Werfel's last drama, *Jacobowsky and the Colonel*. Davidheiser argues that the parallels between the politics of the Young Turks and the rise of German National Socialism are striking, an aspect of the novel that the Nazi authorities must have recognized because they banned it (although, of course, it was also banned because Werfel was Jewish). Davidheiser believes that Werfel revealed his premonition of Jewish fate when, on a lecture tour of Germany in late 1932, he chose to read from the chapter "Zwischenspiel der Götter," in which Pastor Lepsius begs Enver Pascha to end the annihilation of the Armenians. Davidheiser also cites three of Werfel's letters, the first written in 1933 while he was working on the novel, the other two written in 1938 and 1944, as further evidence of Werfel's concern with the fate of the Jews under National Socialism (13-14). Wagener (1993) writes that it is tempting to make Werfel a prophet of the fate of his own people, but, despite the many parallels between the Turks' treatment of the Armenians and the Nazis' treatment of the Jews, he points out that Werfel finished the work before the active persecution of the Jews began. The parallels between the Young Turks' nationalistic ideology and that of National Socialism are, however, in his opinion, obvious and intentional (121-22).

Interest in the novel as a foreshadowing of the Holocaust led some critics to conclude that the novel revealed Werfel's own attitude toward Judaism at the time. Bach (1957), for example, writes that Bagradian's participation in the fate of the Armenians suggests Werfel's confession of belonging to his own Jewish community of fate (195). Williams (1970) also believes that the novel expresses Werfel's identification with the Jews in the face of the threatening persecution (92). More recently, Steiman (1985) argues that it reveals Werfel's complex identity as a Jew amid a host culture and his ambivalent relationship to that culture and its dominant religion. He believes that the characters and the issues in the book reflect Werfel's perspective as a central European Jew (76).

Much of the interest has revolved around the question of Werfel's attitude to politics and political activism in the novel. Puttkamer (1952) points out that Werfel presents the need to fight as a question of dignity and freedom (87). She believes that the tiny group of Armenians on Musa Dagh who fight against overwhelming Turkish forces symbolizes for Werfel a people's spiritual desire for freedom. Williams (1970, 1974) is also interested in this question. For him, the novel represents a turning point in Werfel's attitude to political activism since, through Bagradian, activism is depicted positively. For the first time since the First World War, Williams argues, Werfel suggests the possibility of reconciling political action with personal integrity; he no longer equates activism with self-aggrandizement and the ruthless pursuit of power, as he did in *Barbara*. Williams believes that Werfel's reappraisal of activism stemmed from his awareness of the threat of Hitlerism to the Jews of Central Europe. According to Williams, for most of the novel, Werfel's affirmation of activism is matched by a grasp of the political process that is far superior to anything the author had previously attempted. Even though Werfel still felt that social reform was only a palliative for human ills, his attitude toward activism had changed from one of intransigent condemnation to one of qualified approval (1970, 91-94).

Nyssen (1974) develops this argument further. She acknowledges that the novel can be interpreted from many different points of view, but for her it is most significant as an example of antifascist literature. Central to the novel, she believes, is the problem of the form and possibility of active resistance, and she argues that in the figure of Bagradian Werfel examines the part that the individual can play in the fight against a dictatorial regime. In the novel, Werfel shows active resistance as a human necessity and makes clear that the Armenian people can be saved only by violent resistance. Thus, in her opinion, the novel not only warns against the Nazis but also suggests a model of resistance (80-83). Pirumowa (1992) too points out Werfel's stress on an active struggle against force (94).

Other critics called attention to other aspects of Werfel's political thinking in the novel. For Bach (1957), it reveals Werfel's attitude toward the community. In the novel, she observes, Werfel wants to show that although community is important, it is not a goal in itself (195). In contrast, Enright (1957) argues that Werfel's depiction of persecution is central to the novel. In his view, the novel is not a debate about the rights and the wrongs involved but simply a painfully detailed "psychology" of persecution since Werfel brings the reader face to face with the victim by systematically breaking down the defenses of false logic, cultivated skepticism, and sentimentality through which we try to deny unpalatable knowledge. Werfel describes how persecution begins, how irritation at another's lack of conformity leads gradually to murder, looting, and rape. The novel thus warns us that man's recognition of humanity, of the worth of human life, is easily lost. Enright argues that Werfel depicts the Armenians as they are. Far from turning them into heroic, idealized figures, he shows that suffering on this scale does not strengthen or refine but dehumanizes (155-58). Like Enright, Wimmer (1973) points out that through the Armenian example Werfel shows how a world can sink into evil, and he argues that Werfel assigns the blame for the terrible massacres to erroneous ideas about progress and to antihuman, nationalistic, and racist theories (179).

In a perceptive discussion of Werfel's political thinking in the novel, Steiman (1985), like Enright, stresses that the historical phenomenon of genocide is central to it. He argues that Werfel explores in this work the question of the personal and collective identity of individuals and peoples who resist conventional geographic, cultural, and religious criteria of definition. Steiman is particularly interested in what Werfel views as the roots of the persecution because they illuminate his political thinking. Werfel, Steiman argues, projects onto the Levant the main ills that he saw in Europe. Thus he shows that the underlying causes of the persecution were not specific to Turkish or Armenian society but were such "poisons" as nationalism, racism, and a belief in progress that were imported from Europe. Since Werfel believed that modernism and nationalism were to blame, he exonerated the Turkish people (although not their government). For this reason also, Werfel did not hold Islam responsible for the genocide of the Armenian Christians, just as he did not believe Christianity was responsible for the persecution of the European Jews. The novel also indicates Werfel's response to the political developments of the 1930s. Steiman argues that Werfel believed Armenian security could be maintained only through a supranational Ottoman ideal, just as he believed that the security of the Jews in Europe depended on such supranational entities as the Hapsburg state.

Steiman points out that the novel is essentially religious, rather than political, in nature. In his analysis, it is religion and not a political or social program that plays a vital role in the success of the Armenian resistance. Although Werfel recognized the importance of political mechanisms and principles, he was most interested in the cultural values that must sustain political organizations. Steiman argues that if one reads the novel from the perspective of political discourse, its conclusion is seriously flawed because the appearance of the French squadron at the end is a deus ex machina, and Bagradian's failure to take advantage of it makes his death meaningless. But, Steiman points out, this is the case only if one is looking for a political meaning, whereas through the entire work Werfel presents all major developments in the life of an individual and community in religious, cultural, and psychological terms. Steiman argues that it is both the strength and the weakness of the novel that, although its major problems and conflicts are clearly political, Werfel's handling of them is resolutely nonpolitical. Although Werfel is no theologian, throughout the novel he uses theological categories to support and sanction a particular political analysis (75-87). Metzler (1988), however, in his Marxist reading of the novel, strongly disagrees with this analysis and argues instead that it depicts imperialistic politics and their hostility to people and to life (337). Wagener (1993) agrees with Steiman that Werfel analyzes political developments not in political but in cultural and religious terms. As he points out, Werfel is not interested in economic or political issues but only in their deeper theological significance (120).

The religious dimension of the novel that Steiman and Wagener discuss was a topic of critical interest from the beginning. Like several early critics, Schulz-Behrend (1951) points out the many biblical allusions in the work. For example, Werfel changed the number of days that the siege lasted to forty to give the novel the many associations that cluster around this biblical number, including the forty years that Israel wandered in the wilderness and Christ's forty days in the wilderness. Like Moses, he remarks, Bagradian is unable to enter the Promised Land (123). Many other critics viewed Bagradian as a Moses figure and the Armenians as the people of Israel and stressed the religious nature of the novel (Puttkamer 1952, 86, Klarmann 1961, 29, Arnim 1961, 124, Lea 1965, 46, Wimmer 1973, 179, and Nyssen 1974, 81).

Blumenthal (1976), in particular, was interested in the religious nature of the work, which he calls a metaphysically dramatized passion of the Armenian people. Like other critics, he points out that the biblical inferences are obvious in the title and that the connection to the New Testament is reinforced by the quotations from the book of Revelation that introduce the three parts. He sees the relationship between Bagradian and his son Stephan in metaphysical terms, as symbolic of the metaphysical relationship between God the Father and God the Son. In his view, Bagradian fulfills his divine mission as father and as son and transforms himself in the novel from a Moses figure to a Christ figure (75-78).

Most critics praised this work and thought it was Werfel's most successful novel. Schulz-Behrend (1951), in fact, calls it one of the great novels of the first half of the twentieth century (123). Enright (1957) is impressed with the power of Werfel's writing here, and he also points out that irony is an integral part of the novel. In his view, Werfel uses irony as his most effective stratagem in his attack on the reader's muffled sensibilities (158). Lea (1965) believes that in this novel Werfel achieved a complete harmony of design and execution (46). From his Marxist perspective, Metzler (1988) views the book as Werfel's major work, although he regrets its religious aspects. Not only is this historical novel, in his estimation, Werfel's most important work, but it is also one of the great achievements of late bourgeois humanistic literature and the most significant antifascist novel of the First Austrian Republic (340). Wagener (1993) also praises the novel. He admires the symmetry of its construction and its rich prose. For him, its most striking stylistic elements are the conversations in which friends and enemies of the Armenians clash, since it is here the battle of principles occurs. These conversations make clear that Werfel is not interested primarily in political history and its implications but in the underlying cultural and religious values (118).

Not all critics, however, viewed the novel so positively. Early on, Brunner (1955) voiced some reservations. He sees the novel as an admirable, epic achievement because it is original, suspenseful, and dramatic. He praises it for giving a vivid and convincing account of the events and for its colorful and graphic depiction of the people and the landscape. He faults the novel, however, for Werfel's typical artistic, stylistic, and grammatical mistakes, a result, in his view, of the author's indifference to purely artistic questions and his lack of a will to form. In Brunner's estimation, these problems occur in all Werfel's works, but especially in his prose. According to Brunner, there is never any doubt about Werfel's genius, but he only rarely achieves the artistic expression that would allow a comparison of his works with the great works of world literature (101). Like Steiman, Williams (1970) is disturbed by the novel's ending, which several reviewers and critics found vexing. He thinks the pattern is too neat and the rescue lacks conviction, and he criticizes the novel for verging on the miraculous. Salvation is bestowed, as he puts it, with the knowing connivance of the novelist rather than against the greatest odds that his imagination could devise (93). Wagener (1993), however, disagrees; he finds the conclusion emotionally satisfying (124).

In his next two works, *Twilight of a World* (1937) and *Höret die Stimme* (1937), Werfel was unable to duplicate the fame he reached with *Musa Dagh*. When *Twilight of a World* appeared in English in 1937, reviewers strongly criticized the framing piece, "An Essay upon the Meaning of Imperial Austria," because of what they saw as its conservative if not reactionary politics. They thought that some of the stories in the collection were good, however. The reviews of the novel *Höret die Stimme* were mixed when it was translated into English as *Hearken unto the Voice* (1938). As some critics noted, it was too intensely religious to achieve wide popularity. Most critics have virtually ignored it, although recently Davidheiser (1991b) and Auckenthaler (1992b) reexamine its importance in Werfel's oeuvre.

Most earlier critics focused on the novel's topicality. In an analysis colored by the recent experience of the war, Slochower (1945) points out the theme of exile and argues that such homelessness should not be viewed as tragic since it is God's way of saving man's spirit from making itself at home in the wrong world. Exile is thus an alternative to enslavement. In his view, the Old Testament prophet Jeremiah, who finds himself surrounded by a rapacious materialism, hears the call of God and chooses alienation as his home in an age when status means servility and humiliation (77). Puttkamer (1952) and Arnim (1961) also see in the novel the many parallels with Werfel's own time.

Brunner (1955) views the novel as Werfel's most monumental poetic tribute to the history and faith of his people (102). Unlike Puttkamer and Arnim, he believes that Werfel's goal here is to create a comprehensive picture of a specific biblical past, although he agrees with them that in its conception Werfel had in mind the tyrants of his time. He contrasts Werfel's handling of the biblical theme with Thomas Mann's treatment of the Joseph story. In his opinion, Mann analyzes the biblical legend ironically through the prism of modern psychology, and the reader is constantly aware of the author and his times. In contrast, Werfel is not concerned with being topical but tries to exclude his own time with its problems and interests. Werfel's Jeremiah is seen theologically rather than psychologically (115-16). Brunner believes, however, that it is one of Werfel's most unified works; a colorful, convincing historical novel (116-17).

Most later comments about the novel consisted of brief mentions in surveys of Werfel's works. Günther (1965), however, was one of the first critics to notice the important role played by the frame, set in the present. (Alma Mahler-Werfel disliked the frame and had it deleted in subsequent printings.) Günther argues that the frame is important because it prevents us from reading the work only as a historical novel. He considers the novel a roman à clef on the theme of Israel in Werfel's works. He also points out its topicality (285-86). Like Günther, Lea (1965) focuses on the frame, which, he believes, contains a further example in Werfel's works of the prodigal son theme. According to Lea's argument, Jeeves has lost contact with Judaism through assimilation, but through persecution and inner transformation he is able to rediscover his religious heritage. Like several of Werfel's Jewish characters, Lea observes, Jeeves show signs of inhabiting a spiritual no-man's-land, but when he goes to the Holy Land his faith begins to reassert itself and to fill his spiritual void. Through Jeremiah's example, Lea shows, Jeeves achieves his own salvation and emerges from his vision as a man reborn, healed of his illness. He now knows that it is his mission on earth to proclaim Jeremiah's message, and he has found the inner freedom to accomplish this. Lea argues that Jeeves's story demonstrates Werfel's belief that the Jews, however hard they try, cannot assimilate because they cannot destroy the roots of their heritage (49-52).

Critics in the 1980s stressed two different aspects of the novel. Steiman (1985) believes that its center is the tragedy of Israel's persecution. More explicitly here than before, he argues, Werfel depicts this fate as the result of the Jews' rejection of spiritual values. Through Jeremiah's experiences, Werfel expresses his conviction that the spiritual alone has reality and all the rest is show (171-72). Jungk (1987), who thinks the novel contains some of the most compelling scenes Werfel ever wrote, sees in it a coded call for resistance. For him, Jeremiah is a symbol of those who resist and question the power of the state and the smugness of the mighty. Like other critics, Jungk stresses that Werfel, who was deeply disturbed by the political events at the time, intended his novel as a warning (160-61).

One of the most thorough analyses of *Hearken unto the Voice* to date is by Davidheiser (1991b), who tries to rescue it from the near oblivion to which critics have consigned it. He argues that this novel, in which Werfel takes a prophetic stance to his times, is one of his most significant prose works. Davidheiser points out perceptively that for the modern reader the subject matter is daunting because, like its Old Testament source, Werfel's book is filled with warnings and forebodings, a reason perhaps that readers are not willing to recognize its merits. In his reassessment of the novel, Davidheiser focuses on three areas in which he believes the novel has been misunderstood. The first is the modern frame. Davidheiser argues that Werfel integrates the frame into the plot and uses it as a forum for commenting both on the role of the writer and particularly on Jewish destiny. In his view, the frame is about what it means to be Jewish in the 1930s, namely to suffer and be set apart from the rest. In the frame, Jeeves and Jewish destiny become one, and this fore-shadows the depictions of Jewish suffering in the main body of the novel. Because the frame links individual and communal fate, it is an important part of the novel, though it is one that critics overlook. Davidheiser criticizes what he calls the fleeting analyses by Puttkamer, Zahn, and Steiman for failing to discern Werfel's modern application of the plot, although, as we have seen, some critics such as Günther (1965) and Lea (1965) pointed out the topicality of the frame earlier. In Davidheiser's view, the frame is a skillfully drawn mixture of authenticity and fiction whose goal is to awaken the twentieth-century reader just as Jeremiah tried to awaken his people. The second aspect on which he focuses is the mixture of authenticity and fiction in the novel. In *Verdi* and *Musa Dagh*, Davidheiser observes, Werfel honed the art of historical narration. In this novel, he argues, Werfel is faithful to the message of the prophecies but embeds them in a plot, characterized by psychological realism, in which he indicts his times. The third area that Davidheiser discusses is the focus of Werfel's statements before and after the publication of the novel that throw light on his notion of his role as a novelist and the prophetic stance he assumes. Davidheiser concludes that these remarks demonstrate that, although Werfel was primarily narrating Jeremiah's life in a mixture of history and fiction, he was also challenging his readers through his depiction of Jeremiah's experiences to reflect on the direction of their own times (51-64).

Like Davidheiser, Auckenthaler (1992b) believes the novel is one of the best that Werfel wrote. He too stresses the importance of the frame since Jeeves's vision and his rebirth at the end of the novel suggest that God's message can still be powerful today. Auckenthaler views the biblical period that is characterized by personal and cultural death and moral decline as an allegory of Werfel's time. The relevance of the novel encourages the reader to question the meaning of life and history. He concludes that the novel has a lasting validity (81-89).

Wagener (1993), who acknowledges that Werfel is successful in invoking the biblical past, is nevertheless critical of the philosophical dimension of the novel. He believes this novel is probably one of the most conservative that Werfel ever wrote since in it he rejects a rational approach to solving political problems in favor of listening for the voice of God. Such an approach, as Wagener observes, "would hardly place the people of the twentieth century in an advantageous position to fight contemporary dictatorships" (130).

Werfel's next novel, *Der veruntreute Himmel* (1939), which was translated into English as *Embezzled Heaven* (1940), became a best-seller and a Book-of-the-Month-Club selection soon after Werfel's arrival in the United States in October 1940. Its success led to a later dramatization by Ladislas Bush-Fekete and Mary Helen Fay that was performed by the Theater Guild in New York on 31 October 1944. The play was not a success because of its poor adaptation, although critics praised the performance of Ethel Barrymore as the protagonist, Teta. Reviews of the novel when it was published in the United States praised its lyrical beauty, Werfel's narrative skills, and his powerful depiction of Teta. Some Catholic and non-Catholic reviewers objected to the way Werfel depicted Teta's religious views in the novel and to what they viewed as his moralizing, but many critics admired his strong expression of faith. Although the novel was a popular success, critical response to it has been sparse, consisting primarily of brief mentions and plot summaries in studies of Werfel's life and works like those by Braselmann (1960) and Zahn (1966). The few discussions that exist tend to focus on Werfel's portrayal of Teta or on what the novel indicates about Werfel's religious and philosophical views at the time he wrote it.

Although many reviewers saw Teta positively, later critics viewed her more negatively. Slochower (1945), for example, believes that Teta is a selfish person, concerned only about her own salvation. He remarks that she never consults her nephew's inclinations but regards him solely as an anonymous intermediary (76). Like Slochower, Wildenhof (1960) stresses Teta's selfishness. He notes that she retires into her small world of order and rejects contacts with people around her, creating an isolation that tempts her to be preoccupied with herself and how to save herself for eternity. According to

Wildenhof, her plan to make her nephew a priest, and thus her intermediary, indicates her great selfishness because in thinking only of herself she forgets the commandment to love others. Only on her pilgrimage at the end does she realize that through her treatment of her nephew she bears responsibility for his failed life (177-84). Steiman (1985), who points out that Werfel intended Teta to represent the soul of humanity in its naive yearning for immortality, argues that Teta's success at the end comes not from any rational purposive design but rather from utter exhaustion and submission (119). Wagener (1993) observes that, although Teta's character has positive features, she is neverthe-less flawed because she believes that by buying herself a priest she can pay God off for any sins she commits (135).

The philosophical dimension of the novel also aroused some critical interest. Brunner (1955) argues that, despite what he calls its anachronistic material, which gives the impression of escape or indifference, the novel is a conscious critique of the religious nihilism of Werfel's time (119). In his perceptive analysis, Steiman (1985) concludes that the novel is a serious attempt to relate spirituality to action, to transform a moral attitude into a practical program. As he observes, its action has no political or social dimen-sions but is an individual's attempt to secure the future by prudential action in the present. For Werfel, Steiman argues, life's value and fulfillment were not in rational action but in the unquestioning devotion of genuine piety (117-19). Kiss (1992) stresses the existential situation of exile that is already apparent at the outset and the significance of Werfel's treatment of the recent past, which he sees as the center of the novel (155). Wagener (1993) argues that Teta's story is lifted to the level of a parable about the ills of the age, its lack of faith, and its loss of metaphysical ties to the divine (139).

In one of the few extensive discussions, Smith (1988) calls the novel inco-herent and sentimental. His main criticism is that it lacks a clear structure. For him, the novel is interesting because it shows a case of aesthetic indecision: Werfel cannot decide whether he wants to convey a feeling of ambiguity and possibility or of definite commitment. During the course of the novel, Smith argues, Werfel introduces elements that could have contributed to a far more serious work, but he fails to pursue them. In the first part, for example, Teta appears at times in a mysterious and ironic light, but in the following parts Werfel suppresses systematically the ironic alternatives he introduced. Smith believes that even in the first part of the novel Teta's character is not entirely successful. In his view, the whole aim of the plot seems to be to test Teta's faith and prove that it is deeply rooted and genuine, but he criticizes Werfel for failing to create a tension between our sense of absurdity in Teta and any sense that her inner life represents genuine religious possibility. The aesthetic problems that develop in the course of the novel are basically twofold: not only does Werfel smother tendencies opposed to Teta's beliefs, but her beliefs also appear naive and cannot bear the weight Werfel places on them. Werfel begins to suggest her weaknesses but does not allow our impressions of them to sink in. An example of this problem is when Philipp, the son of the Argan family for whom Teta works, dies. Smith argues that Werfel clearly wants to stress in this situation Teta's composure and her religious faith. But of all the scenes in the novel, this one illustrates, for him, the weakness of Teta's characterization most strongly since her religious response seems trivial and almost empty; there is no hint that she is disturbed in any way by his death. Her response raises the question of whether she is too narrow and insensitive. Smith observes that this should open up the possibility that her faith is rooted in self-centeredness and thus radically question it. Werfel, however, fails to follow up on such ironic possibilities as these. Another central weakness of the novel, in Smith's estimation, is that Werfel fails to integrate the story of the Argans with Teta's. He concludes that up to a certain point the characters and many of the incidents in the novel are believable, interesting, and even intriguing. But through its course, Werfel selects and isolates certain qualities of the characters and certain possible responses and favors them over others, thereby eliminating the ironic alternatives. Smith dislikes the novel's ending. In trying for a triumphant conclusion, he believes, Werfel succeeds in creating merely cloying sentimentality (222-42).

Werfel's unfinished novel, *Cella oder die Überwinder*, which he wrote in 1938 and 1939 in France, was not published until 1954 when it appeared in the third volume of *Erzählungen aus zwei Welten* in the *Gesammelte Werke*. Although it sparked virtually no critical response at that time, it has been considered more recently to be one of his strongest works. Beginning with Lea (1970) it has attracted surprisingly favorable critical responses and has been widely considered to be one of the few works in which Werfel deals directly with the political events of his time (Wagener 1993, 12). Most of the critical attention has revolved around Werfel's portrayal of the *Anschluß*. The other major trend in the criticism of the work has focused on what it tells us about Werfel's attitude to the persecution of the Jews.

Lea (1970), who wrote the first major article on the novel, deserves most of the credit for bringing it to critical attention. For him, this requiem for Austria is particularly significant because of how it addresses the Jewish question and what it shows about Werfel's attitude toward his own Jewishness. According to his thesis, the novel deals with the situation of the marginal Jew in a time of mortal danger. Through Bodenheim's ambivalent attitude to his Jewishness, which, for Lea, is the central question in the work, Werfel depicts the social and psychological position of a Jewish family that has left the ghetto but has not been accepted into the gentile world. Lea argues that their attempt to emancipate themselves has led to a limbo existence that results in serious personality disturbances. Their attempt to assimilate fails because of social ostracism. Throughout the work, Lea points out, Bodenheim demonstrates that being an Austrian means more to him than being a Jew, which he considers a burden. While Bodenheim's claim to regard Austria as his own seems valid, especially because of his former military service, Werfel's manner of presentation suggests, in Lea's estimation, that a Jew is fated not to acquire a national identity and that if he tries to do so, he deceives himself and refuses to accept his biblical destiny. Lea believes that Werfel's handling of this complex problem is vivid in many details but suffers from the novel's mixture of fiction and opinion and the author's attempt to make his tale a theological statement (105-9).

Although Lea appreciates the strengths of the novel, he is disturbed by Werfel's definition of Judaism in this work (as well as in some of his later ones) as a blood order in which membership is permanent and involuntary. Lea shows that almost all the Jewish figures in the plot fall into various patterns of alienation from the Jewish tradition. In Lea's view, Werfel suggests that persecution comes as a punishment for worshipping false idols. Yet this cause-and-effect relationship between assimilation and persecution, he feels, is not convincing on a political level. Lea shows that the novel suggests various reasons why Werfel strongly rejects assimilation. Werfel believes that it causes negative psychological pressures and does not appease—and may even pro-voke—anti-Semitism. Moreover, close Judaeo-Christian collaboration, an essential tenet of Werfel's theology, is possible only if each faith maintains its own identity. Finally, Werfel believes, assimilation jeopardizes the messianic mission of Judaism as defined in his view in the Old Testament (105-14).

Although Lea is disturbed by Werfel's treatment of Jews in the novel, he believes that the fragment is written with evocative power, despite some weaknesses. Structurally, for example, the connections between the beginning, Cella's preparation for her recital, and the political events remain to be worked out. Lea also notices an occasional editorializing, caused perhaps by Werfel's closeness to the events he was depicting. He remarks that one can only be grateful that the work remained a fragment since the planned ending, a concert by Cella in Carnegie Hall, would have been an almost operetta-like anticlimax (Lea 1982, 250). Despite such weaknesses, Werfel gives a masterly depiction of the German invasion and the resulting mass hysteria. Lea believes that it is one of Werfel's best prose works, one in which he demonstrates a sure feeling for atmosphere and local color.

Other critics developed the historical aspect of the work that Lea touches on at the end of his article. Williams (1974), for example, believes that the recreation of the atmosphere in Austria before and after the *Anschluß* is a considerable narrative achievement because Werfel displays so well his ability to convey the essence of the political crisis through its impact on individual characters (87). Reffet (1984), who calls the novel the most political of all Werfel's works, agrees with Williams. In his view, it is the best literary docu-ment about the end of Austria (91).

Like Williams, Steiman (1985) is interested in the historical dimensions of the work. He calls it a poignantly evocative novel of an Austria caught in the Nazi takeover, and he believes that Werfel effectively depicts the whole tragedy of the time. In his estimation, Werfel manages to avoid here much of the cloying spirituality and annoying anti-intellectualism that mar so much of his work and instead manages to recreate through representative, individual personalities the political and social realities of Austria in the 1930s. For Steiman, it is significant that the work remained a fragment, an indication that Werfel's strength here is in evoking and recreating what was happening rather than in suggesting a way out of the crisis. Steiman regards *Cella* as the most sustained and integrated expression of Werfel's vision of a society in which he lived all his life and whose disintegration he records here.

Yet, as usual, Steiman is critical of Werfel's political beliefs. Werfel, he writes, diagnoses the inner vitality of fascism as natural and mechanistic and thereby abdicates the task of analyzing its specific political and ideological aspects; he sees it only as a force of darkness. Steiman regrets that, given his perceptive insights into the psychological dimensions of Austria in transition to Nazism during the *Anschluß*, Werfel did not extend his analysis to include political categories of human relationships. For example, the only thing that *Cella* offers by way of resistance to the Nazis is a monarchist restoration. It is, he believes, characteristic of Werfel's strengths and weaknesses that he recreates the Austrian situation of 1938 with a powerfully evocative and penetrating realism but resorts to a quasi-mystical transcendentalism for his analysis of the events that caused it. The result is an impression of both fearless realism and mystic escapism (103-15).

Like other critics, Wagener (1993) calls *Cella* Werfel's most political novel since he deals in it with the concrete past, with actual events and realities, rather than with spiritual alternatives to a false reality (140). In Wagener's view, the main theme is the fate of the assimilated Jews in Austria, their mistaken belief of being accepted, and their realization in 1938 that they have not made any progress. In this novel, he believes, the exiled, assimilated Jew Franz Werfel comes to terms with his own Jewishness and his mistaken former faith in the brotherhood of mankind (145). Wagener points out that, as usual, Werfel is not interested here in just presenting reality or providing his reader with social or political analysis. Rather, reality for him plays a role only in terms of its theological and metaphysical significance (147).

Werfel's greatest popular success by far was *Das Lied von Bernadette* (1941), translated as *The Song of Bernadette* (1942), which was a best-seller in the United States in 1942 and 1943. It was a Book-of-the-Month-Club selection in 1942, and the film rights were sold to 20th Century-Fox for $100,000 (Krispyn 1978, 139). The film, starring Jennifer Jones, won five Academy Awards after its release at the end of 1943. The sales of the book in the United States reached over a million copies. Major newspapers published articles about it, radio conversations with Werfel were broadcast nationally, the *Ladies Home Journal* published an abridged form of the novel in 1943, and it was featured in *Life* in 1943. This success, which made Werfel much in demand as a speaker, also made his exile years considerably easier for him because of both the recognition he received in his country of asylum and the resulting financial security. The novel also made him into a kind of popular hero for the nation's Catholics (Steiman 1985, 146). Many readers, especially Catholic ones, appreciated the religious faith and the spiritual power of the book. Others, however, objected to the way Werfel portrayed thinkers of Bernadette's time as radical nihilists (Steiman 1985, 151).

Despite the novel's enormous popular and commercial success and the almost uniformly superlative tone of the reviews, it has received surprisingly little critical attention until recently, except for brief mentions and summaries of the plot. Like the reviewers, the critics who have dealt with the novel have been particularly interested in its religious dimension. Slochower (1945) writes that the novel is Werfel's most recent homage to regeneration by metaphysical faith, and he criticizes this strongly because, in his view, Werfel purports to do nothing more than restate poetically Bernadette's visions and the miraculous cures at Lourdes, but he presents the visions as unquestionable matters of fact and through labored verisimilitude tries to convince the reader of their veracity. Werfel's method of countering a sophisticated rational age of disbelief, he complains, is disingenuous here (77-78).

Other critics viewed the religious aspects of the work more positively. According to Grenzmann (1950), a man of faith had written this novel. He argues that Werfel appeared to believe in the miracles, a question that caused lively speculation among the reviewers. In his view, the novel demonstrates that Werfel understood the Catholic world deeply (245-49). Puttkamer (1952) and Streicher (1958) also stress the religious aspects and the deep faith evident to them in the novel. Streicher (1958), for example, focuses on the piety in the work. For him, the work is gripping because of its sense of miracle and its depiction of holiness. McCrossen (1961) argues that through Bernadette Werfel makes his plea for people to renounce pride, conceit, and spiritual blindness (39). Klarmann (1973) sees the novel as a clear example of the allegorical quality of Werfel's art. It is not only the story of the saint, he argues, but it also expresses allegorically Werfel's notion of the high mission of art because, like the poet, Bernadette is allowed to see what others cannot (49). Krispyn (1978) also stresses the pronounced religious nature of the work. For him, the novel reflects Werfel's growing preoccupation with Roman Catholicism, and he suggests that Werfel was drawn to Catholicism because its pomp and ritual struck a responsive chord in his essentially operatic heart (139). These responses typify the trend of enthusiastic and uncritical rhapsodizing in both the reviews and the early criticism of the novel.

Brunner (1955) also acknowledges the novel's expression of genuine piety. He points out that, like *Der veruntreute Himmel*, *Bernadette* expresses Werfel's passionate rejection of the agnostic realism of his time. He discusses the differences between Werfel's novel and Zola's novel *Lourdes*. Werfel, for example, is interested in the apotheosis of the miracles while Zola negates them by subjecting them to rationalistic and psychological analysis (129). Brunner is disturbed by Werfel's prose, however, which he finds here even more careless than usual. Yet he remarks that, despite these flaws, the novel has the power to move the reader (136).

Steiman (1985) sees the work as a further example of Werfel's increasing antimodernism and antirationalism in that Werfel attacks human reason, science, and socialism, which, for him, were at the root of the contemporary crisis. Although the theme is Catholicism, Steiman remarks, the novel's message is not about dogma but about faith, which is characterized by the simple inarticulate piety that Werfel saw rooted in the sources of our being. For this reason, Steiman views Werfel's faith in the novel as more expressionist than Catholic (151).

Some critics addressed the realism and irony that reviewers touched on briefly at the time of the book's publication. Streicher (1958), for example, calls Werfel an excellent observer in this work. For him, Werfel is a realist in the old sense of the word, one who creates characters of flesh and blood (8-10). McCrossen (1961), who, like Brunner, explores the influence of Zola's novel *Lourdes* on *Bernadette*, suggests that the stark realism, even naturalism, with which Werfel describes the daily life of Bernadette's family, if not directly inspired by Zola, can be considered as a lineal descendant from the technique of the French naturalist. Despite Werfel's sincerity and his reverence for his subject, however, McCrossen believes that he did not really understand Bernadette because he made her into a romantic figure (40).

Later work by such critics as Koepke (1976) and Steiner (1987) has focused on the novel as an exile work, particularly on its success in the United States and the reasons for this success. In addition to his interest in the exile aspects of the work, Steiner points out that its structure, based on the rosary, reinforces the religious theme. He observes that the story is not only about the religious impact of Bernadette on the common people but also about the contrast between Bernadette's religiousness and the skeptical lack of faith and agnosticism that characterize officialdom in the novel. Steiner credits Werfel's novel with helping to free American Catholicism from its long-time stigma as a foreign faith of a foreign underclass and making it more comprehensible to non-Catholic readers (71-73).

In the recent collection of essays on Werfel edited by Nehring and Wagener (1992), two of the eleven articles are devoted to *Bernadette*, an indication of the desire among critics to take a fresh look at the novel. Hadda (1992) approaches it psychoanalytically. As her theoretical base, she uses the work of Heinz Kohut and his colleagues, the formulators of self-psychology, to interpret the figure of Bernadette. As she points out, Kohut constructed a model that shows that the growing child has two essential psychological needs from the parenting figures, a mirroring need and an idealizing need. Hadda argues that psychoanalysis is above all an exploration of unique meaning. People and literary characters, she asserts, do not fit into categories based on another person's experience or into theoretical assumptions. Approaching them with the expectation that they should do so is the problem with much psychoanalytical criticism, in her opinion.

Hadda focuses on what Bernadette's visions mean to her. From the self-psychological perspective, she argues, this is Bernadette's first experience of being treated as special and cherishable. The Lady's attention provides her with a sense that she is not alone. According to Hadda's thesis, Bernadette's experience with the Lady is one of deep and satisfying mirroring in which the Lady communicates to Bernadette that she finds her delightful and valuable. Hadda suggests that Bernadette has never received such attention before; she has never received from her mother the reciprocal gaze that is the essence of mirroring. Because of the mirroring she now receives, Bernadette blooms like a well-tended plant. Her internalization of the Lady's benevolent influence allows her to lead a healthier, more inwardly secure life. In addition, the Lady satisfies Bernadette's desperate longing for a tender and affirming mother. Hadda also explores what the story of Bernadette meant for Werfel. She points out his early warm relationship to Roman Catholicism and suggests that he saw in Bernadette the strength and calm that he needed to maintain his own cohesion during this time of radical change and danger. Thus, for him, Bernadette "fulfilled a self-object function, granting him hope, purpose, and, in a strange way, even a buffer against despair and morbidity" (85-98).

Zeman (1992) takes a different approach. He points out that, although there is no doubt that a practiced writer was at work in the novel, critics were suspicious of one who offered hope and consolation through traditional ethical and aesthetic means. He observes correctly that the aesthetic quality of the novel has been overlooked, something that he hopes to rectify in his analysis. According to his thesis, the story of the miracle of Lourdes, not the life of Bernadette, is the central focus of the novel. This focus leads Werfel to employ an episodic technique, a series of pictures and scenes, and he makes no attempt to develop and connect the different strands of the action. In Zeman's view, the schematic characters lend themselves easily to being adapted to film, a possibility that he suggests Werfel may have had in mind. Zeman discusses the realistic language and the detailed depictions of the urban scenes and the different classes. This language contrasts so sharply, however, with the miraculous that the language in the novel suffers from a singular lack of unity. Thus Zeman points to the artistic limitations of the work, although he appreciates the novel for its stress on love in a time of hatred (99-109).

Wagener (1993) sees the work as a historical novel in which the author's conservative style and approach to narration complement the plot and its underlying belief structure. Nowhere else, in Wagener's estimation, is Werfel so antimodern in his presentation. Wagener argues that the author wanted indirectly to attack Zola's treatment of the Bernadette theme. His attack on naturalism fits in well with the novel because naturalism was the style in which the attempt was made to apply scientific principles to art. Since Werfel attacks here the scientific spirit of the nineteenth century, he must logically also attack the photographic realism of naturalism. Wagener believes that Werfel must be defended against the accusation of having written a sweetish, religious novel, the purpose of which was to further belief in mystical visions and miracles. That is simply not the case, Wagener says firmly. At no point does Werfel state that he believes in the apparitions. Instead, he reports them in a seemingly factual, often ironic manner and leaves readers to draw their own conclusions. In Wagener's opinion, Werfel is not concerned with proving the validity of the miracles. What is at stake for him is Bernadette's truthfulness and the genuineness of her faith and belief. He wants to demonstrate the victory of faith over science, the victory of the spiritual world view over intellectual reasoning (151-54).

Surprisingly, *Stern der Ungeborenen* (1946) (*Star of the Unborn*, 1946), which was, as Wagener (1993, 1) points out, a critical disaster when it first appeared, later aroused lively critical attention. When it was published shortly after Werfel's death, reviews of the novel in the United States were almost uniformly negative, and even the few reviews that acknowledged some positive aspects of the novel were highly qualified. The novel was attacked for its theorizing and preaching; it was called a monstrosity, a dud, and a monumental blunder. Yet Alfred Werner, writing in the *Jewish Frontier* in April 1946, remarks that it reveals a great deal about Werfel and his thinking. It contains, in his view, a gold mine of information and is a valuable key to Werfel's soul—although, like other reviewers at the time, Werner criticizes Werfel for cramming all his opinions of life, death, religion, society, politics, and love helter-skelter into the novel without any aesthetic considerations.

Werner's view that the novel was a summary of Werfel's thinking at the end of his life was echoed by critics such as Grenzmann (1950), who calls it Werfel's swan song and the last conclusions of his wisdom. Puttkamer (1952), Bach (1957), and Braselmann (1960, 73) share these views. Samuelson (1983) sees in the novel a summing up of Werfel's defiance of all secular materialism (1808), and Steiner (1987) observes that it can be seen as Werfel's last intellectual will and spiritual testament. In his opinion, Werfel sensed his approaching death and tried to compress all he had to say about the state of the past, present, and future into one last epic tale of nearly monumental proportions (73-74).

Some critics were interested in the novel as an example of the utopian or dystopian tradition and for the literary models they detected in it. Like several of the early critics, Braun (1948-49) stresses this aspect of the novel when he calls it a cosmic, utopian satire. Puttkamer (1952) sees Werfel's utopia as a new conjuration of the tower of Babel, with, however, a twist since here man's hubris has succeeded (130). For Werner (1955), the work belongs with such novels as Samuel Butler's *Erewhon* and George Orwell's *1984* (145). Rolleston (1979) argues that the novel shows that Werfel had absorbed the Anglo-American tradition of H. G. Wells, Aldous Huxley, and Olaf Stapledon. In his view, many of the science fiction components that Werfel employs in the novel, such as telepathy and mental travel, can be found in Stapledon's work (59-60). Samuelson (1983) views it as a mixture of utopia and dystopia, as both a scientific and antiscientific romance. For him, it is both a metaphysical vision of the far future and a critique of it. Samuelson concludes that the novel is not Werfel's greatest work, but he believes that it is a significant part of his oeuvre and a useful addition to the literature of fantasy (1812). Lippelt (1984) sees it as literary science fiction of the highest level. In his view, the original way in which Werfel mixes past, present, and future time makes his work superior to other respected examples of modern science fiction (295).

Several critics focused on the novel's sustained critique of American life—particularly of life in California—and the American dream. Parrington (1947), for example, argues that the novel reflects the confused motivation of the day; the search for intellectual justification; and the feeling, shared by many, that mankind is on the last lap of progress, that the discovery of atomic power holds the key to self-annihilation, a view shaped by the dropping of the atomic bomb on Hiroshima. Parrington believes that Werfel had become skeptical about progress. Thus he considers the novel in certain respects a critique of the American dream, in which progress plays an integral part (214-16). Similarly, Werfel's translator, Gustave O. Arlt (1951), stresses that the novel is strictly an American one. He argues that the wish to simplify material existence through labor-saving devices, the thirst for comforts and luxuries, and the hedonism that impels people to shrink from anything unpleasant are characteristic of America rather than Europe. Samuelson (1983) also argues that Werfel criticizes the insidious hedonism of Southern California with its glorification of youth and beauty and its complacent faith in an endlessly improving future.

What the novel reveals about Werfel's philosophy of life and his view of the world in his last years was, however, the main topic of critical interest. Grenzmann (1950) notes that it suggests a pessimistic view that, despite the developments in the "astromental" world, people remain basically the same. The novel thus expresses the paradox of all progress, that people cannot change (251-56). Puttkamer (1952) also stresses the pessimism that underlies the work. Although at first there appears to be an immense cultural optimism about the possibility of progress, this changes during the course of the novel.

For Puttkamer, the novel demonstrates that even if we attain the highest level of spirituality and human capabilities, we will never be quite at home in this world (130-33). Like Grenzmann, Bach (1957) sees in the novel a parody of many unmistakable aspects of the twentieth century. In Werfel's depictions of an endlessly refined humanity whose only occupation is the cosmetic conservation of appearance, she points out, the reader recognizes his ironic depictions of the despairing attempts of modern society to banish suffering and make light of death (199).

Rolleston (1979) was one of the first critics to explore in depth the novel's debt to Werfel's exile experience. In the novel, he argues, Werfel sought to isolate and magnify the polarities of modern man's fate, his cosmological potential, and his obsessive destructiveness by propelling the reader into the vantage point of exile. According to him, the style of the novel represents Werfel's attempt to create a fiction that combines modern astrophysics and that radical uprooting of humanity known as exile. Like other critics, Rolleston discusses at length Werfel's polemical view of the world in the novel, the combative dualism that had characterized such essays as "Realismus und Innerlichkeit," and that he believes is an integral part of this work.

In Steiman's (1985) view, the novel is, in some respects, Werfel's most important work. He notes that what is clear from the start is that Werfel is attempting to invoke the authority of time, of 100,000 years of "history," to strengthen his indictment of such old enemies as materialism, modernism, and intellectual activism. Although the novel takes the form of an exploratory tour, Steiman observes that there is no sense of wonder or spirit of inquiry. Instead there is an almost smug satisfaction in the process of confirming the author's prejudices. Steiman argues that Werfel's reactionary petulance is clear from the outset. He points out the many pages of schoolmasterly hectoring that mar the novel and observes that for a reader who is more interested in the novel than the author, these passages give this otherwise fascinating work of escapism pointless ballast. They are, however, an essential indicator of the intellectual rendering of accounts that Werfel provides. Steiman remarks that Werfel's publisher tried to produce it as a kind of instant classic at the end of his life, but he suspects that the novel would probably not have been published at all, if Werfel had not already been famous, and that only the vogue of the irrational can account for attempts made to revive it in the mid-1970s (153-59).

Another area of critical interest in the novel has been its religious aspects. Braun (1948-49), for example, used this work and Thomas Mann's *Doktor Faustus* as examples of the turn to religious themes in the modern novel, an aspect of the work that Puttkamer (1952) and Werner (1955) also stress. Many critics such as Bach (1957) consider the role of the Jew and the Bishop as the central focus of the novel, since through these figures, they argue, Werfel reiterates his religious views and his belief in the close connections between Judaism and Christianity.

Klarmann, as usual, was most intrigued by the religious aspects of the work. In two articles in 1946 he calls it a profound new *Divine Comedy* in which Werfel creates a dazzling cosmogony. He believes that the novel contains Werfel's final thoughts about God, the cosmos, and man. In a 1973 article Klarmann stresses as always Werfel's awareness of his messianic mission, noting that in this novel he rejects all intellectual-materialistic dreams of salvation in this world and reaffirms at the end the simple faith of Barbara. Klarmann believes that Werfel's most important goal here is to persuade people to turn away from materialism, to remind them again of their divine origin and divine goal. Werfel wanted people to understand that they are on the earth only briefly and that they do not live by bread alone.

The religious aspects of the novel continued to interest later critics. Schoy-Fischer and Haumann (1984), for example, stress that the search for God lies at the center of the novel. They argue that through the sacrificial death of Io-Knirps the world finds salvation since this symbolic act confirms the end of the astromental age and the beginning of a new future. Like other critics, they point out the important role played by the Jew and the Church in the novel (311-13).

Like most of Werfel's novels, the aesthetic aspects received very little attention. Puttkamer (1952) was one of the first to appreciate the novel not only for the thoughts Werfel presented in it but also the way he presented them. She particularly mentions Werfel's use of suspense, humor, irony, and biting wit. Stöcklein (1954) stresses the book's baroque elements. He argues that in this novel, in which he also detects traces of Swift, Werfel consciously used the model of the baroque fantastic, entertaining, and didactic travel novel, even to the chapter headings (271). Werfel's religious-didactic goals are particularly reminiscent of the baroque, in his view.

Rolleston (1979) was one of the few critics to explore in depth the structure and technique of the novel. He points out in particular the fragmentation of the narrative, the unusual closeness and independence—even arbitrariness—of the narrator, and the narrative posture that seems clumsy and at times tiresome. He argues that the fragmentation and the narrator's insistent presence are the basis of Werfel's technique in the novel. Werfel wants to incorporate into his fiction, he believes, both the rationalist tone of modern science and its thematic randomness. Thus, instead of truth, he presents us with fragments; he accumulates layers of apparent meaning while constantly shifting the bottom layer. Rolleston points out that Werfel's technique of narrative repetition slides into reiteration of cyclical rhythms that undermine a situation's uniqueness. He raises the question of whether this technique is successful in the novel. Judging by its respectful but somewhat detached reception, he believes the answer is no. In general, Werfel's manner, his jovial conservatism, his vulgarities, and the almost indiscriminate richness of his material did not endear him to the critics of the 1950s when some of the basic work on Werfel was done. In the age of the nonfiction novel and other forms of overflow from fiction into life and vice versa, Werfel's intentions in the novel can, he believes, be assessed more fairly. In his view, the novel is a compendium of sophisticated fictional methods, but they are all out in the open, thrusting themselves at the reader. He concludes that form and content are as well matched in *Star of the Unborn* as the New Criticism could desire (66-79).

Critics in the early 1980s were much less positive about the novel. Samuelson (1983), for example, calls it a mixture of the silly and the profound, a view that can be influential since his article appeared in a reference work, the *Survey of Modern Fantasy Literature*, and thus can shape a reader's early response to the novel. He rejects Klarmann's comparison of the novel with the *Divine Comedy*, deeming it incongruous because of the lightweight material of Werfel's novel (1811). Steiman (1985) sums up a typical reaction to the novel. Those who were chiefly concerned with the book as literature rather than autobiography responded to it very negatively. Those who did not share Werfel's spiritual proclivities were repelled by it (159-60).

More recently, however, several critics have taken a fresh look at the novel. Steiner (1987) argues that it is full of subtle and open irony and even good old-fashioned humor, which Werfel conveys with the epic gusto for which he is renowned. Many of his futuristic visions, which are told tongue in cheek, are witty and meant to induce chuckling and laughter. Although Steiner stresses the satirical aspects of the novel, he also points out its serious core (74). Binder (1992a) is most interested in the autobiographical aspects of the work, especially the impact of Werfel's exile and his sense of his impending death. Although he points out that, unlike many exiles, Werfel did not look down upon American culture and loved the colorfulness of American life, he shows that the pain of exile was present, nevertheless. In contrast, Strelka (1992a and b) investigates the political, social, and religious utopias in the novel. His essay is particularly useful for his discussion of Werfel's use of concepts from Tibetan Buddhist philosophy, such as the notion of rebirth. Wagener (1993) agrees with earlier critics that the novel is, in many respects, the sum total of Werfel's religious and humanistic thinking. His remarks about Werfel's style in the novel are helpful. In his view, Werfel uses a number of playful stylistic elements to loosen up the often theoretical, theological-mystical discussion. Humorous reference to Greek and classical mythology is, for example, one of the most marked stylistic elements. Wagener stresses the role of humor in the novel, although, as he notes, it is not always successful. He also points out the many parallels in the novel to Werfel's own time. The Wintergarden, for example, is reminiscent, in his view, of the annihilation camps. Wagener believes that the future world that Werfel depicts in the novel is a negative one: thus the novel is a dystopia rather than a utopia. The underlying tone is pessimistic; despite the many changes in the astromental world, people have not changed, and their hubris has carried them even farther from God (158-67).

Werfel's reputation as a novelist has undergone several changes. Like many reviewers and members of the reading public, early critics such as Kohn-Bramstedt (1934) often viewed Werfel's talents as a novelist very positively. In his view, Werfel had mastered the methods of modern realism and had, in addition, a clear understanding of the dark regions of the subconscious and the determining power of social conditions. He argues that through error and suffering many of Werfel's characters reach a higher level of human worth and maturity, and he likens their development to that of the characters in Dostoyevsky's novels (66-67). For Puttkamer (1952), Werfel's narrative strengths are the suspense he creates, the liveliness of his characters, and his novels' ability to entertain, despite their serious content.

In a lengthy conclusion to his monograph about Werfel's prose works, Brunner (1955) points out Werfel's strengths and weaknesses as a novelist. He notes that Werfel's prose causes difficulties for the critic because of its incommensurability. All attempts to discern a unifying principle fail because of the variety of Werfel's material and themes (142). Unlike other critics who have detected recurring themes in Werfel's prose works, Brunner argues that there is no basic theme that connects Werfel's novels: instead there is thematic discontinuity and heterogeneity, together with a formidable narrative genius. That makes Werfel's epic, in his view, a literary peculiarity. Brunner writes that critics consider Werfel's prose to be a second-class achievement. He notes that in literary histories, for example, it is treated unkindly, almost contemptuously, unlike his early lyric poetry. He observes that, in contrast to the intensity and the avant-garde nature of his poetry, Werfel's prose remains traditional, partly because the author is too contemptuous of form to experiment with new directions. This faithfulness to tradition reflects Werfel's basic conservatism, in Brunner's opinion (146). Although Brunner admires Werfel's narrative talents in creating interesting and entertaining stories, he faults him for his aesthetic weaknesses. For example, in Werfel's prose, the characters are never completely developed. Brunner believes that such weaknesses can be attributed to Werfel's impatience; he rarely took the time to develop his work carefully and thoroughly or to think his thoughts through to the end. This lack of artistic perfection is evident most clearly in his style. In Brunner's view, Werfel writes perhaps the most lively and dynamic prose of his time, but his use of language reveals little discipline or critical self-control. Werfel's indifference to pure art and its rules makes his prose questionable from an aesthetic point of view (142-50). Zahn (1966) raises the question of why, after initially enthusiastic responses to many of his novels, Werfel's fame as a novelist began to fade after his death, and he reaches similar conclusions. He believes that Werfel is considered old-fashioned because he is a narrator of the old school. In his view, Werfel wanted to entertain the reader and not be concerned about form: he was, in fact, contemptuous of *l'art pour l'art* aesthetes (84-85).

Nowadays, however, with the revival of critical interest in Werfel's novels, critics no longer treat them with the contempt Brunner detected in 1955 but, on the contrary, increasingly recognize the power of Werfel's writing, although they are not blind to its flaws. Steiman (1989) summarizes best both its weaknesses and its strengths. Among the weaknesses that he perceives are an aloof and omniscient tone, ideological moralizing, and prolixity. As he points out, Werfel mixes scenes of brilliant dramatic intuition with endlessly detailed bits of melodrama. Moving passages of intense action and powerfully evocative characterization are followed by preachy didacticism and melodrama. Above all, his prose demonstrates a lack of discipline. Steiman concludes that Werfel's lasting achievement lies in those novels and stories in which he powerfully evokes the world of old Austria. He argues that the passage of time has rendered the philosophical ballast in his work less irritating, while the best of his writing retains the quiet and absorbing power that once enthralled millions of readers ( 306-11).

# 5: The Importance of Geography and Culture

MANY CRITICS HAVE been interested in the various geographic, intellectual, and literary forces that contributed to shaping Werfel's thought and works. From early on, critics pointed out that Prague and Czechoslovakia, specifically Bohemia, played a significant role in Werfel's works, and this has continued to be a topic of interest (Abels et al. 1990, 73-78). Others noticed Werfel's debt to the baroque Austrian tradition. More recently, critics have investigated both Werfel's reactions to the United States when he was in exile and the impact that the United States exerted on his works. Another topic of interest has been the great variety of literary forces that shaped Werfel's works. These include the Czech writers with whom he was familiar, his relationship with writers of the Prague circle, the influence of Walt Whitman on his poetry, and the lasting impact of Dostoyevsky.

Almost immediately, critics such as Specht (1926) noticed that Prague was a significant force in Werfel's development as a writer. Specht focuses in particular on the influence of Prague's heritage of mysticism and magic, the medieval and the fantastic, and the occult and superstition, an influence that he does not view totally positively since, together with Werfel's Jewishness, he holds it responsible for what he sees as the non-German elements in his work (26). In Specht's view, Werfel's personality contained a faint Slavic suggestion that he defines as the conflict among hesitant tenderness, indecisive melancholy, a certain fatalism, and vehement outbursts of contemptuous anger, rebelliousness, and recklessness. This Slavic influence, Specht believes, derives from his native city (27).

Later critics explored Werfel's connections not only to his native city but also to Bohemia and the later state of Czechoslovakia. This topic was of particular interest to such Czech critics as Goldstücker. Politzer (1974) mentions that Goldstücker organized two conferences at Castle Liblice near Prague, one in March 1963, dedicated to Kafka, and one in November 1965, called "Weltfreunde," a title obviously taken from Werfel's first poetry collection. Politzer points out the political significance of these conferences, particularly the one in 1965, since the Prague German authors discussed at it had been previously banned. The conference thus served not only to mark the rediscovery of these authors, including Werfel, but was also, as Politzer remarks, one of the early groping attempts to follow Alexander Dubcek's reforms: it was one of the first signs of the Prague Spring (31-32).

Among those who have looked at the impact of Prague and Bohemia on Werfel, there is a great deal of agreement about their significance for Werfel's works and his philosophy of life, although different critics underscore different aspects of the relationship. They argue that the tradition of mysticism and the occult, and the variety of literary movements and ideas from all over Europe that characterized the literary life in Prague, provided Werfel with an important intellectual climate. Some point out that the political climate in Prague shaped Werfel's political views, and others attribute the sense of isolation and alienation in many of Werfel's works to the isolation of the Germans and the Jews as a minority in Prague.

Hyrslová (1958) was one of the first critics to analyze in detail Werfel's close connection to Prague and Bohemia. In her view, these places shaped what she sees as one of the most important aspects of Werfel's works, the notion of belonging somewhere. This sense of belonging gives Werfel and the characters in his work a crucial anchor to their lives. According to Hyrslová, Werfel's characters can be grouped according to whether or not they have a home. She also points out that Werfel's memories of his childhood in Bohemia play a significant role in many of his works. She argues further that Prague was important for shaping Werfel's notion of a people and of *Heimat*, and that such characters as Barbara in *Barbara oder die Frömmigkeit* exemplify for Werfel this notion of *Heimat*. Hyrslová believes, in fact, that Werfel's strong attachment to the Czech people helped him overcome his loneliness. But she makes clear that the Czechoslovakia to which Werfel returns in his memories is not that of the post-First World War period but rather the old Bohemia of the Hapsburg era. She stresses that Werfel refused to abandon his notion of *Heimat* as he knew it and was determined to continue to preserve it, even when it no longer existed (727-32).

Foltin (1960) agrees with Hyrslová that Werfel's work is deeply rooted in Prague. She discusses how the city, its people, its landmarks, and its spiritual and intellectual climate pervade Werfel's writing; and she observes that, even though Werfel left the city in his youth, he continued to evoke it in many of his works throughout his creative life. Its influence can be seen in Werfel's choice of characters and names. Barbara (Babi), for example, is a Czech diminutive for grandmother, and Teta is Czech for aunt. Furthermore, Czechs and Slovaks people many of Werfel's stories, and his play about the Hussite wars, *Das Reich Gottes in Böhmen*, demonstrates his interest in Czech history. Foltin points out that in many personal remarks, such as in his letters to Alma Mahler before their marriage, Werfel attests to the impact that Prague had on him. Another example of it is the local color of the German language of Prague, which was mixed with Czech and Yiddish expressions. Even Werfel's closeness to Catholicism, Foltin believes, has its roots in Prague, a city of massive churches and spires. Foltin concludes that throughout his life, despite his wanderings, Werfel remained a child of Prague and never lost his love for his native city (190-93).

In 1926 Specht pointed out briefly that Werfel's military service decisively influenced him by giving him an opportunity to get to know the Bohemian people. Through this experience, Werfel came to love simple people and to hate all compulsion (38). In an article in which he discusses the short prose piece "Die Stagione," written in 1912 and collected in *Zwischen Oben und Unten* (1975), Goldstücker (1966) develops this point and argues that this early piece is a result of an important widening of Werfel's experience. The Czech environment that Werfel experienced in the provinces, according to Goldstücker, provided him with a model of simple people and aroused his love for them. After this experience, Werfel began to create simple people like those found in Dostoyevsky's works. Goldstücker concludes that his contact with the ordinary Czech people enabled Werfel to use Dostoyevsky's influence on him productively (72).

Thomke (1972) further analyzes the influence of the cultural and spiritual traditions of Prague that Specht had observed. In his view, Werfel's work would be unthinkable without the specific heritage that Prague literature offered. He shows that the intellectual and cultural diversity of Prague was essential both to Werfel and to the other Prague expressionists. This rich intellectual and cultural diversity included such literary and cultural movements as the new romanticism of the turn of the century, the Austrian baroque tradition, *Heimatkunst*, Slavic literature, and, above all, French and German symbolism, Berlin decadence, and *Jugendstil*. In no other city within the German-speaking area, in his view, did so many influences from east, west, north, and south cross, and these diverse trends are evident, above all, in Werfel's lyric poetry. Thomke believes that Werfel was particularly open to the Eastern European spirit. Like Specht, Thomke emphasizes that the city's mystical traditions, especially the *Kabbala*, shaped Brod, Werfel, and other Prague writers. For example, the fantastic, the grotesque, and an obscure mysticism, all of which are evident in Werfel's works, had characterized Prague German literature since the turn of the century (205-18).

In a 1980 article, Goldstücker focuses on Werfel's nostalgia for a lost childhood that derives, in his view, from his connection to Prague. Goldstücker points out that this sentiment is not limited to Werfel's early poetry but appears throughout his works. In the early poems, Werfel is preoccupied with his lost and disappearing childhood, and he recreates childhood experiences to give them at least an illusory continued existence (403). But also as a grown man Werfel tried to hold on to the child's fresh and original ability to experience. This is true even in the works he wrote during his exile years, most of which are filled with nostalgic memories of his childhood in Prague. Following Hyrslová's earlier argument, Goldstücker sees in Werfel's works a recurring sense of homelessness and homesickness and a longing for the lost home that has become idealized in his memory.

Like Thomke, Steiman (1985) stresses that the mystical aspects so fundamental to the novels of Werfel's later period were shaped by Prague's rich spiritual and ethnic textures (9). He disagrees, however, with the majority view that Werfel had warm and uncritical feelings toward Prague, recalling the author's insistence that, for a non-Czech, the city had no reality but was a daydream, a paralyzing ghetto, a hollow world of sham and hallucination. More than other critics, Steiman thus emphasizes Werfel's ambivalence to his native city. He remarks that although Werfel disliked nationalism, he was surprised by the sense of community he felt with the people of Bohemia when they fell victim to the Nazis. Like Hyrslová, Steiman shows that it is the old Bohemia of the Hapsburg era that Werfel evokes since it was not the Bohemia of the Czech state but rather that of the Hapsburg empire to which Werfel's heart went out when the Nazis occupied the Sudetenland. It was the Hapsburg ideal of a supranational, monarchical state that had been Werfel's true home, Steiman argues. Werfel hated nationalism, and nationalism had changed Bohemia into the modern Czech state. Steiman concludes that there was a dual focus to Werfel's attachment to his home: one part of it was the world of simple humanity that his nurse Babi epitomized, and the other was the Hapsburg political system, that Steiman terms a humane and benevolently inefficient administration that allowed a rich diversity of cultural expression to flourish (124).

Recently, Schamschula (1989) follows Hyrslová closely when he argues that the national label is very important for Werfel. Like Hyrslová, he believes that the group, whether it is defined linguistically, geographically, historically, or religiously, plays a central role both in Werfel's private life and in his works; and this reflects, in his opinion, the position of a person in the midst of the ethnic variety of Central Europe. According to his argument, national identity is a determining factor for many of Werfel's characters and an integral part of Werfel's cultural universe. Like Foltin, Schamschula observes that Werfel derives his leaning toward Catholicism from Prague, especially from his nurse Babi. He downplays the ambivalence that Steiman observes in Werfel's feelings about his native city. According to him, Werfel had an almost sentimental relationship to Prague and Bohemia, demonstrated by the frequent spontaneous declarations of love for these places even in his later poems, although he sometimes felt that he was a stranger there (345-49). Abels (1990) picks up on the theme of strangeness. Like earlier critics, he believes that the central motif of strangeness in Werfel's work derives from his roots in Prague (7).

In a recent article, Hyrslová (1992) shows the importance to Werfel of his Central European heritage. She argues that because Werfel grew up among ethnic diversity, he was particularly sensitive to the differences of various national groups. Instead of identifying himself closely with a particular national group, he tried to promote contacts among the groups, as his work as cultural mediator demonstrates. His attempts to promote understanding and tolerance provide a model, Hyrslová believes, from which people in Central Europe can learn today (16).

Several critics pointed out that the feeling of strangeness that characterizes Werfel's work is common to other Prague German writers of the time. Klarmann (1961), for example, notes that despite many differences there is a common thread among Prague German authors, a sense of alienation from the world caused by living in Prague (6). Politzer (1974) develops this in more detail in his discussion of the feeling of strangeness that Werfel, Rilke, Kafka, and other Prague German writers experienced in their childhood. For the Prague Germans, he argues, the city was a social and national ghetto, and for Jews like Werfel and Kafka it was also a religious ghetto. Like Rilke and Kafka, Werfel was aware of the national and social abyss that separated him from the Czechs. Although through their Czech nurses all were exposed to Czech songs, fairy tales, and music, all of this was somewhat discredited because it came from servants. Rilke, Kafka, and Werfel, he believes, were able, however, to see that beyond their own isolated existence there was a community that had asserted itself despite oppression. Because of their isolated situation, Prague gave these writers a setting in which they experienced drastically the critical position of modern man. Politzer points out that Prague was not only an important setting but it was also important as a gate to the Slavic world as whose outpost the city had always experienced itself (20-23). In a later article, Horwath (1981) stresses the gloom, despair, and escapism that pervade Prague German literature, a reflection, in his view, of the social and political upheaval that the Prague Germans faced and their spiritual despair and loss of identity because of growing Czech national assertiveness. According to him, however, Werfel differed from the other Prague German writers in that he avoided their fanatic ethnicity and all-pervading pessimism by becoming safely anchored in the metaphysical world of Catholicism (32).

Several critics have looked closely at Werfel's relationship with other Prague writers, particularly Kafka. Bauer (1980), one of the first to explore this relationship in detail, points out that Kafka often mentioned Werfel in his diaries and his correspondence, especially in his letters to Felice Bauer. Bauer believes that Kafka was proud of his connection to the young, successful author through whom he gained contact to the Kurt Wolff and Rowohlt publishing companies. At times, Bauer argues, Werfel became for Kafka an authority whom he followed blindly. Bauer stresses, however, Kafka's mixed feelings toward Werfel. Although he admired Werfel enthusiastically, he also kept his distance from him. Bauer suggests that Kafka's fascination with Werfel was tinged by half-erotic feelings. In his article, Bauer also discusses the reasons for Kafka's rejection of Werfel's play *Schweiger*, which he criticized for depicting an insignificant and trivial case history. Despite this, Bauer believes that Kafka, like Rilke, never stopped viewing Werfel as a true poet. In contrast to Kafka, however, Werfel left little documentation about their relationship, partly because Werfel's letters have never been systematically collected, let alone edited (191-205).

Anz (1984), who is most interested in Kafka's and Werfel's relationship to Otto Gross, whose theories had an impact on their thought at this time, also suggests why Kafka disliked *Schweiger*, a play that Anz believes is now significant only as a document of the time. In his opinion, one character in the play, Dr. Ottokar Grund, the private docent and anarchist, met with Kafka's strong disapproval. Ottokar Grund was a depiction of Otto Gross, with whom both Kafka and Werfel were closely connected at this time and whom Kafka especially admired. Anz believes that in *Schweiger* and *Barbara* Werfel defamed Gross: in the play, in fact, Werfel made him into a monster (190).

Pasley (1989) explores the relationship between Kafka and Werfel most thoroughly. He believes that Kafka was drawn to Werfel's work above all by its vitality, authenticity, and spontaneity of expression. Because of this, Kafka was willing at first to ignore Werfel's vague philosophical-theological and political beliefs and the frequent sloppiness of his writing. Pasley points out that, unlike Kraus, who found Werfel's lack of intellectual and artistic rigor morally objectionable, Kafka was more tolerant of these shortcomings. In particular, Kafka found something magical about the musicality of Werfel's works. Like Bauer, Pasley discusses Kafka's letters to Felice Bauer and his diary entries that reveal, in his view, that the impact of Werfel's early poetry on Kafka was overwhelming. Although Kafka often comments that Werfel's work both inspires and confuses him, his high initial regard for it is clear. Later, however, Kafka begins to express doubts about Werfel's literary works and the seriousness of Werfel's sense of responsibility as a writer. These doubts culminate in Kafka's rejection of *Schweiger*, a play in which he thinks Werfel betrays not only his artistic powers but also his moral and spiritual responsibilities as a writer. Pasley suggests that what appalled Kafka about the play was that it was merely an interesting local anecdote. In Kafka's view, Werfel had cheapened the profound issues that it was his responsibility as a writer to address by presenting his play in terms of an individual psychiatric case history. Pasley goes beyond Bauer and Anz when he argues that not only did Werfel's work have an impact on Kafka, but the reverse was also true: in his opinion, Kafka's works had a powerful effect on Werfel. In *Nicht der Mörder, der Ermordete ist schuldig*, he believes, Kafka's impact is so strong that one can actually talk of a literary influence since not only are there thematic similarities to such works as *Die Verwandlung* but also the descriptive detail and the rhythm and style of expression are reminiscent of Kafka (81-86).

Several critics have argued that Werfel's contacts with the Czech people were decisive in shaping his religious and political views. Foltin (1974), for example, believes that Werfel saw the Czechs as a nation of strong moral character. This is evident in his works; his Czech characters, she argues, command our moral attention and are usually those guided by high ideals and a concern for others. Foltin suggests that both Werfel and Brod, his mentor, sympathized with the Czechs because they perceived their struggle before they became a state in 1918 to be similar to that of the Jews. Like Hyrslová, Foltin points out, however, that the Czechs in Werfel's works are characterized by nostalgic memories since Werfel does not depict those who struggled for a Czech state but rather the elderly, who were passive in the political struggle and whom he depicts idyllically. In her view, Werfel uses the Czechs in his writing as a metaphor for a people whose strength, like that of Barbara, comes from a spiritual source and whose failure stems from alienation from God. Thus the Czechs and Slovaks provide Werfel with a metaphor for the human condition, not as it is, but as it could and should be (12-20).

Reffet (1983) is also interested in how the Czechs shaped Werfel's political thought. He argues that, from the beginning, Werfel was attracted to fringe groups in society, and at that time such groups were Czech. According to him, the Czechs were Werfel's first experience of a suppressed and colonized people, and his later depictions of oppressor and oppressed derive from his experience with them. In Reffet's view, Werfel was politically inspired by the Czechs because he was fascinated with a small people who suffered, fought, and finally prevailed. For Werfel, he concludes, Czechoslovakia was a model of a tolerant, pluralist state (85-90).

Several critics have been interested in Werfel as a cultural mediator of Czech literature, particularly because of his translations of works by Ottokar Brezina and his introduction to the German translation of Petr Bezruc's *Schlesische Lieder* (1916). In a Marxist approach, Hermsdorf (1964) claims that Werfel's familiarity with Czech literature was his closest contact with a plebeian-rebellious literature that was tied to the people. He argues that Werfel's introduction to Bezruc's *Schlesische Lieder* had the effect of a challenge. According to him, Werfel's strong solidarity here with the Czech poet in the middle of an imperialist war was a contribution to the anti-imperialist forces in Germany and Austria: it was a confession of solidarity with those fighting against imperialism. This, in his view, was how the Czechs understood it. Although Hermsdorf overstates his case ideologically, he shows the importance of Werfel's translation in making Bezruc more widely known. Hermsdorf clearly believes that Bezruc's strong stand against social oppression shaped Werfel's later political views. Foltin (1974), however, finds it particularly ironic that Werfel was interested in Bezruc since, of all the Czech poets of the time, he was, in her view, the most consistently anti-Semitic and anti-German (17). Like Hermsdorf, she points out that Werfel's praise of Bezruc in his introduction was seen at the time as a confession of solidarity with the Czechs.

Some critics have explored what they perceive to be specific influences of Czech literature on Werfel's works. Thomke (1972), for example, mentions these influences, although rather briefly. He notes that Ottokar Brezina's influence on Werfel's poetry has not been generally recognized, and he caustically remarks that if it were recognized, Werfel's poetry might lose even more of its appearance of originality. Brezina was a Catholic who tended, like

Werfel, to mysticism. Like Werfel's, Brezina's lyric poetry glorifies the mysterious harmony in the cosmos and the connectedness of all souls, although
Thomke concedes that such themes are also characteristic of Verhaeren and
Whitman, other influences he detects in Werfel's early lyric poetry. Thomke
also mentions that Werfel was influenced by Antonin Sova, especially by his
affirmation of life, and by Petr Bezruc (210-11).

More recently, Schamschula (1989) argues that Werfel's familiarity with
Czech literature went far beyond his work as a translator; it also shaped his
creative work. For example, he points out that in Bozena Nemcova's *Die
Großmutter* (1856), a work that was quickly translated from Czech into German and became one of the most popular books of the nineteenth century,
there is a character that closely resembles Barbara in *Barbara oder die Frömmigkeit*. Another direct influence, he believes, is the figure of the Mittagsgöttin, the Mittagsweib, or the Mittagshexe, which often appears in Czech
literature. In his view, Werfel reworked this figure, which in Czech literature is
usually evil, into a symbol of life (357).

As the discussion of some of the critical response to Werfel's dramas indicated, critics often took on the role of detective in tracking down Werfel's debt
to other literary works and authors. More than any other critic, Thomke
(1972) has pointed out the great variety of literary sources that shaped Werfel's
poetry, and because of these many influences, he finds Werfel too derivative.
According to Thomke, Werfel drew from such sources as the psalms, mystical
and Gnostic traditions, medieval hymns, the poetry of the baroque and Emp-
findsamkeit, the poetry of Klopstock and the young Schiller, Goethe, the
romantics, Mörike, Heine, the folk song, Nietzsche, Liliencron, Holz,
Dehmel, Mombert, Wedekind, Rilke, Brod, Poe, Whitman, Laforgue, Rim-
baud, Kierkegaard, Strindberg, Dostoyevsky, Tolstoy, Brezina, Sova, and
Bezruc. After presenting this long list to support his contention that Werfel's
work lacks originality, Thomke scathingly remarks that it is probably incomplete (300-1). Of this list of sources, however, critics have focused in depth
only on the influence of Dostoyevsky and Whitman on Werfel and have
mentioned the others briefly.

One of the earliest influences detected was that of Walt Whitman.
Although Specht (1926) asserts that Werfel is in no way derivative, he
acknowledges that Werfel's poetry is reminiscent of Whitman's but claims
wrongly that Werfel read him later (91). Bithell (1939) was struck by the
Whitmanesque style of *Der Weltfreund*, in particular by Werfel's use of Whitman's ecstatic apostrophe and the lines of unequal length (423); and others,
such as Puttkamer (1952), Sokel (1959), and Fox (1964), to mention but a few,
shared his opinion. Sokel, for example, observes that Werfel was impressed
with Whitman's ecstatic humanitarianism (19). Recently, Abels (1990) points
out that, after Dostoyevsky, Whitman was Werfel's most decisive literary
experience (26).

Although this influence was frequently noted, it was, surprisingly, not discussed in any depth for many years. Thomke (1972), however, addresses this question more thoroughly. He points out that Werfel read Whitman's *Leaves of Grass* shortly after it was translated into German in 1907 or 1908, and he argues that the indiscriminate love that Werfel proclaims in his early poetry is an essential part of Whitman's influence on German poetry. Thomke believes that the intellectual encounter with Whitman helped determine Werfel's gospel of love. In his estimation, Werfel's stress in his early poetry on the connectedness of all creatures, a theme that is particularly evident in *Der Weltfreund*, is strongly reminiscent of Whitman (234).

More recently, Grünzweig (1988) analyzes Whitman's impact on Werfel in greater depth in an article entitled "Inundated by this Mississippi of Poetry," a quotation from Werfel's later reaction to Whitman in an article called "Thanks" that was published in January 1941 in *Decision*. Grünzweig observes incorrectly, however, that Werfel critics have been reluctant to acknowledge this influence. In his article, he analyzes Werfel's famous poem "An den Leser," from *Der Weltfreund*, which he terms the programmatic poem of early expressionism. For Grünzweig, the similarities between this poem and passages in Whitman's "Song of Myself" are obvious. Like Whitman, who in his poetry projects his persona into the whole world, Werfel extends his "I" to sympathize with all people. Grünzweig points out too the stylistic influence of Whitman's long line. But he perceptively notes some marked differences. He detects in Werfel's poem, for example, a yearning that is not characteristic of Whitman's poetry since Whitman's speaker is certain of his relatedness to the world and does not speak about his desire to be related. In Grünzweig's view, Werfel seems strangely removed from his objects; he expresses his connectedness to the world around him in the past tense, which suggests an isolation of the speaker in the present. Grünzweig believes that Werfel never achieved a union of nature and environment in the way that Whitman did. In contrast to Whitman, Werfel is more hesitant and more alienated by society. Grünzweig wonders whether this is a result of the German-Austrian sociocultural tradition or the bourgeois's inborn sense of hierarchies. He believes that in his poetry Werfel encounters difficulties in achieving a Whitmanesque frame of mind. Rather than retreat in a Whitmanesque fashion and recreate the unity of the world on the level of the senses, Grünzweig concludes, Werfel withdrew in German or European fashion, and this allowed him to stick to his elitist cultural traditions, distrustful of the emergence of modern technological civilizations (56-61).

Another major influence that critics detected not only on Werfel's poetry but also on his prose and drama was the Slavic influence, particularly that of Dostoyevsky and, to a much lesser extent, of Tolstoy. From early on, many reviewers in Germany and the United States noticed this effect. For example, a review of *The Pure in Heart*, the English translation of *Barbara oder die Fröm-*

*migkeit*, by Louis Kronenberger in the *New York Times* on 10 May 1931 was
entitled "Franz Werfel in the Boots of Dostoevsky." Early critics such as
Specht (1926) and Jacobson (1927) were struck by the Slavic influence. As
Jacobson observes, Werfel's Bohemian home was a bridge to the Slavic world,
particularly to the world of Dostoyevsky and Tolstoy. For her, the three pillars
on which Werfel builds are the Slavic world, German idealism, and music
(338).

In the first extensive study of Dostoyevsky's influence on Werfel, Turrian
(1950) argues that Werfel's whole cultural development is unthinkable without
Dostoyevsky. She believes that without this inspiration from the east Werfel's
passion; his obsession with God, which for West Europeans is often incomprehensible; and his fanatical attempt to save the world and himself cannot be
fully understood (39). Turrian stresses the importance of Dostoyevsky in
general for German expressionism: his notion of salvation and of the poet's
calling as prophet and savior were views that shaped both the German expressionist movement as a whole and Werfel in particular. Turrian believes that
Dostoyevsky influenced Werfel's views in several important ways. Werfel's
concept of love, his notion of the purity of childhood, his depiction of the
conflict between father and son, and his stress on salvation through a woman
all owe, in her opinion, an intellectual debt to Dostoyevsky. Another close
parallel is the theme of salvation, which plays a central role in the works of
both authors. Like Dostoyevsky, Werfel shows that all sinners share redemption. In addition, Turrian sees close links between their notion of God as
torment and the dualism of the soul. In virtually all his major beliefs, she
concludes, Werfel owed a strong debt to Dostoyevsky.

Pachmuss (1963) also addresses the question of Dostoyevsky's influence on
Werfel, but, unlike Turrian, she examines not only the parallels between the
two authors but also some crucial differences. For her, the major similarities
are the notion of love as a redeeming power of humanity, the importance of
the fullness of experience in human life, and the propensity for a kind of moral
masochism, expressed in the longing for suffering and the inclination for
martyrdom. Like Dostoyevsky, Werfel often speaks of love as the redeeming
power of humanity, and both hold that people must come to realize their share
of guilt for the sins and suffering of others.

Pachmuss is critical of Turrian's work for focusing only on the affinities
between the two authors. She writes that the similarity in the treatment of
some ideas by both authors should not be overemphasized since the two
writers differed greatly in their aesthetic approaches. Werfel's emphasis on the
mystical and on a person's imaginative and magical relationship to the sur-
rounding world, for example, is alien to Dostoyevsky. Pachmuss sees some of
the greatest differences in their religious attitudes. In her view, Dostoyevsky's
religion, unlike Werfel's, has no trace of mysticism. Despite these differences,
she concludes that Werfel grappled with Dostoyevsky's ideas.

In a later article, Pachmuss (1972) rearticulates and develops these views. She notes that both authors stress such themes as Christian love, people's responsibility for the sins and suffering of others, loneliness, and the duality in the world. Werfel also agrees with Dostoyevsky that intuition is a more reliable guide in life than logic, that truth and spiritual happiness may be attained only through suffering, and that material concerns in life must yield to spiritual pursuits. Like Dostoyevsky, Werfel views all people and all things as revelations of the divine spirit, and both have an antirationalist approach to the world of physical phenomena. In this article, Pachmuss stresses that a major difference between the two authors is in the importance they attribute to spiritual and physical reality. For Werfel, she believes, the divine world of light and goodness comes first and the temporal world second. In contrast, Dostoyevsky viewed both physical and spiritual reality as equally important in human life (419).

Like Pachmuss, Thomke (1972) is critical of Turrian's study, but his criticism is much sharper. He faults Turrian for being superficial in her analysis. For Thomke, Dostoyevsky's strongest impact on Werfel is in his notion that the poet's task is not an aesthetic one; the poet should instead assume the role of prophet and savior. Thomke also believes that the motif of guilt links Werfel to Dostoyevsky since, for both authors, the way to salvation is through guilt and crime (256).

Adams (1975) explores another Slavic impact on Werfel. In her essay, she looks at the similarities between Werfel's and Tolstoy's notions of art and concludes that there is not a direct influence but rather a kinship of spirit. In her view, the most obvious parallel between the two authors is that both were truly religious writers. Like Tolstoy, Werfel considered himself a medium through whom God speaks. Adams points out, however, that Werfel's notion of art is quite different from that of Tolstoy. Werfel views art, she argues, not as an instrument through which to achieve a utopian society of brotherhood of man but as the divine link to man's original happiness before the fall and as a means of communication between God and man (5-18). Pederin (1983) also looks at Werfel's relationship to Tolstoy and Dostoyevsky, and he argues that Werfel managed to link avant-garde Western literary endeavors with the heritage of Russian literature (99).

In addition to the impact of the Slavic tradition, critics have detected a variety of influences in Werfel's works. Werfel's early poetry reminded Naumann (1923) of Stefan George, and he was one of the first to point out Werfel's debt to Klopstock and the young Schiller, a debt that Kohn-Bramstedt (1934) also noticed. Thomke (1972) develops Klopstock's influence on Werfel's early poetry in more depth. In his view, Werfel borrows from Klopstock and the Storm and Stress writers the hymnic form that was popular in the eighteenth century. Like Klopstock, Thomke observes, Werfel wanted to move people (226). He believes that Werfel felt an affinity for Klopstock and the Storm and Stress, but he also remarks that perhaps Werfel was incapable of creating new forms for himself and therefore had to adapt old ones, a comment that underscores Thomke's criticism that Werfel was too derivative. Thomke also points out Werfel's close connections to the young Schiller in such poems as "Vater und Sohn."

As we have seen in the discussion of Werfel's dramas, several critics, especially Klarmann (1959) and Fox (1964), pointed out how the baroque significantly shaped Werfel's views of theater. Thomke (1972) observes how Werfel drew on elements of his baroque heritage in his early lyric poetry. Others have seen this impact not only in Werfel's dramas and poetry but throughout his entire works. Politzer (1961), for example, argues that, like baroque literature, Werfel's work makes a public affair of faith, of the mystery of life and death, of ecstasy and repentance. Like baroque authors, Werfel accomplishes this, he believes, by the seduction and the melody of the language with which he depicts metaphysical problems and experiences (23).

Werfel's relationship to psychoanalysis, specifically to Freud, has been a neglected topic. Although several early reviewers such as Storfer (1931) thought that they detected Freud's influence, especially his notion of the Oedipus complex, in Werfel's work, this area has since then aroused surprisingly little critical interest. Urban (1973) was one of the first to explore in more detail Werfel's relationship to psychoanalysis, and he includes in his article two letters that Werfel wrote to Freud and diary entries in which Werfel mentions Freud, material that was previously unpublished. Urban documents Werfel's familiarity with Freud's work and argues that Werfel had a good knowledge of his theories. Although Urban merely presents his material without analyzing its significance for Werfel's development as a writer, his work was nevertheless important since it brought together previously unpublished documents that shed light on Werfel's attitude toward psychoanalysis.

For several years, interest in this area lagged. Wyatt (1983), in fact, complains about this neglect. Recently, Reffet (1989a) explores in more depth what he sees as Werfel's lifelong confrontation with psychoanalysis. He observes that it is well known that Werfel incorporated into his work a knowledge of psychoanalysis. *Nicht der Mörder, der Ermordete ist schuldig*, for example, was viewed at the time almost as a lecture on psychoanalysis and was reviewed in psychoanalytical journals. Another example of psychoanalytical influence, he believes, is in the play *Spiegelmensch*, in which Thamal acts as a kind of analyst when he frees the country from the monsters, which, in Werfel's own interpretation of the play, represent complexes and suppressed desires (111). According to Reffet, Werfel shows in his early works that psychoanalysis can either free or enslave humanity, depending on the way it is used. In *Schweiger*, for example, the fascist analyst creates tyranny. There is a similar criticism of psychoanalysis in the figure of Gebhart, based on Otto Gross, in *Barbara oder die Frömmigkeit*. In Reffet's opinion, Werfel does not criticize psychoanalysis as a whole in these two works, but rather its excesses. Reffet points out that Werfel later attacked psychoanalysis sharply in such essays as "Realismus und Innerlichkeit" (1931) and "Können wir ohne Gottesglauben leben?" (1932). In his view, however, Werfel did not reject psychoanalysis but only its materialistic one-sidedness (107-20).

Another area of influence that has attracted some critical attention is Werfel's relationship to romanticism. Thomke (1972), for example, points out the strong influences of the romantic period on Werfel's early lyric poetry, and several critics, such as Furness (1989), notice Werfel's critique of romanticism in his novel *Verdi*. In the most thorough article on this topic, Krügel (1967) notes that Werfel displays a puzzling assortment of attitudes toward romanticism, varying from criticism of it as chaotic sentimentality to acceptance of it as the most profound element in the German artistic tradition. In his article, Krügel shows that Werfel's seemingly conflicting statements are in fact not contradictory but arise from his perception of different trends of thought within romanticism itself. Werfel's comments reflect, according to Krügel, two opposing aspects of German romanticism, that of an aestheticism that is hostile to life and that of a sacrificial ethic in the service of life. In his view, Werfel's most significant remarks about romanticism occur in *Verdi*, in his introduction to Verdi's letters, in "Realismus und Innerlichkeit" (1931), and in "Von der reinsten Glückseligkeit des Menschen" (1938). Krügel shows that Werfel's comments on romanticism occur mostly within the context of his attempts to explain himself as an artist. He cautions, however, that Werfel is no dispassionate observer of romanticism. Whether denouncing it or not, his tone is consistently immoderate and personal, as are virtually all of Werfel's pronouncements on culture, religion, and politics in his essays.

Krügel discusses in detail Werfel's kinship with the romantics. For example, a central factor in Werfel's view of life is his mistrust of reason, which had its counterpart in German romanticism. Other close connections are Werfel's use of emotion as an aesthetic criterion, the important position he assigns to music among the arts, and his notion of art as divine manifestation. For Werfel, as for romantics like Wackenroder, Krügel argues, art is significant only if it arises from the heart and appeals to the heart. Form is of no interest if it is divorced from inspiration and emotional effect. Like the romantics, he remarks, Werfel thought that music was preferable to articulate language since music comes from the heart. Of all the romantics, Krügel believes, Werfel was closest to Wackenroder: Werfel's sanctification of art and the pathos with which he communicates artistic experience, for instance, are strongly reminiscent of Wackenroder.

Krügel also discusses Werfel's sharp critique of romanticism. In his estimation, Werfel's main quarrel with it stems from its preoccupation with forces that are hostile to life. Werfel is, for example, opposed to the romantic obsession with death. Unlike the romantics, Krügel stresses, Werfel's cosmic outlook centers on life, not death. For Krügel, the early dramatic piece *Der Besuch aus dem Elysium* is a key work in understanding Werfel's attitude toward romanticism. In this piece, the protagonist embraces death because he cannot face life. Werfel unmasks this romanticism as cowardice and rejects it. Krügel argues that if Werfel attacks romanticism frequently it is because he views it as part of an antiethical tendency in art that is directed against human values and the affirmation of life itself (82-102).

The significance of music in Werfel's life and works has long been a topic of critical interest, although it has not, as yet, been explored in any depth. From early on, critics such as Specht (1926) noticed the musicality of Werfel's poetry, a topic developed by several critics including Klarmann, who stresses the musical nature of Werfel's muse and the enthusiasm that he felt for music. Brunner (1955) gives perceptive insights into the importance of music to Werfel. In his view, Werfel creates out of the spirit of music and considers music the highest and most divine of all the arts (21). As Brunner observes, Werfel glorified, above all, the bel canto as the purest form of music (21-22), hence his enthusiasm for Verdi. Recent critics have agreed with earlier ones about the significance of music and its meaning for Werfel. In the exhibition put on by the Adalbert Stifter Verein, a section was devoted to the ethical and aesthetic function of music in Werfel's life and works. As Abels and others point out, music for Werfel is transcendental: it is the medium for overcoming the rupture between the "I" and the world (Abels et al. 1990, 65-71). Abels (1990) observes that Werfel's forms of expression, even in his prose, are always musical (65).

The impact of Werfel's exile on his works has been a topic of lively interest from the beginning, but especially in more recent years. From early on, several critics pointed out the central theme of exile in many of Werfel's works. Earlier critics generally approached this theme from an existential and metaphysical point of view. For them, the sense of exile was present in Werfel's works long before he was actually forced into exile. It represents, as Klarmann (1973) puts it, Werfel's feeling of cosmic exile, of not belonging in this world; it indicates his sense of homelessness and his longing to return to harmony with God and with the cosmos. With the growing interest in exile studies in the 1970s and 1980s, however, critics turned to the impact of Werfel's actual exile experiences in his host countries. Most attention has been devoted to Werfel's exile in the United States and little attention, as yet, to his exile in France.

Klarmann (1973) was the main spokesman of those who were interested in the metaphysical aspects of the exile theme in Werfel's works. He argues that Werfel's exile was lifelong: from early on, Werfel was deeply familiar metaphysically with the notion of being driven from his home. According to Klarmann's interpretation of this theme, for Werfel, real exile was merely a further radical allegory of what he, like Dostoyevsky, viewed as the predestined instability of life on earth. It was an expression of his belief that when creation was separated from its creator there arose in creation a longing to return from the cosmic exile to its origins (45, 53). Klarmann acknowledges that in the works Werfel wrote during his exile there is a new local color that intensifies the metarealism of his writing but that, in the final analysis, the concerns Werfel addressed remain the same. For example, the experience of being driven out, which is central to *Cella oder die Überwinder* and *Der veruntreute Himmel*, which Klarmann views as Werfel's most important exile works, is evident in such earlier works as *Die Geschwister von Neapel* and in *Musa Dagh*.

In the published version of his 1977 dissertation at the Johannes Gutenberg-Universität Mainz, Weber (1990) agrees with Klarmann that Werfel understood exile not as a political condition but as an existential one that expressed the essential loneliness of people. Unlike Klarmann's religious interpretation of Werfel's notion of exile as exile from God, of which Weber is critical, Weber uses instead a sociopsychological methodology to interpret Werfel's exile stories. Such an approach to Werfel's biography, he argues, sheds light on the development of models of perception that shape not only the exile stories but Werfel's entire work (138). Like all of Werfel's works, he believes, the exile stories are shaped by Werfel's childhood experiences in his family. For example, he argues that Werfel could not sufficiently assimilate the conflicts of his childhood and integrate them into his personality. In his view, these unassimilated crises and the traces of such early fixations as an Oedipus complex and a longing for emotional security continued to determine Werfel's adult personality and are reflected in his work even though he gives them a metaphysical rather than a psychoanalytical interpretation (85, 115).

Reffet (1984) and Betz (1984) are among the few critics who have been interested in Werfel's exile years in France. Reffet remarks that when Werfel arrived in France he was already well know to the French. As he points out, Werfel was the only German-language writer whom French critics accepted without reservation, and he was the first German expressionist poet to be translated into French (95). Reffet also touches on Werfel's attitude to France as it is depicted in his works. In his article, Betz includes a letter that Werfel wrote from Marseilles in 1940 to Louis Gillet, the art historian and critic, in which he expresses his despair at the terrible situation and the difficulties of getting a visa and begs for Gillet's help.

Not surprisingly, because of his popularity in the United States and because of the years he spent in exile in this country, there has been a great deal of critical interest in Werfel's exile and in the attitude toward the United States that he reveals in his literary works. As many have shown, Werfel was one of the most successful German exile writers, and America offered him not only asylum but also financial and popular success and personal recognition.

Frey (1946) was one of the first to investigate the reception of Werfel's works in the United States. He stresses that no other exile writer who found refuge in this country ever attained such phenomenal success as Werfel, and he concludes his article, which is useful for its discussion of reviews of Werfel's work, by observing that Werfel came to occupy an important place in America's literary life (121-28). Another early critic, Arlt (1951), Werfel's friend and translator, was interested chiefly in exploring the impact that the United States had on Werfel. In his view, Werfel's Americanization was an inner rather than an outer one. Outwardly, he remarks, there was little evidence of it, except in some informality in clothes. He points out that, although Werfel never mastered the English language as a conversational tool and rarely spoke it, he nevertheless could read English easily. He read a variety of magazines and newspapers, and he also loved movies, which he attended frequently. In Arlt's opinion, because of Werfel's exposure to these media of various cultural levels, his inner acclimatization to America progressed rapidly since his consciously uncritical attitude allowed him to be open to a wide variety of ideas and language, ranging from Thomas Wolfe and John Steinbeck to Humphrey Bogart and Mickey Mouse. Arlt points out that Werfel made many American friends and absorbed their point of view. Werfel was also fascinated by American history, particularly that of the American West. Another significant factor in shaping Werfel's attitude to the United States, according to Arlt, was the honorary degree that the University of California at Los Angeles awarded him in 1943. Arlt observes that Werfel had never received such recognition in Europe and was deeply moved by it (3-4).

With the growing interest in exile studies in the 1970s, critics began to reassess Werfel's attitude to the United States, as the article by Foltin and Spalek (1976) demonstrates. They argue that in the essays he wrote and the interviews he gave in the United States Werfel attempted to give the oppressed hope by encouraging people to turn inward and to trust in God. In their view, Werfel's political engagement in American exile is firmly anchored in his strong religious convictions, and these explain why he was never bitter, despite his illness and his exile. They believe that Werfel's attitude to the United States differed from that of many exiles who criticized America for its lack of culture and its materialistic consumer society and often reacted to their exile here with sarcasm or resignation. Although Werfel had gone through an anti-American stage in the 1930s and was not free of prejudices, his comments about America during his exile were never bitter or disappointed but rather were characterized by humor. They also note that exile ushered in a fruitful period for Werfel, and they believe that several of the works he wrote in exile—for example, the play *Jacobowsky und der Oberst*, the novel *Stern der Ungeborenen*, some of his stories, and, above all, his late poems—are among the best he ever wrote (646-63).

Critics addressed a variety of aspects of Werfel's experiences in the United States. Moore (1976), for example, includes Werfel in her discussion of exile in Hollywood and stresses the comfortable life that he was able to live. In his discussion of the relationship between exile writers and the American book market, Koepke (1976) focuses on the success of *The Song of Bernadette*. His article is useful for its analysis of reviews of the novel at the time it was published and insights into its reception (106-9). Sándor (1976) sheds light on Werfel's relationship with his American publisher, Ben Huebsch (126-28). According to Steiner (1987), Werfel left an indelible imprint on the American consciousness. As he points out, America was a kind host country, a safe haven for Werfel and for his spiritual and intellectual quest. Werfel's stay in the United States was beneficial, he believes, both to Werfel and to his host country (71-78).

Other critics were interested in exploring Werfel's changing attitude toward the United States. Moeller (1974) believes that his most positive assessment of this country was made around 1920. In *Nicht der Mörder, der Ermordete ist schuldig* and in *Bocksgesang*, for example, Werfel portrays America as the golden frontier, a land of openness and freedom. In the mid-1920s and into the 1930s, Werfel became critical of the United States for its materialism and lack of spiritual values. In "Realismus und Innerlichkeit" (1931), for example, he turned against the United States. As Moeller observes, Werfel had come to see the United States as a country that changed its citizens into soulless, collective beings who work on assembly lines and fulfill their roles as consumers in a gigantic industrial mass production system. After his move to California, however, Werfel's image became concrete and conciliatory (43-48).

Foltin (1982) rearticulates and develops these views. In her opinion, Werfel's image of the United States changed significantly during the course of his stay in this country. She points out that from early on, Werfel had a special relationship to America, in particular in his early years because of the influence of Whitman on his works and his interest in Edgar Allan Poe, whom he considered the greatest architect of lyric poetry. This youthful enthusiasm for Whitman and Poe later broadened to include Sinclair Lewis, Eugene O'Neill, Hemingway, Pearl S. Buck, and Thomas Wolfe. Foltin agrees with Moeller that in such early works as *Nicht der Mörder, der Ermordete ist schuldig* and the drama *Bocksgesang*, Werfel portrays America in a positive light through the image of rural America and freedom. Like Moeller, she notes the shift in Werfel's attitude toward the United States in "Realismus und Innerlichkeit," in which Werfel condemns the country for its materialism and loss of subjective values. Foltin argues, however, that when Werfel was an exile, he came to see the United States as the most reliable ally of those fighting for the salvation of the world, and he began to look at the country in an increasingly friendly light. At the end of his life, in fact, he thought of it with both humor and appreciation. Foltin points out that the exuberant parody of American life in *Stern der Ungeborenen* can be read as the judgment of an author who knows the weaknesses of America and criticizes them but does not reject the country. Foltin concludes that America was intellectually a mixed experience for Werfel, as it

may have been for many exiles, but it was undeniably the environment that
brought him great literary triumph and personal recognition (300-7).

More recently, several critics have turned to Werfel's letters, most of which
still remain unpublished, to gain insights into Werfel's exile and his relationship to America. Berlin (1988) and Berlin, Daviau, and Johns (1991) look at
Werfel's and Alma Mahler-Werfel's correspondence with Ben Huebsch,
Werfel's American publisher, who was the editor and vice-president of Viking
Press. In the 1988 article, Berlin published a selection of letters from the
period 1936 to 1941, which include Werfel's comments about the *Anschluß* and
his early exile. The later article brings the correspondence from 1941 to the
end of Werfel's life, covering both the business relationship and friendship.
The authors observe that the letters contained in the second article read almost
like a cram course in how books are marketed and show that Werfel was
keenly interested in every aspect of the handling of his books and prepared to
complain whenever he thought his interests were not being properly served. In
their opinion, this correspondence provides an unusual perspective on the exile
experience and on Werfel as a writer in general. Although primarily part of a
business correspondence, these letters are informative, they conclude, since
they document Werfel's extraordinary success, which contrasts so sharply with
the plight of the average exile (124).

In an insightful discussion, Steiman (1991) explores Werfel's letters for
what they reflect about his attitude to exile. In the letters he discusses, he sees
certain paradoxes. One of these, he believes, is that in some ways Werfel was
more at home in his American exile than he had been in Europe. As Steiman
points out, Werfel loved California for both its culture and its climate, and he
was not patronizing and contemptuous toward the United States as other
exiles were. In fact, he genuinely enjoyed the movies, magazines, and radio and
delighted in the company of stars, directors, and ordinary people. As Steiman
stresses, America was good to Werfel. He did not have to struggle with the
language since he already had translators, and he had a protector and a friend
in his American publisher before he came. In Steiman's opinion, Werfel's exile
was one of the happiest and most productive periods of his life, despite his
reluctance to leave Europe and despite his serious illness. Steiman argues that
it was not only the material security he enjoyed that enabled him to adapt with
such apparent ease. More important, he stresses, was the fact that because
Werfel's identity was not tied exclusively or even primarily to any national
homeland, the loss of the one in which he lived for twenty years did not affect
him so severely as it might otherwise have done. Steiman also discusses
Werfel's dependence on Alma Mahler-Werfel, and he remarks that, in one
sense, Werfel was never really an exile since his real home was Alma, and he
never lost her (69-80).

Wagener (1992), who traces representative reviews of Werfel's works in
the United States, explores how American reviewers contributed to Werfel's

success in this country. As he aptly observes, German Germanists have had a distanced attitude to Werfel that grew partly out of their reluctance to consider him a serious author, even though they recognized individual achievements. In Wagener's view, German criticism has been too rigidly locked into the dichotomy between art and kitsch, between modern "elite" literature and popular mass culture, a dichotomy that does not exist to the same extent in American criticism. In contrast to their German counterparts, American literary critics did not believe that if a work was entertaining, it was weak. American critics wanted, in fact, a plot that was gripping and suspenseful. They also did not become skeptical of an author just because a work was widely read. Reviewers in the United States were, however, critical of Werfel's religious views, his sentimentality, his "piety," his antirationalism, and his mysticism (1-19; see also Michaels 1992).

Nowadays there is a much greater appreciation and understanding of the rich geographic, cultural, and literary forces that shaped Werfel's works, although some, such as his debt to the Czech literary tradition and the importance of music in his works, still need more critical attention. Because of the interest in exile studies, we also have now a much clearer picture of Werfel's exile years in the United States and the impact of exile on his works, although his exile in France would merit further analysis. As is typical of Werfel criticism, however, there is controversy since some, like Thomke, see Werfel's debt to his literary, cultural, and geographic heritage as further evidence of his lack of originality, while others appreciate how he draws on such diverse sources to create original literary, dramatic, and poetic works.

# 6: Franz Werfel's Religious and Political Thinking

FROM THE BEGINNING, critics recognized the central importance of religion in Werfel's life and works, and its significance is still acknowledged today. In the Werfel exhibition that the Adalbert Stifter Verein organized in 1990, a section was devoted to Werfel and religion (Abels et al. 1990, 59-64), and Karlheinz Auckenthaler is at work on a monograph about Werfel and religion. Like earlier critics, Wagener (1993) believes that it is the strength of Werfel's religious convictions that unifies his work and fills it with an inner spirit of humanity (173). Werfel's religious views were, however, highly controversial and led to heated critical debate. Many of the early reviewers as well as such influential critics as Adolf Klarmann admired what they saw as Werfel's deep religious convictions and treated him respectfully as if he were a philosopher or even a theologian. From the beginning, however, some reviewers saw these religious views as an aesthetic problem that marred Werfel's entire writing. As Werfel's religious views became more pronounced, especially in the works he wrote in the 1930s and during his exile, more voices were raised in protest. Some complained that Werfel's religious writing in several of his works verged on religious propaganda. Even within Catholic circles, where many praised his strong depiction of faith in such novels as *Embezzled Heaven* and *The Song of Bernadette*, there were some serious reservations; some accused him of only a superficial understanding of Catholic faith. Several Jewish critics were even more disturbed by Werfel's religious beliefs and viewed his Catholic sympathies as apostasy and some of his religious ideas as anti-Semitic. Although there is general agreement that Werfel was a religious writer, there have been widely diverging views about how to situate him within a specific religious tradition. For some, especially the earlier critics, Werfel was a Christian and specifically a Catholic writer, whereas others argued that he remained Jewish. More recently, critics have focused on how Werfel tried to reconcile Christianity and Judaism.

Of the critics who focused on Werfel's religious thinking, Adolf Klarmann was for many years the most influential. According to his thesis, religious thinking permeates all of Werfel's works. In a 1939 article, Klarmann explores Werfel's theology and eschatology in his early works; he expands this discussion to include Werfel's later works in an article in *Modern Language Quarterly* in 1946. In Klarmann's view, Werfel's theology and eschatology did not change in any significant way during his life: his views merely deepened with his growing wisdom and experience. In the 1939 article, Klarmann argues that Werfel openly confesses in his early works his belief in Christ as the Messiah. In his opinion, the Christian experience of pity is evident in Werfel's early poetry. Klarmann remarks that Werfel's notion of the poet as the mediator between God and his creation in *Die Versuchung* reflects the views of Thomas Aquinas, although other critics see in this notion the influence of Dostoyevsky. As Klarmann points out, Werfel later rejected the poet's role as a self-appointed redeemer, evident in *Die Versuchung* and the early poetry, since he came to regard this savior complex as the highest form of vanity. Another characteristic of Werfel's religious thinking at this time, according to Klarmann, is his focus on the separation between God and the world, a theme that Werfel often expresses symbolically in the relationship between father and son. Klarmann observes that, unlike other expressionist writers who saw the relationship between father and son as a generational struggle, Werfel viewed it metaphysically. This is evident in the poem "Vater und Sohn," for example, in which Werfel contrasts the original condition of bliss and harmony before creation with the later tragic separation of man from God. In many of his early works, Klarmann argues, Werfel expresses his longing to return to the original harmony with God. Other Christian ideas that pervade Werfel's early works, according to Klarmann, are his belief in salvation through love, penance, and suffering and his conviction that salvation cannot be attained on earth but only at the end of the world when the separation between the creator and the created no longer exists (207). These are all questions, Klarmann remarks, that were the focus of theological debate within Christianity.

In the later article (1946a), Klarmann focuses on several religious themes that permeate Werfel's entire works. One such theme is the role of the poet. In his earliest writing, Klarmann observes, Werfel expresses a strongly pronounced missionary, even messianic, concept of art and the poet. For Werfel, the poet's mission is to reveal in symbols a divine truth that is imparted to him beyond his own control or his desire. In *Die Versuchung* the poet accepts this mission joyously, but later it threatens to become an oppressive burden because it leads to ostracism and to torments within the poet's mind as he struggles to find the solution to man's happiness and final redemption. Klarmann argues that Werfel formulates this dispute between God and his unwilling prophet in *Höret die Stimme* and presents his view of the high mission of art allegorically in *Bernadette*. In Klarmann's opinion, this novel is not only the moving story of a saint; Werfel symbolically depicts divine poesy in the person of Bernadette. Klarmann also sees Werfel's frequent use of the childhood motif as another religious theme because, in his view, it indicates Werfel's longing for pure religious faith. For Werfel, childhood is the stage of pure faith: it is a time when a person is in complete harmony with the universe and its creator and is therefore truly happy. Werfel's longing for such a faith thus accounts for the recurring theme of childhood in his works. As Klarmann points out, the faith that such characters as Bernadette and Barbara possess is that of a child.

Klarmann summarizes what he considers to be some of Werfel's most significant religious beliefs. He argues that Werfel believed that the separation of creation from the creator left a void in both. Thus there arose in creation an "epistrophe," a longing to return to the source from where it came. Klarmann sees this longing in many of Werfel's works. According to Klarmann, Werfel believed that man's soul, which came from God, would return to God from the exile into which all creation was thrown by this separation. Werfel saw the earth as the predestined theater of the drama of redemption and man as the main actor. Since the earth had been chosen for such an exalted mission, it must, in Werfel's view, be the center of cosmic action. Klarmann stresses that Werfel believed that God gave people free will to choose between good and evil and that original sin stemmed from man's choice of evil. Klarmann observes that the belief in the Madonna was an essential element in Werfel's Christianity, and this reverent acceptance of the Virgin led to the final stage of his religious philosophy, his Catholicism, to which he was also attracted because it was supranational and nonsectarian.

Throughout both these articles, Klarmann stresses that Werfel's mission was always a religious one, and he concludes that Werfel at no time wavered in his belief in God. He even attributes Werfel's temporary excursion into radical politics at the end of the First World War to his religious faith, which with its deep compassion and love for all creation made him long to turn the world into a place of happiness for everyone. In Klarmann's view, Werfel misunderstood the political-materialistic eschatology of such politics, and this explains why his political activism was temporary. According to him, Werfel's religious beliefs embraced from the beginning both the Old Testament and the New Testament as divine revelation. He argues that in Werfel's speculations about God and creation the author reiterated his complete acceptance of Christianity but did not abandon his Jewish faith because the divine plan encompassed both (1946a, 392). Klarmann concludes that, at the end of his life, Werfel arrived back at the same station from which he started out: from the naive, unquestioning, intuitive faith of a child, he progressed through intellectual search to a final humble acceptance and confession of pure faith again (1946a, 385).

Lea (1965) shares Klarmann's conviction that religion plays a central role in Werfel's works. In his article he shows that the parable of the prodigal son, a recurring theme in Werfel's works, allegorically expresses Werfel's belief that man is destined to become estranged from God before he can return to Him. He points out that whereas the biblical prodigal son became alienated by yielding to wastefulness and carnality, Werfel's prodigal sons experience worldliness primarily as separation from spirituality. Lea remarks that the rebellious son who breaks away from the father and abandons his ancestral faith is for Werfel a symbol of man's apostasy. He believes that the loss and recovery of spiritual identity that many of Werfel's characters experience has religious significance because it gives their lives the form and substance of a Dantean cycle of sin and redemption. In his view, Werfel's characters must pass from the innocence and belief of childhood through spiritual confusion before they return to a faith that has been challenged by materialism and thereby strengthened and reaffirmed. Lea points out that one form of apostasy to which Werfel's characters are susceptible is the attempt to change the existing social order by revolutionary methods, which Werfel viewed as vain and self-aggrandizing. In Lea's opinion, Werfel's prodigal sons are singled out for the special mission of prefiguring the path that mankind must take, but this mission requires them to be apart. Lea believes that Werfel applied his interpretation of the prodigal son theme to man's entire theological history, which was characterized for Werfel by an ever-widening gulf between God and man (41-53).

Although critics agreed that religious beliefs inform Werfel's works, they were less sure about what religion to situate these beliefs in. For many of the earlier critics, Werfel was one of the most important advocates for a revitalization of Christian ideals, and they admired him as a passionate seeker of God. Paulsen (1938) sees Werfel as a Catholic writer, and he argues that Werfel's religion was close to that of the original Christians in its stress on boundless love (416). Werner (1955) believes that, for most of his life, Werfel was hypnotically attracted to the teachings of Rome. In Werner's view, Werfel's philosophy strikingly resembles orthodox Catholicism in its stress on life as guilt because it is separation from man's metaphysical origin and thus a departure from God. Werner is, however, critical of Werfel's closeness to certain groups in the Catholic Church. Because of Werfel's dislike for revolutionaries, he argues, he allied himself with the most reactionary near-fascist wing of the Catholic Church (142-44). For Grenzmann (1950), Werfel is a religious poet whose works are saturated with a religious feeling for the world. Like many other critics, he finds Werfel's religious beliefs a paradox: he was permeated with the Christian Catholic faith but did not take part in its sacraments; he was a non-Catholic, a non-Christian poet, whose loyalty to persecuted Judaism did not allow him to convert but who became one of the most impressive witnesses of Catholic faith (245).

Other critics were interested in Werfel's relationship to his Jewish faith. Siemsen (1945), for instance, thought that in *Jacobowsky und der Oberst* Werfel affirmed his Jewishness and accepted his Jewish fate (162). For Slochower (1945), Werfel was an example of a Jew who wanted to be a Catholic but could not. In his view, this was because Werfel was conditioned by the very scientific attitude and the analytic procedure that he repudiated. Thus, even when Werfel espouses primitiveness, metaphysics, and Catholic permanence, he also questions them (76). Of the early critics, Brunner (1946) is the most perceptive in his discussion of Werfel's attitude to his Jewish heritage. He explores this in the context of the passage in the *Theologumena* that many critics have considered to be a key passage for understanding Werfel's attitude to Christianity and Judaism. In it Werfel stresses the interdependence of the Jewish and Christian religions and the need for Jews to act as negative witnesses to Christ.

Brunner points out Werfel's belief that, without such negative witnesses, Christ would sink into mere myth. Thus, according to Werfel, salvation could be achieved only through the working together of Christians and Jews. Brunner rightly observes that this is an important concept to Werfel and one to which he returns again and again. Although Brunner acknowledges Werfel's critical distance from Judaism, he concludes that, despite his Christian eclecticism, Werfel remained what he had been all his life, a Jew (220-29).

Using a similar argument, Puttkamer (1952) addresses in detail the relationship between Christianity and Judaism in Werfel's works. She argues that the more deeply the Christian drama of salvation was revealed to Werfel, the more strongly he felt himself to be a Jew. Like Brunner, Puttkamer agrees that the nucleus of Werfel's Christian-Jewish theology is that the Church and Israel must witness for each other, the Church through its positive witness, and Israel through its negative witness, marked by suffering and persecution. In her view, although Werfel believed all his life in Christianity, he could not convert because of this need to witness. Puttkamer suggests how Werfel's position between the two religions brought him a lot of misunderstanding from all sides: many Jews saw him as an apostate; assimilated Jews were annoyed with his Jewish radicalism; Christians complained about his lack of consistency; and unbelievers did not understand the importance of the question (153-64).

One of the best and most thorough articles on Werfel's attitude to Judaism is by Grimm (1985). At the beginning of his article, Grimm takes issue with the many critics, such as Grenzmann (1950), Puttkamer (1952), and Arnim (1961), who view Werfel as a Christian poet. In Grimm's opinion, even critics like Brunner (1946) and Rengstorf (1974), who are more just to the double nature of Werfel's beliefs, nevertheless put the role of Christian belief in the foreground. At the outset, Grimm stresses the difficulties of situating Werfel's religious position. He argues that Werfel was neither dogmatic nor was he concerned with fixing his position within the "petrified" religions. Instead, he sought a lively debate with religion. From the standpoint of the Church, however, Grimm observes, Werfel's attempts at debate had something dilettantish (or poetic) about them.

After his overview of the previous critical literature on Werfel's religious thinking, Grimm turns to an analysis of the role that Jewish issues play in Werfel's life and thought. According to his argument, Werfel's relationship with Judaism shows from early on the tendency for the symbiosis of Christian and Jewish elements that he expresses so forcefully in his later works. Grimm discusses Werfel's negative feelings toward Judaism and his suspicion of Zionism because it seemed to him to revert to a nationalism that he believed the Jews should have long ago overcome. He points out the many times that specifically Jewish themes or Jewish characters appear in Werfel's works, and he agrees with other critics that from 1933 on, such themes come to the foreground. *Theologumena* represents, for Grimm, the last step in Werfel's lifelong reflection upon these issues.

Grimm then turns to an analysis of Werfel's religious beliefs and stresses that belief in God is central to Werfel's works and worldview. From the start, Werfel's belief in the trinity separated him from orthodox Judaism. Grimm cautions, however, that Christianity and belief in Christ were not identical for Werfel, a point that he believes many critics have misunderstood. In Grimm's opinion, the mutual dependence of Christianity and Judaism that is central to Werfel's religious thinking is based on Werfel's remaining in the Jewish faith. Like Brunner (1946), Grimm agrees that Werfel believed that, in order not to sink into myth, Christianity needs those who deny it and who through their suffering testify to its truth. Grimm emphasizes that Werfel viewed anti-Semitism as a metaphysical phenomenon, and, for the same metaphysical reasons, he rejected Zionism. As he points out, it was unthinkable for Werfel to convert since he believed that the positive contribution of Israel to the divine plan was in its suffering participation in the process of salvation. Thus, in order to remain faithful to the task ordained by God, the Jew could not belong to any other religion or nation. Grimm concludes that Werfel did not make a decision for either religion, nor did he try to synthesize them since he thought that the salvation of mankind lay in the dialectic relationship between these two religions, in bearing positive and negative witness to the same truth. Grimm concedes that such a metaphysical interpretation of Jewish history is problematic in the twentieth century, especially after Hitler (259-73).

In his perceptive but highly critical analysis of Werfel's religious beliefs, Steiman (1985) argues that the vision that sustains Werfel's work is neither Christian nor Jewish in any conventional sense, nor is it a mixture of the two: "it is rather, almost iridescent, with a creatively dynamic tension born of the conflicting elements in his origin" (2). Steiman notes that Werfel's notion of Christianity is often the opposite of what Christianity is usually thought to be. In Werfel's estimation, Christianity affirms rather than denies the self; it celebrates rather than denies the world; it rejects all abstraction; and it considers individuality sacred. In Werfel's understanding, Christianity was thus not in any way ascetic but was rather the only genuine hedonism (27). Steiman points out that even while Werfel was becoming something of a propagandist for Roman Catholicism, he could never bring himself to convert to Christianity, a move that he knew would mean deserting his people. Instead, in Steiman's view, Werfel evolved a prolix but shallow theology that gained increasing prominence in his last years (98-99). Steiman believes that even though Werfel continued to affirm the fundamentals of Christianity while remaining firmly ensconced in Judaism, he did not attempt a syncretic reconciliation of the two religions because their distinct historicity was fundamental to his conception of them. In Steiman's view, it was not so much the need to decide or reconcile theological issues but rather the need to elucidate the historical relations between the two that informs Werfel's works. He believes the source of this need, however, to be more aesthetic than analytical. It was a need to affirm in all its painful reality that which is, to see love and beauty in everything, and to reveal the presumptuous and myopic folly of attempting to alter the order of being (166). In Steiman's estimation, *Theologumena* contains Werfel's most important statement of his religious views. Werfel believed that the man Jesus was God incarnate. He also believed that it was historically and theologically necessary for Jews to reject the doctrine of this incarnation. In attempting to resolve this contradiction, Werfel adopted the old notion that the Jews were negative witnesses to the truth of Christianity and that their ostracism and suffering validated this act of negative witnessing. Steiman believes that Werfel's religious views were no conventional faith, and he dismisses them as "an aestheticism and humanism dressed up in philosophical and theological garb" (192), a conclusion that is far removed from the reverent approach taken by Klarmann and others who were convinced of the depth and complexity of Werfel's religious thinking.

In contrast to those critics who believed that Werfel remained Jewish for metaphysical reasons, Schwarz (1992), who uses a sociopsychological approach, argues that Werfel belonged to a generation of Jews that, unlike their parents' generation, could no longer ignore the failure of Jewish attempts to assimilate into Christian society. Werfel refused to convert to Catholicism, according to Schwarz, not only because he thought of it as betrayal but also because he had long since come to realize that he could not escape from being Jewish (165-76).

In a recent article (1992), Steiman rearticulates his criticism of Werfel's religious beliefs and also addresses Werfel's attitude toward anti-Semitism. As Steiman observes, Werfel always insisted that he was a Jew, but a Jew who believed in Christ, and he stresses that Werfel's attachment to Christianity was not to any formal confession. Rather, Werfel saw it as a bulwark of the inner world of the spirit against materialism in all its forms. Steiman points out that, although Werfel understood anti-Semitism in its political and social forms, he obscured this understanding by using quasi-theological language (51). He is critical of Werfel's notion that the Jews are doomed to wander the earth as persecuted aliens and eternal witnesses to a truth they denied since in these ideas "Werfel was adapting the theological currency of medieval antisemitism, according to which divine justice doomed the Jews to homelessness and persecution for their crime of deicide" (58). Thus Werfel believed that anti-Semitism was divinely ordained and historically necessary (59). Steiman argues that where Werfel differs from these anti-Semitic notions, however, is in his emphasis on the merit of the Jews continuing as negative witnesses to Christian belief and the Jewish origin of that belief (58-59).

Wagener (1993) takes a much kinder approach to Werfel's religious views. Like others, he argues that Werfel's religious orientation, his quest for metaphysical values, and his belief in the mission of Christians and Jews are evident throughout his works. As he points out, Werfel was not a systematic thinker; his ideas grew out of his rich experiences in life. For this reason, many of them are assailable from both the Christian and the Jewish perspective (25). Wagener believes that the strength of Werfel's work stems from his "unwavering plea for humanity, for the reestablishment of man's relationship to God, his plea not to succumb to the powers of godlessness, the powers of the modern machine age, the powers of secularism" (173).

Although many critics admired Werfel's confession of religious faith— Braselmann (1960), for example, went so far as to say that his theological message, not his poetic offering, was what would last (78)—some were unhappy about critics' preoccupation with Werfel's religious thinking. Lippelt (1984), for example, notes provocatively that this has been the most obvious trend in Werfel criticism since his death, and he accuses such critics as Grenzmann (1950, 1955), Puttkamer (1952, 1955), Keller (1958), and Braselmann (1960) of turning Werfel into their literary sacristan. He decries this critical direction since he believes that it has hampered Werfel criticism. Werfel criticism that is not theologically oriented, he caustically observes, can not find in its garden any effective antidote to this trend (290-91). Grimm (1985) has similar reservations when he remarks that the number of theological interpretations of Werfel's works in the critical literature could make one think Werfel was a philosopher rather than a creative writer (259).

Werfel's political thinking aroused as much controversy as his religious views. Critical reaction has ranged from a reverent appreciation of these views to accusations that they were reactionary. In the 1930s and 1940s, reviewers in the United States were disturbed by these political ideas, which they considered dangerous at a time when the Allies were fighting against Nazism, and they criticized Werfel for not taking a more active role in the struggle against Hitler as other exile writers were doing.

One aspect of Werfel's political thinking that aroused interest was his attitude toward Austria. Klarmann (1946b) staunchly defends Werfel from the accusation expressed by several critics that his views of the old Hapsburg empire were reactionary; he calls this charge unwarranted. Klarmann argues that Werfel thought of the old Hapsburg monarchy as a model of how many different nationalities could live together successfully. Out of the Hapsburg empire, Werfel saw arise a true cosmopolitanism, a symbiotic culture and civilization of grace and beauty, and a tolerance and understanding among different peoples, all of which was destroyed in 1918 (115-16). Unlike most later critics, Klarmann does not accuse Werfel of painting an idealized picture of the Hapsburg past.

Williams (1974) agrees with Klarmann that Werfel came to see the imperial past as an era of humaneness, tolerance, and integrity that was thrown into sharp relief by the barbarity of the 1930s. In his discussion of *Twilight of a*

*World,* Williams points out that in contrast to his stories, which originally presented a negative picture of Austria under the Hapsburgs, Werfel's remarks in his introductory essay to the collection demonstrate how his attitude to the old world of Austria had mellowed. Williams accuses Werfel of even misinterpreting his own stories to stress the civilized ambiance of the Hapsburg monarchy that he conjures up in his essay on imperial Austria. Werfel's account of the Hapsburg monarchy, Williams concludes, wavers between idealization and perceptiveness: it is an amalgam of insight and wishful thinking (83-90)

Like Williams, Lea (1982) points out Werfel's glorification of Austria. He argues that Werfel's love for his Austrian home is an important motif in many of his works. Like many other Jews who moved from the provinces to Vienna, he remarks, Werfel idealized and romanticized old Austria as a land that united many different peoples, that was not ruled by nationalistic tendencies, that played the role of mediator between East and West. Central to Lea's argument is a discussion of Werfel's piece, "An Essay upon the Meaning of Imperial Austria," which introduces the English translation of Werfel's story collection *Twilight of a World.* This essay, which Lea calls Werfel's swan song for Austria, provides, in his opinion, a good example of what Claudio Magris (1966) calls the Hapsburg myth because in the essay Werfel praises a land that exists only in his imagination. Lea argues, however, that despite Werfel's glorification of old Austria, he was not in favor of monarchism and nationalism but considered nation states to be basically demonic. In the Hapsburg empire, Werfel saw a higher universal principle and a noble ideal that transcended nationalism. Lea points out that, despite Werfel's idealistic views of Austria, he is at times critical and satirical, for example in his depiction of Austria's role in the *Anschluß* in *Cella oder die Überwinder* and his satirical depiction of the opportunistic Austrian bureaucrat Leonidas in *Eine blaßblaue Frauenschrift* (1941). As Lea observes, however, these works satirize the Austrian state that came into existence after the First World War, not the old Hapsburg state (242-50).

Steiman (1985) gives a perceptive analysis of Werfel's attitude toward Austria. He points out that it was the Hapsburg ideal of a supranational, monarchical state that Werfel considered his real home. In Steiman's opinion, Werfel felt a dual attachment to this home. One part was to the world of simple humanity, represented by his childhood nurse, Babi, and the other was to the political system, which Steiman defines as the humane and benevolently inefficient administration in which potentially destructive national conflicts were suspended, creating an atmosphere that allowed a rich multiplicity of cultural expression to flourish (124). Steiman argues that both aspects of Werfel's early world, the human and the political, were undermined and then transformed by what he saw as the modern disease of nationalism into new states after 1918, the reason for Werfel's nostalgia. Steiman stresses that it was the embodiment of the pre-1918 world that Werfel celebrated in the 1930s. The stories in *Twilight of a World*, for example, are not marred by the same nostalgic tendentiousness as the introductory essay, but the essay blends history with nostalgic reverie. Steiman points out that Werfel's political nostalgia for a mythical Austrian past increased during the 1930s, and he emphasizes that Werfel's works from the late years of that decade are celebrations of a past spiritual ideal rather than its political order.

Steiman believes that, although Werfel's preoccupation with the Hapsburg imperial ideal was clearly stimulated by the political events of the late 1930s, it was no mere romantic refuge for the Jewish exile from Central Europe. As he points out, Werfel had been supportive of a supranational concept for years. An example of this is in *Musa Dagh*, where Werfel portrays the Ottoman empire favorably in comparison with its successor state, a modern republic that is poisoned, according to Werfel, by the heresies of progress and nationalism. The old Ottoman empire provided, in Werfel's view, a supranational framework, based in the religion of Islam, in which its different peoples could live together in harmony. Steiman calls attention to the clear parallel in Werfel's views between the Ottoman imperial ideal and Islam and that of the Hapsburg empire and Catholicism. In Werfel's thinking, in both cases a political and religious ideal coalesced in fruitful symbiosis for the benefit of all they enveloped (127-36).

Reffet (1986) focuses on the change in Werfel's attitude to the Austrian empire. In his view, the rallying call "Down with the Hapsburgs" in 1918 accurately reflects Werfel's position at the time. According to Reffet, Werfel wanted not the defeat of Austria but that of the monarchy and the aristocracy. He points out that in such stories as "Das Trauerhaus," "Kleine Verhältnisse," and "Die Entfremdung," Werfel has no word of regret for the passing of the old order. Reffet argues that, beginning with *Barbara*, Werfel's perspective changed as he came to reject revolution, and he also remarks that Werfel avoided writing about politics in Austria at the beginning of the 1930s for fear of offending Kurt von Schuschnigg, who was often the guest of Werfel and his wife (353-55).

Werfel's involvement in the revolution in Vienna in 1918 and his attitude to political activism in general have aroused lively interest. Most critics viewed Werfel's early essay "Die christliche Sendung" (1917) as a key document in the development of his political views, although some critics, such as Klarmann (1946a), dated Werfel's rejection of political activism from the play *Die Versuchung* (1913). After the publication of the 1917 essay, many were dismayed by the attitude toward political activism that Werfel expresses in it. Max Brod (1916-17), for example, who attacked Werfel's essay for characterizing activism falsely, charged that Werfel's attack on Kurt Hiller's activism was a caricature of activism (717).

Most critics agree that "Die christliche Sendung" is a key work for understanding Werfel's critique of political activism. They point out that here Werfel clearly rejects the possibility of creating human happiness through social action. For him, activism implies a desire for power, and power is always evil. They emphasize that, in Werfel's opinion, all political parties have a similar goal: they seek power to ensure human happiness, but power is corrupting, and thus the revolutions of today become inevitably the establishment of tomorrow. All attempts to change the world are doomed since the reformer of today turns into the tyrant of tomorrow. Werfel thus rejects activism because it is an attempt to reform society rather than to transform the individual from within. Most agree that, for Werfel, the regeneration of the individual must precede the regeneration of society (Klarmann 1939 and 1969, Lea 1968, Foltin and Spalek 1969, Williams 1974). Steiman (1985), who notes that this essay demonstrates the religious, metaphysical, and structural framework that characterizes all of Werfel's subsequent social and political thought, points out that its implication is conservative and reactionary (23, 28), a view with which Wagener (1993) agrees.

Lea (1968) was one of the first to analyze in detail the significance of Werfel's political thought as he expressed it in his works. He believes that the failure of political activism is central to many of Werfel's works, but particularly to his dramas, in which Werfel's conviction that messianic aspirations are heresies is most evident. Werfel's view of political activism as an ultimately self-serving scheme for world salvation seems, in Lea's view, to rule out any means of improving society by political means (331). Lea concludes that Werfel equates any kind of political activism with political radicalism, a view that the lack of political moderates in Werfel's dramas supports.

Pfeifer (1971) was interested in Werfel's changing attitude to revolution and to the Hapsburg monarchy. According to him, Werfel was physically and intellectually touched by the events of 1918 and the destruction of the Danube monarchy. In Pfeifer's view, the most important reasons for Werfel's political involvement at this time were his reaction to his war experiences and his pacifism. He observes, however, that Werfel's dislike of patriarchal society also played a part since Werfel transferred his criticism of patriarchy to the military and to the state. In Pfeifer's opinion, there were several reasons Werfel changed from a supporter of the revolution to its opponent. In part, he was influenced by Alma Mahler, who was strongly against rebellion, but he also disliked the bloodthirstiness of some of the revolutionaries. Pfeifer stresses that Werfel was disturbed by his observation of the psychology of revolution; he believed that the technique of revolution required the control of the masses through hypnosis and their reduction to an easily influenced matter that could be molded by leaders who were seducers (194-205).

Although critics agreed that Werfel rejected all political activism early in his career, Williams (1974) thought that this rejection did not last throughout his life. In his opinion, a marked change in Werfel's attitude toward political activism is expressed in *Musa Dagh*. Here, he believes, Werfel no longer equates activism with self-aggrandizement and the ruthless pursuit of power, as he typically did in his earlier works, but suggests that political action might be a proper course. According to Williams, Werfel's reappraisal of activism came from his awareness of the threat of Hitlerism to the Jews of Central Europe, and this made him change his earlier view that social reform could never be more than a palliative for human ills (76-90).

Werfel's strong opposition to materialism, rationalism, and nihilism, which he expresses in such essays as "Realismus und Innerlichkeit" (1931), "Können wir ohne Gottesglauben leben?"(1932), and "Von der reinsten Glückseligkeit des Menschen" (1938), sparked a great deal of controversy. Some respected him for his emphasis on revitalizing spiritual values, while others attacked him for his conservatism. In a scathing response to "Realismus und Innerlichkeit," for example, Braune (1932), from his left-wing perspective, called the essay reactionary and naive and charged that its author lacked knowledge of the sociological, political, and economic questions he attempted to address. In his view, Werfel's attacks on capitalism and Marxism differed little from those of the Nazis: one could hear the same thing from Hitler and his followers every day (20). Such caustic dismissal of Werfel's political thinking was typical of much of the response at the time, and similar reservations have continued to today. In his discussion of Werfel's essays, Wagener (1993), for example, observes that Werfel's denial of social and historical forces demonstrates the inherent conservatism and politically abstinent spirit of his thinking (21), and he terms it escapist philosophy (22).

Although many critics have addressed different aspects of Werfel's political thinking at various times, a clear, if rather negative, picture did not appear until Steiman (1985) addressed Werfel's political and social views in his discussion of Werfel's major prose works and his essays. I can only highlight certain aspects of Steiman's argument; I can in no way do justice to his extensive and thorough analysis. As Steiman observes, beginning in 1931 Werfel was impelled by the political and economic crisis to speak out more directly about social and political issues, but, in his view, Werfel expresses his comments in a quasi-theological language whose thrust is undeniably conservative. Steiman points out that Werfel's political thinking offered only a spiritual prescription for ills whose political symptoms were becoming acutely critical (123).

Like other critics, Steiman emphasizes Werfel's hatred of nationalism, which he considered a disease that he blamed for destroying the old Hapsburg empire. As he shows, nations and nationalism were Werfel's archenemies. In Werfel's view, nations are demonic while empires are organic (129). According to Steiman's thesis, Werfel used an empire like that of the Hapsburgs as a model for his political thinking. For example, he proposed as a successor to the many nation states in Europe a free assembly of national states in a sort of Central European union (125-26). In Steiman's opinion, Werfel sensed the practical problems confronting the reestablishment of a supranational state but did not attempt in any way to delineate them, much less come to grips with them. Although Werfel knew that the political institutions he advocated could not be easily adapted to modern industrial society, he did not attempt to refine and elaborate his political ideas to facilitate such an adaptation but simply accelerated his attack on the foundations of modern industrial society. Werfel's essentially antimodernist attack on reason and his diagnosis of the world's greatest evils as radical realism and naturalistic nihilism are, for Steiman, expressions of the cultural malaise of his class and the limitations of its critical apparatus (132-33).

Although like other critics Steiman stresses that Werfel was not a systematic thinker or writer, he believes that the maxims and aphorisms in *Theologumena* (1944) contain the closest approximation to a systematic and explicit basis for Werfel's psychotheological concept of society. Steiman summarizes Werfel's thinking here in the following way. According to Werfel, the state is inherently an enemy of the individual. It is a theological hydra from which there is neither escape nor appeal. In Werfel's view of the state, Steiman detects the shrill shriek of the bourgeois screaming to be delivered from taxation (133). Steiman stresses that throughout these aphorisms Werfel's thinking is conservative and reactionary because Werfel did not conceive of society, history, and life as the interacting, interpenetrating maze of obligations, sanctions, responsibilities, and powers within which human beings live with one another. For Werfel, the action of the individual tells us only about the individual: it has no meaning for anyone else. Steiman believes that Werfel's notion of radical individualism projects his vision of society onto a quasi-theological plane. In fact, Werfel reduces the whole socioeconomic process to a cycle whose fundamental dynamic is theological. War, totalitarianism, and capitalism were all part, in Werfel's view, of a vicious cycle that began with the fall from God. Steiman points out that although Werfel's sympathies were with ordinary people, the political implications of his thinking favored those established in wealth and power (134). Even though much of Werfel's writing sounds more like a plea for detached individualism than a brief for the existing order, Steiman observes, the aspects of social behavior he cites as illustrations reveal his petit bourgeois anxieties, which serve again and again to support the status quo. In Steiman's view, Werfel's social critique tends to be psychological rather than social, formal and a priori rather than substantial and analytical (135).

Despite his sharp criticism of Werfel's political views, Steiman shows that Werfel manages to retain an acute power of observation and an analytical insight that are surprising in light of the ideological and reactionary nature of his writing. He believes that Werfel's analysis of social problems shows the division of his loyalties and the theoretical limitations of his thinking. In Steiman's view, what prevented Werfel's pursuit of a consistent and conse- quential political analysis was his mystical, metaphysical past and Alma. Both deflected his concern with present political realities to other spheres. Steiman argues that if it had not been for Alma Mahler-Werfel, Werfel's political analyses would have been pursued to less equivocal conclusions (62) because Werfel genuinely believed that the writer should be an active and enlightened critic of society, not its uncritical supporter (67-68).

From his sociopsychological approach, Weber (1990) comes to a similarly negative assessment of Werfel's political views. He points out that all Werfel's political statements are characterized by his use of unhistorical, unpolitical, "eternal" categories. Because of this, Weber argues, Werfel's political views give more insights into his personal needs than into the concrete political situation and the possibility of changing it (130). Like other critics, Weber shows how Werfel suppresses and reinterprets his brief period of antiauthori- tarian, antibourgeois rebellion. This distancing from his radical political past was caused, in Weber's estimation, by his relationship with Alma Mahler and his acceptance through her into the Catholic upper class of Vienna with its conservative political and cultural values (8). Werfel's 1938 story, "Die arge Legende vom gerissenen Galgenstrick," collected in the third volume of *Erzählungen aus zwei Welten* in the *Gesammelte Werke* in 1954, is set in the Spanish Civil War and exemplifies for Weber the problems of Werfel's treatment of political events. He accuses Werfel here of making the cruelty of fascist reality disappear in a metaphysical mist (179).

Recently, several critics have explored Werfel's attitude to fascism. Steiman (1985) points out that Werfel was no admirer of fascism. He sees Werfel's unwillingness to mention Hitler's name as an expression of his repugnance, his refusal to accord reality to something repulsive by naming it, and, more importantly, an expression of his belief that Hitler and his movement were generalized, metaphysical evils rather than specifically individual, political phenomena. For Steiman, Werfel's perception of Hitlerism in theological or metaphysical terms is central to his evolving response to that phenomenon (68-69). Steiman comments that it is tempting to indulge in sarcasm as one assesses the responses of writers like Werfel or Stefan Zweig to the political situation, but he points out that, although the Austria of Dollfuss and Schuschnigg could be called semifascist and clericofascist, in comparison with its neighbors the Austrian state of the 1930s was moderate and liberal, the context on which Werfel based his judgments (71). Steiman notes that neither in Europe nor in his exile in the United States did Werfel emerge as a signifi- cant spokesman for the antifascist cause but instead wrote articles in praise of the cultural and historical importance of various European peoples threatened by fascism, and he continued to address literary groups on the moral crisis of contemporary European culture (5).

Davidheiser (1991a) explores the question of why, when Werfel clearly had a premonition of the Holocaust, he did not take an active role in fighting against the Nazis. As Davidheiser points out, Werfel's public stance during the Second World War vacillated between outspoken criticism and optimistic restraint. He argues that there were four reasons for this restraint. Werfel's basic optimism prevented him from seeing the severity of the situation. He was also preoccupied with completing his works, and thus his attention was distracted from events in Europe. Another reason was his nonpolitical nature. Lastly there was his financial stake in the publication of his works (15). Davidheiser thus implies that at least one reason for Werfel's lack of activity was a self-serving one.

Like Davidheiser, Wagener (1994) points out Werfel's naiveté about the Third Reich. He stresses that Werfel's attitude toward nationalism—and fascism and National Socialism were for Werfel contemporary forms of nationalism—scarcely changed throughout his life. As Wagener argues, Werfel believed that nationalism was a heresy caused by the loss of religious ties, and this religious understanding of nationalism accounts for the metaphysical language that Werfel uses in his works to confront it, National Socialism, and fascism. Nationalism was a further manifestation for Werfel of the radical nihilism of this century, marked by the intellectualism, abstraction, and belief in science, technology, and collectivism that he despised. Because Werfel viewed National Socialism as an expression of the disrespect for religious and spiritual values, he believed that the guilt for the crimes of National Socialism rested not just with a small leadership group but with the whole German people.

Several critics have shown that Werfel's notion of community was an integral part of his political thinking. In an important article, Bach (1957) explores Werfel's attitude to community and to the collective. She argues that Werfel views the problem of community and the collective from a religious or metaphysical point of view. She defines Werfel's notion of community as one that stems from personal contact, friendship, love, and ties of the family, clan, or people. For him, community includes the brotherly connection of people with one another and the religious community. In contrast, he sees the collective as a grouping for a specific purpose such as work or political connections. Bach argues that all such collectives, in Werfel's opinion, limited the rights of the individual and were thus threatening to the individual (189). Williams (1974) agrees with Bach that the notion of community is central to Werfel's political thinking. In his opinion, Werfel's social ideal is the community, which, as a spontaneous association of like-minded individuals joined together in love and harmony, is the exact opposite of the modern state. For Williams, the weakness of Werfel's argument lies in his denigration of social conflict and political organization and in his exclusive emphasis on spiritual regeneration (70).

Recently, Keith-Smith (1989), in an article in which he discusses Schreyer and Werfel, rearticulates and broadens the discussion of the importance of community in Werfel's works. As he points out, Schreyer and Werfel, as central figures in expressionism, were both concerned with the nature of self and the possible establishment of a new society in which the concept of community would play a determining role (93). In his view, one of the clearest definitions of Werfel's mistrust of the state is to be found in the early dialogue "Euripides oder über den Krieg" (1914). Here Euripides makes the distinction between an individual who can sacrifice him or herself for others and a nation that can never do that. Keith-Smith points out that the claim that a nation has a divine mission to destroy or subjugate other nations is a theme that Werfel employs in *Juarez and Maximilian* and *Das Reich Gottes in Böhmen* to explore the ruthlessness of the demagogue and to reveal where the major flaw lies, namely in the use of power in the service of ideology rather than for the benefit of individual and communal rights. Werfel distinguishes in his works between a nation whose success is measured by quantitative amounts and a people whose quality of life matters more. Keith-Smith points out that, in all cases, Werfel shows the problem of forming or relating to a community as a challenge, whether it is the ecstatic emphases of the early poetry or the more controlled spirituality of the later works. In Werfel's works, a sense of community can be engendered by love, as it is in *Barbara*; through the awareness of the split between Judaism and Catholicism, as it is in *Cella*; or as a response to defend racial identity, as in *Musa Dagh*. Werfel also presents community as a means to individual development. Keith-Smith concludes that in *Stern der Ungeborenen*, for example, Werfel attacks the features of modern society that mitigate against the development of true community, such as the banishment of suffering, the degeneration of death into a taboo, the stockpiling of weapons, and the leveling of human struggles and dignity into mediocrity. As he observes, the need for suffering to sustain the humanity of an individual and/or community is an essential feature of Werfel's idea of an enriched existence. Above all, he argues, it is the recognition of guilt and redemption, responsibility and self-sacrifice that marks the notion of community in Werfel's works (94-103).

Although the critical literature that deals with Werfel's religious and political thinking is helpful for the insights it gives into the development of Werfel's views, it has some shortcomings. As Buck (1961) points out, Werfel is first and foremost a storyteller, a man to whom the world appeared in richly detailed and profuse images. The artistic vision is primary in all his works, and it is necessary to understand this thoroughly before trying to understand the involved and even contradictory logic of his philosophical writings (84-85). Foltin and Spalek (1969) caution that Werfel's essays were not intended as systematic philosophy or theology but rather express his intuitive grasp of the problems (179). Steiman (1985) also stresses that systematic thinking is not

Werfel's strong point. In his view, Werfel tends to litter his pages with some-times humorous but mostly ill-tempered and preachy polemic against the evils of "abstraction" (24). Several critics who were interested in Werfel's political thinking have been tempted to try to impose an order on what are often highly contradictory and unsystematic views. Of main interest to these critics is how Werfel typifies certain social and cultural attitudes of his time. As Steiman points out, for many, the interest in Werfel is in the complexity of his social and cultural positions in a historic period of significance. Werfel the creative writer is, however, often forgotten in the desire of certain critics to use his works as documents of their time.

# 7: Conclusion

IN 1972, TWENTY-SEVEN years after Werfel's death, Lore B. Foltin concluded her monograph on Werfel by pointing out what she thought was the sorry state of Werfel scholarship and criticism. In her opinion, there were many areas of critical and scholarly neglect. For example, there was no reliable bibliography of Werfel's works, a situation she tried to remedy in her monograph, and there was no satisfactory critical account of Werfel's oeuvre since the monographs that had been written all had certain weaknesses, which she accurately detected: Specht's (1926) monograph went only up to 1925 and was too verbose; Puttkamer's (1952) was valuable but left out some works and fragments; Braselmann (1960) was too one-sided in his conviction that Werfel's lasting contribution was theological and not poetic; and Zahn (1966) based his work uncritically on Alma Mahler-Werfel's *Mein Leben*. For Foltin, there was an urgent need for a critical discussion of Werfel's oeuvre that would focus on Werfel the poet, not on Werfel the thinker and the theologian. In addition to this complaint, Foltin listed a variety of other neglected topics: Werfel's lyric poetry needed a more thorough interpretation; the intellectual and cultural impact on Werfel of Bachofen, Bergson, Schopenhauer, and Nietzsche should be investigated; and Werfel's relationship to Tolstoy, Dostoyevsky, and Turgenev, the Russian authors he so greatly admired, needed further study. She was also surprised that Werfel's relationship to music had not been more thoroughly explored. For example, Werfel's adaptations of the three Verdi libretti aroused virtually no critical attention. Other neglected areas were Werfel's poetic language, particularly the development of his use of metaphors and symbols; the connections of his dramas to the epic theater; his relationship to expressionism; his view of history; and the development of his narrative technique and dramaturgy. Like other critics, Foltin noted inadequacies in the *Gesammelte Werke* that Klarmann edited and the lack of work on Werfel's essays and letters (113-15). Thomke (1972) regretted the absence of a reliable edition of Werfel's lyric poetry and pointed out the need for further discussion of Werfel's connections to Prague German literature and to Bohemia and Czechoslovakia. Over a decade later, Wyatt (1983) thought critics still owed Werfel a more thorough analysis of his works and accused them of being reluctant to look at his writing with critical impartiality. He also observed a decrease in interest in Werfel in the scholarly journals.

Although much has changed in Werfel criticism since these critics voiced their concerns, several of the aspects that Foltin mentioned are still neglected today. Critics still tend to be most interested in Werfel the thinker and theologian rather than Werfel the poet, and this interest is in many ways justified. Werfel's thought, unsystematic as it is, provides fascinating insights into his reactions to social and cultural issues in this turbulent period of history and is central to an understanding of his creative works. For example, Steiman (1985) says candidly that he is concerned with assessing not Werfel's literary merit but instead "his faith, the faith of an exile, the ground from which it rose, and its expression in his work" (189). Wagener (1993) discusses various aspects of Werfel's development as a creative writer, but he also stresses the importance of Werfel's religious convictions in unifying his work. We thus have nowadays a good sense of Werfel's development as a thinker but not as good a sense of the development of his poetic, narrative, and dramatic techniques and his language and imagery. Many of the other neglected areas that Foltin detected are still neglected today. Werfel's intellectual debt to such thinkers as Bergson, Bachofen, Schopenhauer, and Nietzsche has not been explored, and no recent critic has reexamined in any detail Werfel's debt to Slavic literature, to mention but two examples.

In other ways, however, there have been encouraging developments in Werfel criticism and scholarship. After many years of neglect, some critics have become interested in Werfel's letters and essays. The work done by Berlin (1988), Berlin and Lindken (1991), Berlin, Daviau, and Johns (1991), and Steiman (1991) may spark further interest in Werfel's neglected correspondence. Recent work done on Werfel's essays is particularly encouraging. Steiman (1985) and Wagener (1993), in particular, recognize in their discussions the significance of Werfel's essays for an understanding of his thought. Werfel's connections to Bohemia and Czechoslovakia have been explored in greater depth since Thomke made his observation in 1972, although his connections to Prague German literature still need further analysis. Recent critics also deal, at least in part, with Werfel's dramaturgy (Huber 1989b, Warren 1989, Reffet 1989c) and to a certain extent with his narrative technique (Zeman 1992, Wagener 1993), although still more work is needed in this area.

Although certain earlier topics such as Werfel's religious and political thinking still continue to fascinate some critics, several recent critics have been most interested in addressing previously neglected areas or works. The early lyric poetry for which Werfel became so famous has attracted relatively little critical interest in recent times in contrast to his exile poetry. One of the most significant developments in Werfel criticism has been a growing interest in his previously neglected dramas. In the last decade, critical interest has turned to Werfel's two last plays, *Der Weg der Verheißung* and particularly *Jacobowsky und der Oberst*. Werfel's expressionist dramas have attracted more critical attention recently, as discussions by Huber (1989b), Abels (1992), Reffet (1992), and

Wagener (1993) indicate. Articles by Schalk (1988), Warren (1989), and Reffet (1989c, 1992) demonstrate a renewed interest in Werfel's historical dramas of the 1920s. Another encouraging sign in this area is the growing critical interest in Werfel's theatrical techniques and his debt to the Austrian and German dramatic traditions and to Max Reinhardt. Thus today we have a much clearer picture of Werfel's contributions to the stage than was previously the case, although more work still needs to be done. Werfel's novels have also attracted more critical attention recently, for which Steiman (1985) deserves much credit. At the time he was writing his monograph, he complained that Werfel as a prose writer was ignored. This is no longer true. In addition to discussions of such works as *Der Tod des Kleinbürgers* and *Musa Dagh*, which are generally acknowledged to be amongst Werfel's most successful and compelling prose works, there has also been a tendency to take a fresh look at such critically neglected works as *Verdi* (Furness 1989), *Höret die Stimme* (Davidheiser 1991b, Auckenthaler 1992b), and *Bernadette* (Zeman 1992, Hadda 1992). *Stern der Ungeborenen* has continued to attract critical attention. Another change in the critical response to Werfel since Foltin expressed her concerns is that Werfel is now generally recognized as an important figure in German and Austrian exile literature. In addition to the greater appreciation of his novels, dramas, and exile poetry, there is a better understanding of how the rich and varied cultural traditions he drew on shaped his works. The most significant change in Werfel criticism in recent times, however, is the more professional stance critics assume. Unlike some of the earlier critics such as Specht and Klarmann, who were strong advocates for Werfel, more recent critics do not blind themselves to the many weaknesses that are all too evident in many of Werfel's works. The older partisan approach that afflicted much of the earlier criticism has given way to a more balanced weighing of strengths and weaknesses.

Wyatt's (1983) complaint that critical interest in Werfel was waning is not valid at the moment. From the beginning of the 1980s, and especially in the last five years, Werfel has been the focus of renewed and lively critical and scholarly activity. Pirumowa (1992) recently concludes in fact that interest in Werfel's works is constantly growing and observes that as long as there is violence in the world, Werfel's books will be indispensable (97). Although this activity can be mostly attributed to the centennial of Werfel's birth, it promises to continue at least for the next few years, during which Karlheinz Auckenthaler's various projects will appear. Despite the recent critical interest in Werfel, most Germanists in Germany and Austria still tend to neglect him.

Werfel remains, however, a controversial figure in the critical literature. There is little agreement on how his works should be evaluated aesthetically, whether, as Thomke (1972) suggests for his early lyric poetry, they should be relegated to the archives, interesting only as documents of their time, or whether they have real literary merit. Nikics's (1992) summary of the lively discussion at the Franz Werfel symposium in Szeged in 1991 expresses this continuing critical controversy well. It is clear that much work remains to be done to complete the picture, especially of Werfel's literary development. In the recent critical literature, however, there is a sense of rediscovery and a desire to reassess Werfel's contributions to German and Austrian literature, typical reactions to the centennial of any writer's birth. Although it seems unlikely that Werfel will ever enjoy the popular and critical acclaim that was accorded him for much of his life, it also seems unlikely that he will suffer the relative neglect that occurred after his death. The pendulum will no longer swing so wildly between acceptance and rejection if critics continue the trend of the last few years to treat Werfel seriously as a significant, if not great, figure in twentieth-century German and Austrian literature.

# Works Consulted

BIBLIOGRAPHIES

Pell, David L. 1971. "Franz Werfel: A Bibliography of Works and Criticism." *Philological Papers* 18: 58-78.

Foltin, Lore B. 1972. *Franz Werfel.* Stuttgart: Metzler.

WORKS BY FRANZ WERFEL

1911. *Der Weltfreund: Erste Gedichte.* Berlin: Juncker.

1913. *Wir sind: Neue Gedichte.* Leipzig: Wolff.

1913. *Die Versuchung: Ein Gespräch des Dichters mit dem Erzengel und Luzifer.* Leipzig: Wolff.

1915. *Einander: Oden, Lieder, Gestalten.* Leipzig: Wolff.

1915. *Die Troerinnen des Euripides.* German adaptation by Franz Werfel. Leipzig: Wolff.

1917. *Gesänge aus den drei Reichen. Ausgewählte Gedichte.* Leipzig: Wolff.

1919. *Der Gerichtstag: in fünf Büchern.* Leipzig: Wolff.

1919. *Der Dschin, Ein Märchen, Gedichte aus dem Gerichtstag; Blasphemie eines Irren.* Vienna: Genossenschaftsverlag; Leipzig: Klemm.

1919. *Die Mittagsgöttin: Ein Zauberspiel.* Munich: Wolff.

1920. *Der Besuch aus dem Elysium: Romantisches Drama in einem Aufzug.* Munich: Wolff. (First published in *Herder-Blätter* 1 (3), 1912.)

1920. *Nicht der Mörder, der Ermordete ist schuldig: Eine Novelle.* Munich: Wolff.

1920. *Spiegelmensch: Magische Trilogie.* Munich: Wolff.

1920. *Spielhof: Eine Phantasie.* Munich: Wolff.

1921. *Bocksgesang: In fünf Akten.* Munich: Wolff. Published 1926 as *Goat Song: A Drama in Five Acts.* Trans. Ruth Langner. Garden City, N.Y.: Doubleday.

1921. *Arien.* Munich: Wolff.

1922. *Schweiger: Ein Trauerspiel in drei Akten.* Munich: Wolff.

1923. *Beschwörungen.* Munich: Wolff.

1924. *Juarez und Maximilian: Dramatische Historie in 3 Phasen und 13 Bildern.* Berlin, Vienna, Leipzig: Zsolnay. Published 1926 as *Juarez and Maximilian: A Dramatic History in Three Phases and Thirteen Pictures.* Trans. Ruth Langner. New York: Simon and Schuster.

1924. *Verdi: Roman der Oper.* Berlin, Vienna, Leipzig: Zsolnay. Published 1925 as *Verdi: A Novel of the Opera.* Trans. Helen Jessiman. New York: Simon and Schuster; London: Jarrolds.

1926. *Paulus unter den Juden.* Berlin, Vienna, Leipzig: Zsolnay. Published 1928 as *Paul Among the Jews (A Tragedy).* Trans. Paul P. Levertoff. London: Diocesan House; Milwaukee: Morehouse.

1926. *Die Macht des Schicksals.* Opera by F. M. Piave and Giuseppe Verdi. Adapted by Franz Werfel. Leipzig: Ricordi.

1926. *Briefe,* by Giuseppe Verdi. Ed. Franz Werfel, trans. Paul Stefan. Berlin, Vienna, Leipzig: Zsolnay.

1927. *Gedichte.* Berlin, Vienna, Leipzig: Zsolnay.

1927. *Der Tod des Kleinbürgers. Novelle.* Berlin, Vienna, Leipzig: Zsolnay. Published 1927 as *The Man Who Conquered Death.* Trans. Clifton P. Fadiman and William A. Drake. New York: Simon and Schuster, republished as *The Death of a Poor Man.* London: Benn.

1927. *Geheimnis eines Menschen. Novellen.* Berlin, Vienna, Leipzig: Zsolnay. Contains "Die Entfremdung," "Geheimnis eines Menschen," "Die Hoteltreppe," "Das Trauerhaus."

1928. *Der Abituriententag. Die Geschichte einer Jugendschuld.* Berlin, Vienna, Leipzig: Zsolnay. Published 1929 as *Class Reunion.* Trans. Whittaker Chambers. New York: Simon and Schuster.

1928. *Neue Gedichte.* Berlin, Vienna, Leipzig: Zsolnay.

1929. *Barbara oder Die Frömmigkeit.* Berlin, Vienna, Leipzig: Zsolnay. Published 1931 as *The Pure in Heart.* Trans. Geoffrey Dunlop. New York: Simon and Schuster, republished as *The Hidden Child.* London: Jarrolds.

1929. *Simone Boccanegra: Lyrische Tragödie in einem Vorspiel und drei Akten.* Opera by F. M. Piave and Giuseppe Verdi. Adapted by Franz Werfel. Leipzig: Ricordi.

1930. *Das Reich Gottes in Böhmen: Tragödie eines Führers.* Berlin, Vienna, Leipzig: Zsolnay.

1931. *Realismus und Innerlichkeit.* Berlin, Vienna, Leipzig: Zsolnay.

1931. *Kleine Verhältnisse.* Berlin, Vienna, Leipzig: Zsolnay.

1931. *Die Geschwister von Neapel.* Berlin, Vienna, Leipzig: Zsolnay. Published 1932 as *The Pascarella Family.* Trans. Dorothy F. Tait-Price. New York: Simon and Schuster; London: Jarrolds.

1932. *Don Carlos.* Opera by J. Méry, C. Du Locle, and Giuseppe Verdi. Adapted by Franz Werfel. Leipzig: Ricordi.

1932. *Das Geheimnis des Saverio.* Leipzig: Reclam.

1932. *Können wir ohne Gottesglauben leben?* Berlin, Vienna, Leipzig: Zsolnay.

1933. *Die vierzig Tage des Musa Dagh: Roman.* 2 vols. Berlin, Vienna, Leipzig: Zsolnay. Published 1934 as *The Forty Days of Musa Dagh.* Trans. Geoffrey Dunlop. New York: Viking, and as *The Forty Days,* London: Jarrolds.

1935. *Schlaf und Erwachen. Neue Gedichte.* Berlin, Vienna, Leipzig: Zsolnay.

1935. *Der Weg der Verheißung: Ein Bibelspiel.* Vienna: Zsolnay. Published 1936 as *The Eternal Road: A Drama in Four Parts.* Trans. Ludwig Lewisohn. New York: Viking.

1937. *In einer Nacht: Ein Schauspiel.* Vienna: Zsolnay.

1937. *Höret die Stimme.* Vienna: Zsolnay. Published 1938 as *Hearken unto the Voice.* Trans. Moray Firth. New York: Viking; London: Jarrolds.

1937. *Twilight of a World.* Trans. H. T. Lowe-Porter. New York: Viking; London: Jarrolds.

1938. *Von der reinsten Glückseligkeit des Menschen.* Stockholm: Bermann-Fischer.

1939. *Cella oder Die Überwinder.* First published in Adolf D. Klarmann, ed. *Franz Werfel: Erzählungen aus zwei Welten.* Vol. 3. *Gesammelte Werke.* Frankfurt am Main: Fischer, 1954.

1939. *Der veruntreute Himmel: Die Geschichte einer Magd.* Stockholm: Bermann-Fischer. Published 1940 as *Embezzled Heaven.* Trans. Moray Firth. New York: Viking; London: Hamilton.

1939. *Gedichte aus dreißig Jahren.* Stockholm: Bermann-Fischer.

1941. *Eine blaßblaue Frauenschrift.* Buenos Aires: Editorial Estrellas.

1941. *Das Lied von Bernadette.* Stockholm: Bermann-Fischer. Published 1942 as *The Song of Bernadette.* Trans. Ludwig Lewisohn. New York: Viking; London: Hamilton.

1942. *Die wahre Geschichte vom wiederhergestellten Kreuz.* Los Angeles: Pazifische Presse.

1942. *Verdi: the Man in his Letters.* Ed. Franz Werfel and Paul Stefan, trans. Edward Downes. New York: L. B. Fischer.

1944. *Jacobowsky und der Oberst: Komödie einer Tragödie in drei Akten.* New York: F. S. Crofts, 1945; Stockholm: Bermann-Fischer, 1944 (the New York edition appeared first). Published 1944 as *Jacobowsky and the Colonel. Comedy of a Tragedy in Three Acts. The Original Play by Franz Werfel.* Trans. Gustave O. Arlt. New York: Viking.

1944. *Between Heaven and Earth.* Trans. Maxim Newmark. New York: Philosophical Library; London: Hutchison.

1945. *Poems.* Trans. Edith Abercrombie Snow. Princeton: Princeton University Press.

1946. *Stern der Ungeborenen: Ein Reiseroman.* Stockholm: Bermann-Fischer. Published 1946 as *Star of the Unborn.* Trans. Gustave O. Arlt. New York: Viking.

1946. *Zwischen Oben und Unten.* Stockholm: Bermann-Fischer.

1946. *Gedichte aus den Jahren 1908–45.* Los Angeles: Pazifische Presse.

1948-75. *Gesammelte Werke.* Ed. Adolf D. Klarmann. Vol. 1, Stockholm: Bermann-Fischer, 1948; vols. 2-7, Frankfurt am Main: Fischer, 1948-74; vol. 8, Munich and Vienna: Langen-Müller, 1975.

1975. *Zwischen Oben und Unten. Prosa, Tagebücher, Aphorismen, Literarische Nachträge.* Ed. Adolf D. Klarmann. Munich: Langen-Müller.

1986. *Das Franz Werfel Buch.* Ed. Peter Stephan Jungk. Frankfurt am Main: Fischer.

1989ff. *Gesammelte Werke in Einzelbänden.* Ed. Knut Beck. Frankfurt am Main: Fischer.

WORKS ABOUT FRANZ WERFEL IN CHRONOLOGICAL ORDER

Polgar, Alfred. 1916. "Franz Werfel: *Die Troerinnen des Euripides.*" *Schaubühne* 12 (25): 599ff. In Polgar, *Kleine Schriften,* ed. Marcel Reich-Ranicki. Vol. 5. Reinbek bei Hamburg: Rowohlt, 1985. 116-17.

Brod, Max. 1916-17. "Franz Werfels 'Christliche Sendung.'" *Jude* 1: 717-24.

Buber, Martin. 1917-18. "Vorbemerkung über Franz Werfel." *Jude* 2: 109-12.

Luther, Arthur. 1922. *Franz Werfel und seine besten Bühnenwerke.* Berlin and Leipzig: Franz Schneider.

Polgar, Alfred. 1922a. "Franz Werfel: *Spiegelmensch.*" *Weltbühne* 18 (25): 626-29. In Polgar, *Kleine Schriften,* ed. Marcel Reich-Ranicki. Vol. 5. Reinbek bei Hamburg: Rowohlt, 1985. 235-40.

Polgar, Alfred. 1922b. "Franz Werfel: *Bocksgesang.*" *Weltbühne* 18 (29): 60-64. In Polgar, *Kleine Schriften,* ed. Marcel Reich-Ranicki. Vol. 5. Reinbek bei Hamburg: Rowohlt, 1985. 227-33.

Naumann, Hans. 1923. *Die deutsche Dichtung der Gegenwart: 1885-1923.* Stuttgart: Metzler.

Polgar, Alfred. 1923. "Franz Werfel: *Schweiger.*" *Weltbühne* 19 (23) 666ff. In Polgar, *Kleine Schriften,* ed. Marcel Reich-Ranicki. Vol. 5. Reinbek bei Hamburg: Rowohlt, 1985. 284-89.

Deutsch, Babette. 1924. "Jewish Poets of Germany." *Menorah Journal* 10: 157-63.

Polgar, Alfred. 1925. "Franz Werfel *Juarez und Maximilian.*" *Weltbühne* 21 (35): 339ff. In Polgar, *Kleine Schriften,* ed. Marcel Reich-Ranicki. Vol. 5. Reinbek bei Hamburg: Rowohlt, 1985. 380-85.

Specht, Richard. 1926. *Franz Werfel: Versuch einer Zeitspiegelung.* Berlin, Vienna, Leipzig: Paul Zsolnay.

Jacobson, Anna. 1927. "Franz Werfel: Eine Würdigung." *Journal of English and Germanic Philology* 26: 337-49.

Kaufmann, F. W. 1927. "Franz Werfel." *Modern Language Journal* 11 (7): 427-33.

Drake, William A. 1928. "Franz Werfel." *Contemporary European Writers*. Freeport, N. Y.: Books for Libraries Press, rpt. 1967. 28-42.

Chandler, Frank W. 1931. *Modern Continental Playwrights*. New York and London: Harper & Brothers. 431-37.

Karsch, Walther. 1931. "Werfel theoretisiert." *Weltbühne* 27 (51): 926-29.

Schumann, Detlev W. 1931. "The Development of Werfel's 'Lebensgefühl' as Reflected in his Poetry." *Germanic Review* 6: 27-53.

Storfer, A. J. 1931."Der Ödipuskomplex bei Werfel und bei Wassermann." *Psychoanalytische Bewegung* 3: 474-78.

Braune, Rudolf. 1932. "Herr Werfel zieht in den Krieg." *Linkskurve* 4 (2): 18-21.

Hitschmann, Eduard. 1932. "Franz Werfel als Erzieher der Väter." *Psychoanalytische Bewegung* 4: 57-61.

Kutzbach, Karl. 1932. "Franz Werfel als geistiger Führer." *Neue Literatur* 33: 13-17.

Kohn-Bramstedt, Ernst. 1934. "Franz Werfel as Novelist." *Contemporary Review* 146: 66-73.

Slochower, Harry. 1934. "Franz Werfel and Alfred Döblin: The Problem of Individualism versus Collectivism in *Barbara* and in *Berlin Alexanderplatz*." *Journal of English and Germanic Philology* 33: 103-12.

Lenz, Harold. 1936. "Franz Werfel's *Schweiger*." *Monatshefte für deutschen Unterricht* 28: 168-72.

Paulsen, Wolfgang. 1938. "Franz Werfel." *Monatshefte für deutschen Unterricht* 30 (8): 409-23.

Bithell, Jethro. 1939. *Modern German Literature 1880-1950*. London: Methuen. 3rd. ed. revised 1959. Page references in the text are to the 1959 edition.

Block, Anita. 1939. *The Changing World in Plays and Theatre*. Boston: Little, Brown. 134-37.

Klarmann, Adolf D. 1939. "Gottesidee und Erlösungsproblem beim jungen Werfel." *Germanic Review* 14: 192-207.

Stamm, Israel S. 1939. "Religious Experience in Werfel's *Barbara*." *PMLA* 54: 332-47.

Hofe, Harold von. 1944. "German Literature in Exile: Franz Werfel." *German Quarterly* 17: 263-72.

Hofe, Harold von. 1945. "Franz Werfel and the Modern Temper." *Christian Century*, 10 Jan. 1945, pp. 47-49.

Klarmann, Adolf D. 1945. "Allegory in Werfel's "Das Opfer" and *Jacobowsky and the Colonel*." *Germanic Review* 20: 195-217.

Lange, Victor. 1945. "Coherence Gone." *Modern German Literature 1870-1940*. Ithaca, N. Y.: Cornell University Press. 79-91.

Siemsen, Anna. 1945. "Zwei Dichter der jüdischen Emigration: Franz Werfel und Alfred Döblin." *Judaica* 1 (2): 157-68.

Slochower, Harry. 1945. "Franz Werfel and Sholom Asch: The Yearning for Status." *Accent* 5 (2): 73-82.

Willibrand, W. A. 1945a. "Franz Werfel's *In einer Nacht, Eine blaßblaue Frauenschrift* and *Jacobowsky*." *Monatshefte für deutschen Unterricht* 37: 146-58.

Willibrand, W. A. 1945b. "The Sermon-Lectures of Franz Werfel." *Books Abroad* 19 (4): 350-55.

Brunner, Robert. 1946. "Franz Werfels theologisches Vermächtnis." *Judaica* 2: 209-29.

Frey, John R. 1946. "America and Franz Werfel." *German Quarterly* 19: 121-28.

Klarmann, Adolf D. 1946a. "Franz Werfel's Eschatology and Cosmogony." *Modern Language Quarterly* 7 (4): 385-410.

Klarmann, Adolf D. 1946b. "Franz Werfel, the Man." *German Quarterly* 19 (2): 113-20.

Werner, Alfred. 1946. "Werfel's Last Search for God." *Jewish Frontier* 13 (April 1946): 76-81.

Parrington, Vernon Louis, Jr. 1947. *American Dreams: A Study of American Utopias*. Providence, R. I.: Brown University Press. 214-16.

Puckett, Hugh W. 1947. "Franz Werfel's Mission." *Germanic Review* 22: 117-25.

Kahler, Erich. 1948. "Franz Werfel's Poetry." *Commentary* 5: 186-89.

Braun, Hanns. 1948-49. "Die Wendung zum Religiösen im modernen Roman: Thomas Mann: *Doktor Faustus*, Franz Werfel: *Stern der Ungeborenen*." *Hochland* 41: 174-80.

Politzer, Heinz. 1949. "Zur Prosa des jungen Franz Werfel." *Neue Rundschau* 60: 283-87.

Grenzmann, Wilhelm. 1950. "Franz Werfel: Im Vorraum der christlichen Welt." In Grenzmann, *Dichtung und Glaube: Probleme und Gestalten der deutschen Gegenwartsliteratur*. Bonn: Athenäum. 241-57.

Politzer, Heinz. 1950. "Franz Werfel: Reporter of the Sublime." *Commentary* 9 (3): 272-74.

Turrian, Marysia. 1950. *Dostojewskij und Franz Werfel: Vom östlichen zum westlichen Denken*. Berne: Paul Haupt.

Arlt, Gustave O. 1951. "Franz Werfel and America." *Modern Language Forum* 36 (1/2): 1-7.

Kolb, Annette. 1951. "Gelobtes Land, gelobte Länder." *Hochland* 43: 274-87.

Schulz-Behrend, George. 1951. "Sources and Background of Werfel's Novel *Die vierzig Tage des Musa Dagh*." *Germanic Review* 26 (2): 111-23.

Puttkamer, Annemarie von. 1952. *Franz Werfel: Wort und Antwort*. Würzburg: Werkbund.

Klarmann, Adolf D. 1954. "Das Weltbild Franz Werfels." *Wissenschaft und Weltbild: Zeitschrift für Grundfragen der Forschung und Weltanschauung* 7 (1/2): 35-48. This article is essentially the same as the 1946 "Werfel's Eschatology and Cosmogony."

Lambasa, Frank. 1954. "Mythological and Supernatural Elements in Four Early Plays of Franz Werfel." Diss. University of Iowa, Iowa City.

Stöcklein, Paul. 1954. "Franz Werfel." In *Deutsche Literatur im zwanzigsten Jahrhundert*, ed. Hermann Friedmann and Otto Mann. Heidelberg: Wolfgang Rothe. 269-87.

Brunner, Franz. 1955. *Franz Werfel als Erzähler*. Zürich: Buchdruckerei Neue Zürcher Zeitung.

Grenzmann, Wilhelm. 1955. *Deutsche Dichtung der Gegenwart*. Frankfurt am Main: Hans F. Menck. 266-78.

Puttkamer, Annemarie von. 1955. "Franz Werfel." In *Christliche Dichter der Gegenwart*, ed. Hermann Friedemann and Otto Mann. Heidelberg: Rothe. 333-44. Also in *Christliche Dichter im 20. Jahrhundert*, ed. Otto Mann. Berne and Munich: Francke, 1968. 360-70.

Werner, Alfred. 1955. "The Strange Life and Creed of Franz Werfel." *Judaism* 4: 142-48.

Bach, Anneliese. 1957. "Die Auffassung von Gemeinschaft und Kollektiv im Prosawerk Franz Werfels." *Zeitschrift für deutsche Philologie* 76: 187-202.

Enright, D. J. 1957. "The Ghosts of Apes: Franz Werfel's *The Forty Days of Musa Dagh*." In Enright, *The Apothecary's Shop: Essays on Literature*. London: Secker and Warburg. 145-67.

Fox, W. H. 1957. "The Problem of Guilt in Werfel's *Nicht der Mörder...*" *German Life and Letters* 11: 25-33.

Reichert, Herbert W. 1957. "The Feud between Franz Werfel and Karl Kraus." *Kentucky Foreign Language Quarterly* 4: 146-49.

Hyrslová, K. 1958. "Zur Frage der Heimat im Werke Franz Werfels." *Zeitschrift für Slawistik* 3: 727-36.

Keller, Ernst. 1958. *Franz Werfel: Sein Bild des Menschen.* Aarau: Buchdruckerei Keller.

Streicher, Siegfried. 1958. "Bernadette und der Dichter." *Schweizer Rundschau* 58: 4-13.

Wiese, Herbert F. 1958. "The Father-Son Conflict in Werfel's Early Works." *Symposium* 12 (1/2): 160-67.

Klarmann, Adolf D. 1959. "Franz Werfel und die Bühne." *German Quarterly* 32 (2): 98-104. Published as "Franz Werfel and the Stage." In Foltin, *Franz Werfel,* 1961a, 50-56.

Sokel, Walter H. 1959. *The Writer in Extremis: Expressionism in Twentieth Century German Literature.* Stanford, Calif.: Stanford University Press.

Braselmann, Werner. 1960. *Franz Werfel.* Wuppertal-Barmen: Emil Müller.

Foltin, Lore B. 1960. "Prague, A Background to Franz Werfel's Work." *Kentucky Foreign Language Quarterly* 7: 188-95.

Günther, Joachim. 1960. "Franz Werfels glückliche Unentwegtheit." *Zeitwende* 31: 740-48.

Mahler-Werfel, Alma. 1960. *Mein Leben.* Frankfurt am Main: S. Fischer.

Scharbach, Alexander. 1960. "Irony in Franz Werfel's Expressionistic Drama *Bocksgesang.*" *Modern Drama* 2 (4): 410-16.

Wildenhof, Ulrich. 1960. "*Der veruntreute Himmel* im Deutschunterricht." *Wirkendes Wort* 10: 176-84.

Arnim, Hans von. 1961. "Franz Werfel." In Hans von Arnim. *Christliche Gestalten neuerer deutscher Dichtung.* Berlin: Wichern. 117-34.

Buck, George C. 1961. "The Non-Creative Prose of Franz Werfel." In Foltin, *Franz Werfel,* 1961a, 83-95.

Foltin, Lore B., ed. 1961a. *Franz Werfel 1890-1945.* Pittsburgh: University of Pittsburgh Press.

Foltin, Lore B. 1961b. "Introduction: A Biography of Franz Werfel." In Foltin, *Franz Werfel,* 1961a, 1-7.

Foltin, Lore B. 1961c. "Prague: Background to Franz Werfel's Work." In Foltin, *Franz Werfel,* 1961a, 8-18.

Guthke, Karl S. 1961. *Geschichte und Poetik der deutschen Tragikomödie.* Göttingen: Vandenhoeck & Ruprecht.

Klarmann, Adolf D. 1961. "Einleitung." Franz Werfel, *Das Reich der Mitte.* Ed. Adolf D. Klarmann. Graz and Vienna: Stiasny. 5-41.

# Works Consulted                161

Lambasa, Frank. 1961. "Franz Werfel's *Goat Song*." In Foltin, *Franz Werfel*, 1961a, 69-82.

Loram, Ian C. 1961. "Franz Werfel's *Die Mittagsgöttin*." In Foltin, *Franz Werfel*, 1961a, 57-68.

McCrossen, Vincent A. 1961. "Zola, Werfel, and the *Song of Bernadette*." *Renascence* 14 (1): 34-40.

Merlan, Wilma Brun. 1961 "Franz Werfel, Poet." In Foltin, *Franz Werfel*, 1961a, 26-38.

Politzer, Heinz. 1961. "Franz Werfel: Reporter of the Sublime." In Foltin, *Franz Werfel*, 1961a, 19-25.

Polzer, Anne. 1961. "Leader of the Renaissance." *Opera News* Feb. 18: 21-23.

Wood, Frank. 1961. "The Role of 'Wortschuld' in Werfel's Poetry." In Foltin, *Franz Werfel*, 1961a, 39-49.

Klarmann, Adolf D. 1962. "Zu Werfels *Besuch aus dem Elysium*." *Herder-Blätter*. Hamburg: Freie Akademie der Künste. ix-xii. Reprint of 1912 edition.

Muschg, Walter. 1963. *Von Trakl zu Brecht: Dichter des Expressionismus*. Munich: R. Piper.

Pachmuss, Temira. 1963. "Dostoevskij and Franz Werfel." *German Quarterly* 36 (4): 445-58.

Fox, W. H. 1964. "Franz Werfel." In *German Men of Letters*, ed. Alex Natan. Vol. 3. London: Oswald Wolff, 2nd ed. 1968. 107-25.

Hermsdorf, Klaus. 1964. "Werfels und Kafkas Verhältnis zur tschechischen Literatur." *Germanistica Pragensia* 3: 39-47.

Adel, Kurt. 1965. "Franz Werfel 1890-1945." *Österreich in Geschichte und Literatur* 9: 322-37.

Günther, Vincent J. 1965. "Franz Werfel." In *Deutsche Dichter der Moderne: Ihr Leben und Werk*, ed. Benno von Wiese. Berlin: Erich Schmidt. 280-99.

Kühner, Hans. 1965. "Franz Werfel als religiöse Gestalt." In *Almanach: Das neunundsiebzigste Jahr*. Frankfurt am Main: S. Fischer. 155-66.

Lea, Henry A. 1965. "Prodigal Sons in Werfel's Fiction." *Germanic Review* 40 (1): 41-54.

Reich-Ranicki, Marcel. 1965. "Franz Werfel und S. L. Jacobowsky." The essay appeared first in the program notes for the premiere of the opera *Jacobowsky und der Oberst* by Giselher Klebe at the Hamburg State Opera on November 2, 1965. In Reich-Ranicki, *Nachprüfung: Aufsätze über deutsche Schriftsteller von gestern*. Stuttgart: Deutsche Verlags-Anstalt, Erweiterte Neuausgabe 1980. 229-34.

Tober, Karl. 1965. "Franz Werfel: *Der Tod des Kleinbürgers.*" *Deutschunterricht* 17 (5): 66-84.

Foltin, Lore B. 1966. "The Franz Werfel Archives in Los Angeles." *German Quarterly* 39 (1): 55-61.

Goldstücker, Eduard. 1966. "Eine unbekannte Novelle von Franz Werfel." *Germanistica Pragensia* 4: 65-73.

Magris, Claudio. 1966. *Der habsburgische Mythos in der österreichischen Literatur.* Salzburg: O. Müller.

Zahn, Leopold. 1966. *Franz Werfel.* Berlin: Colloquium.

Goldstücker, Eduard. 1967. "Die Prager deutsche Literatur als historisches Phänomen." In *Weltfreunde: Konferenz über die Prager deutsche Literatur,* ed. Eduard Goldstücker. Prague: Academia; Berlin and Neuwied: Luchterhand. 21-41.

Krügel, Fred. 1967. "Franz Werfel and Romanticism." *Seminar* 3 (2): 82-102.

Trost, Pavel. 1967. "Die dichterische Sprache des frühen Werfel." In *Weltfreunde: Konferenz über die Prager deutsche Literatur,* ed. Eduard Goldstücker. Prague: Academia; Berlin and Neuwied: Luchterhand. 313-18.

Urzidil, Johannes. 1967. "Der lebendige Anteil des jüdischen Prag an der neueren deutschen Literatur." *Bulletin des Leo Baeck Instituts* 10: 276-97.

Karlach, Hanus. 1968. "Werfels Kampf um das Drama." *Germanistica Pragensia* 5: 93-105.

Kunisch, Hermann. 1968. "Franz Werfels *Reich Gottes in Böhmen* im Zusammenhang der österreichischen Staatsdramen." In *Beiträge zur Dramatik Österreichs im 20. Jahrhundert,* ed. Institut für Österreichkunde. Vienna: Ferdinand Hirt. 71-83.

Lea, Henry A. 1968. "The Failure of Political Activism in Werfel's Plays." *Symposium* 22 (4): 319-34.

Rieder, Heinz. 1968. "Die Tragödie der Seele: Franz Werfels *Juarez und Maximilian.*" In *Beiträge zur Dramatik Österreichs im 20. Jahrhundert,* ed. Institut für Österreichkunde. Vienna: Ferdinand Hirt. 85-97.

Foltin, Lore B., and John M. Spalek. 1969. "Franz Werfel's Essays: A Survey." *German Quarterly* 42 (2): 172-203.

Klarmann, Adolf D. 1969. "Franz Werfel." In *Expressionismus als Literatur,* ed. Wolfgang Rothe. Berne and Munich: Francke. 410-25.

Klarmann, Adolf D., and Rudolf Hirsch. 1969. "Note on the Alma Mahler Werfel Collection." *Library Chronicle* 35: 33-35.

Rosenfeld, Emmy. 1969. "Wanderer zwischen den Welten: Else Lasker-Schüler und Franz Werfel." In *Studi e ricerche di letteratura inglese e americana,* ed. Claudio Gorlier. Vol. 2. Milan: Cisalpino-Goliardica. 259-86.

Foltin, Lore B., and Hubert Heinen. 1970. "Franz Werfel's 'Als mich dein Wandeln an den Tod verzückte': An Interpretation." *Modern Austrian Literature* 3 (2): 62-67.

Lea, Henry A. 1970. "Werfel's Unfinished Novel: Saga of the Marginal Jew." *Germanic Review* 45 (2): 105-14.

Williams, C. E. 1970. "The Theme of Political Activism in the Work of Franz Werfel." *German Life and Letters* 24 (1): 88-94.

Bauer, Roger. 1971a. "La querelle Kraus-Werfel." In *L'Expressionnisme dans le Théâtre Européen,* ed. Denis Bablet et Jean Jacquot. Paris: Editions du Centre National de la Recherche Scientifique. 141-51.

Bauer, Roger. 1971b. "Kraus contra Werfel: Eine nicht nur literarische Fehde." In *Sprache und Bekenntnis.* Berlin: Duncker and Humblot. 315-34. This article is essentially the same as 1971a. Republished in Roger Bauer. *Laßt sie koaxen. Die kritischen Frösch' in Preußen und Sachsen! Zwei Jahrhunderte Literatur in Österreich.* Vienna: Europaverlag, 1977. 181-99.

Hautmann, Hans. 1971. "Franz Werfel, *Barbara oder die Frömmigkeit* und die Revolution in Wien 1918." *Österreich in Geschichte und Literatur* 15: 469-79.

Ivernel, Philippe. 1971. "L'abstraction et l'inflation tragiques dans le théâtre expressionniste allemand." In *L'Expressionnisme dans le Théâtre Européen,* ed. Denis Bablet et Jean Jacquot. Paris: Editions du Centre National de la Recherche Scientifique. 77-91.

Pfeifer, Josef. 1971. "Franz Werfel und die politischen Umwälzungen des Jahres 1918 in Wien." *Études Germaniques* 26: 194-207.

Steilen, Irmgard. 1971. "Franz Werfel: 'Veni Creator Spiritus.'" In *Gedichte der "Menschheitsdämmerung,"* ed. Horst Denkler. Munich: Wilhelm Fink. 125-41.

Dolch, Martin. 1972. "Vom 'Kleinbürger' zum 'Übermenschen': Zur Interpretation von Franz Werfels *Der Tod des Kleinbürgers."* *Literatur in Wissenschaft und Unterricht* 5: 127-43.

Foltin, Lore B. 1972. *Franz Werfel.* Stuttgart: Metzler.

Pachmuss, Temira. 1972. "Dostoevsky, Werfel, and Virginia Woolf: Influences and Confluences." *Comparative Literature Studies* 9: 416-28.

Rengstorf, Karl Heinrich. 1972. "Zwischen Sinai und Golgatha: Zum religiösen Weg Franz Werfels." *Tribüne* 11: 4703-20.

Thomke, Hellmut. 1972. *Hymnische Dichtung im Expressionismus.* Berne and Munich: Francke. 203-303.

Horner, Harry. 1973. "Recollections of My Work with Max Reinhardt: *The Eternal Road.*" In *Max Reinhardt 1873-1973*, ed. George E. Wellwarth and Alfred G. Brooks. Binghamton, N. Y.: Max Reinhardt Archive. 53-74.

Klarmann, Adolf D. 1973. "Franz Werfels Weltexil." *Wort und Wahrheit* 28: 45-58.

Mierendorff, Marta. 1973. "Spekulierende Einbildungskraft und historische Analyse. Franz Werfels Exilroman *Stern der Ungeborenen.*" In *Die deutsche Exilliteratur 1933-45*, ed. Manfred Durzak. Stuttgart: Reclam. 480-88.

Urban, Bernd. 1973. "Franz Werfel, Freud und die Psychoanalyse. Zu unveröffentlichten Dokumenten." *Deutsche Vierteljahrsschrift für Literatur- wissenschaft und Geistesgeschichte* 47 (2): 267-85.

Wächter, Hans-Christof. 1973. *Theater im Exil: Sozialgeschichte des deutschen Exiltheaters 1933-1945.* Munich: Carl Hanser Verlag. 157-60, 183-88.

Wimmer, Paul. 1973. *Franz Werfels dramatische Sendung.* Vienna: Bergland.

Adams, Eleonora K., and Ursula Kuhlmann. 1974. "Perspektiven über Werfels dramatisches Schaffen." In *Views and Reviews of Modern German Literature: Festschrift for Adolf D. Klarmann*, ed. Karl S. Weimar. Munich: Delp. 195-212.

Derré, Françoise. 1974. "Militärerziehung und Vater-Sohnkonflikt in österreichischer Sicht." *Modern Austrian Literature* 7 (1/2): 51-67.

Foltin, Lore B. 1974. "The Czechs in the Work of Franz Werfel." In *Studies in Nineteenth Century and Early Twentieth Century German Literature: Essays in Honor of Paul K. Whitaker*, ed. Norman H. Binger and A. Wayne Wonderley. Lexington, Ky.: Germanistische Forschungsketten Nr. 3. 12-21.

Moeller, Hans-Bernhard. 1974. "Amerika als Gegenbild bei Franz Werfel." *Literatur und Kritik* 9 (81): 42-48. Also in *Deutschlands literarisches Amerikabild*, ed. Alexander Ritter. Hildesheim, New York: Georg Olms, 1977. 401-7. Reprinted as "America as a Counterimage in the Works of Franz Werfel." In *Vistas and Vectors: Essays Honoring the Memory of Helmut Rehder*, ed. Lee B. Jennings and George Schulz-Behrend. Austin: Department of Germanic Languages, University of Texas: 1979. 164-69.

Neumann, Karl. 1974. "Franz Werfel's Early Lyrical Work with Four Poems Newly Translated." *Southern Quarterly* 13: 241-63.

Nyssen, Elke. 1974. "Franz Werfel: *Die vierzig Tage des Musa Dagh.*" In Nyssen, *Geschichtsbewußtsein und Emigration: Der historische Roman der deutschen Antifaschisten 1933-1945.* Munich: Wilhelm Fink. 80-83.

Politzer, Heinz. 1974. "Dieses Mütterchen hat Krallen: Prag und die Ursprünge Rainer Maria Rilkes, Franz Kafkas und Franz Werfels." *Literatur und Kritik* 9 (81): 15-33.

Rengstorf, Karl Heinrich. 1974. "Das Bild des Menschen im dichterischen Werk Franz Werfels." *Tribüne* 13 (51): 5913-30.

Sapper, Theodor. 1974. "Expressionismus im Werk Franz Werfels." In Sapper, *Alle Glocken der Erde: Expressionistische Dichtung aus dem Donauraum.* Vienna: Europaverlag. 105-8.

Williams, C. E. 1974. "Franz Werfel: Advocatus Domini." In Williams, *The Broken Eagle: The Politics of Austrian Literature from Empire to Anschluss.* New York: Barnes and Noble. 60-90.

Adams, Eleonora K. 1975. "The Meaning and Mission of Art as Seen by Franz Werfel and L. N. Tolstoy." *Germano-Slavica* 6: 5-20.

Goldstücker, Eduard. 1975. "Ein unbekannter Brief von Franz Werfel." In *Austriaca: Beiträge zur österreichischen Literatur: Festschrift für Heinz Politzer zum 65. Geburtstag,* ed. Winfried Kudszus and Hinrich C. Seeba. Tübingen: Max Niemeyer. 370-75.

Blumenthal, Warner. 1976. "Father and Son in the East: A New Look at Werfel's *The Forty Days of Musa Dagh.*" In *Studies in Language and Literature: The Proceedings of the 23rd Mountain Interstate Foreign Language Conference,* ed. Charles L. Nelson. Richmond: Eastern Kentucky University Press. 75-79.

Foltin, Lore B., and John M. Spalek. 1976. "Franz Werfel." In *Deutsche Exilliteratur seit 1933,* ed. John M. Spalek and Joseph Strelka. Vol. 1. Berne and Munich: Francke. 644-67.

Koepke, Wulf. 1976. "Die Exilschriftsteller und der amerikanische Buchmarkt." In *Deutsche Exilliteratur seit 1933,* ed. John M. Spalek and Joseph Strelka. Vol. 1. Berne and Munich: Francke. 89-116.

Moore, Erna M. 1976. "Exil in Hollywood." In *Deutsche Exilliteratur seit 1933,* ed. John M. Spalek and Joseph Strelka. Vol. 1. Berne and Munich: Francke. 21-39.

Ritchie, J. M. 1976. *German Expressionist Drama.* Boston: Twayne.

Sándor, András. 1976. "Ein amerikanischer Verleger und die Exilautoren." In *Deutsche Exilliteratur seit 1933,* ed. John M. Spalek and Joseph Strelka. Vol. 1. Berne and Munich: Francke. 117-34.

Reffet, Michel. 1977. "Franz Werfel, Romancier. Un Prophétisme." *Austriaca* 3: 79-93.

Bauer, Roger. 1978. "Werfel als Kritiker (Ein Nachwort zu allen Nachworten)." *Canadian Review of Comparative Literature* 5: 178-92.

Guthke, Karl S. 1978. "Franz Werfels Anfänge: Eine Studie zum literarischen Leben am Beginn des 'expressionistischen Jahrzehnts.'" *Deutsche Vierteljahrsschrift für Literaturwissenschaft und Geistesgeschichte* 52: 71-89.

Krispyn, Egbert. 1978. *Anti-Nazi Writers in Exile.* Athens: University of Georgia Press. 138-43.

Gresch, Donald. 1979. "The Fact of Fiction: Franz Werfel's *Verdi: Roman der Oper*," *Current Musicology* 28: 30-40.

Rolleston, James L. 1979. "The Usable Future: Franz Werfel's *Star of the Unborn* as Exile Literature." In *Protest, Form, Tradition: Essays on German Exile Literature*, ed. Joseph P. Strelka, Robert F. Bell, and Eugene Dobson. University: University of Alabama Press. 57-80.

Bauer, Roger. 1980. "K. und das Ungeheuer: Franz Kafka über Franz Werfel." In *Franz Kafka: Themen und Probleme*, ed. Claude David. Göttingen: Vandenhoeck and Ruprecht. 189-209.

Goldstücker, Eduard. 1980. "Franz Werfel, Prag und Böhmen." In *Bild und Gedanke: Festschrift für Gerhart Baumann zum 60. Geburtstag*, ed. Günter Schnitzler, Gerhard Neumann and Jürgen Schröder. Munich: Wilhelm Fink. 402-9.

Meister, Monika. 1980. "Robert Musils Zeitgenossen im Spiegel seiner Kritik." *Maske und Kothurn* 26: 271-85.

Brynhildsvoll, Knut. 1981. "Themen und Motive aus Ibsens *Peer Gynt* in Franz Werfels 'magischer Trilogie' *Spiegelmensch*." *Edda: nordisk tidsskrift for litteraturforskning* 5: 311-34.

Horwath, Peter. 1981. "The Erosion of *Gemeinschaft*: German Writers of Prague, 1890-1924." *German Studies Review* 4 (1): 9-37.

Ash, Adrienne. 1982. "Lyric Poetry in Exile." In *Exile: The Writer's Experience*, ed. John M. Spalek and Robert F. Bell. Chapel Hill: University of North Carolina Press. 1-23.

Brown, Albert H. E. 1982. "Exildramatiker am Broadway." In *Das Exilerlebnis: Verhandlungen des vierten Symposium über deutsche und österreichische Exilliteratur*, ed. Donald G. Daviau and Ludwig M. Fischer. Columbia, S. C.: Camden House. 64-73.

Davidheiser, James C. 1982. "The Quest for Cultural and National Identity in the Works of Franz Werfel." *Perspectives on Contemporary Literature* 8: 58-66.

Foltin, Lore B. 1982. "Franz Werfel's Image of America." In *Exile: The Writer's Experience*, ed. John M. Spalek and Robert F. Bell. Chapel Hill: University of North Carolina Press. 300-10.

Krispyn, Egbert. 1982. "Jacobowsky: It's a Long Way to Broadway." In *Das Exilerlebnis: Verhandlungen des vierten Symposium über deutsche und österreichische Exilliteratur*, ed. Donald G. Daviau and Ludwig M. Fischer. Columbia, S. C.: Camden House. 224-30.

Lea, Henry A. 1982. "Franz Werfels Requiem für Österreich." In *Das Exilerlebnis: Verhandlungen des vierten Symposium über deutsche und österreichische Exilliteratur*, ed. Donald G. Daviau and Ludwig M. Fischer. Columbia, S. C.: Camden House. 242-52.

Reffet, Michel. 1982. "Stefan Zweig et Franz Werfel: Les Deux Jérémie." In *Stefan Zweig 1881-1942*, ed. Pierre Grappin. Paris: Didier. 51-59.

Koopmann, Helmut. 1983. "Franz Werfel: *Jacobowsky und der Oberst*: Komödie des Exils." In *Drama und Theater im 20. Jahrhundert: Festschrift für Walter Hinck*, ed. Hans Dietrich Irmscher and Werner Keller. Göttingen: Vandenhoeck and Ruprecht. 259-67.

Michaels, Jennifer E. 1983. *Anarchy and Eros: Otto Gross' Impact on German Expressionist Writers*. New York, Berne, Frankfurt am Main: Peter Lang. 145-61.

Paulsen, Wolfgang. 1983. *Deutsche Literatur des Expressionismus*. Berne, Frankfurt am Main, New York: Peter Lang. 108-15.

Pederin, Ivan. 1983. "Franz Werfels Beziehungen zu Tolstoj und Dostojewski." *Österreich in Geschichte und Literatur* 27 (2): 91-99.

Reffet, Michel. 1983. "Franz Werfel und die Tschechoslowakei." *Österreich in Geschichte und Literatur* 27 (2): 84-90.

Samuelson, David N. 1983. "*Star of the Unborn*." In *Survey of Modern Fantasy Literature*, ed. Frank N. Magill. Vol. 4. Englewood Cliffs: Salem. 1807-12.

Wessling, Berndt W. 1983. *Alma: Gefährtin von Gustav Mahler, Oskar Kokoschka, Walter Gropius, Franz Werfel*. Düsseldorf: Claassen.

Wyatt, Frederick. 1983. "Der frühe Werfel bleibt: Seine Beiträge zu der expressionistischen Gedichtsammlung *Der Kondor*." *Amsterdamer Beiträge zur neueren Germanistik* 17: 249-74.

Anz, Thomas. 1984. "Jemand mußte Otto G. verleumdet haben: Kafka, Werfel, Otto Gross und eine 'psychiatrische Geschichte.'" *Akzente* 31 (2): 184-91.

Betz, Albrecht. 1984. "'Gegen die vordringende Barbarei': Zu einigen unveröffentlichten Briefen von Heinrich Mann und Franz Werfel an Louis Gillet." *Exilforschung* 2: 381-92.

Lippelt, Thomas. 1984. "Eine astromentale Welt ohne Vögel, Goldgier und Todesangst: *Stern der Ungeborenen*, Franz Werfels kalifornische Romanvision von 1945." *Text und Kontext* 12 (2): 290-303.

Reffet, Michel. 1984. "Franz Werfel en France." *Austriaca* 10: 87-97.

Schoy-Fischer, Irene, and Heino Haumann. 1984. "Zukunftsvorstellung in Franz Werfels *Stern der Ungeborenen*." *Text und Kontext* 12 (2): 304-14.

Grimm, Gunter E. 1985. "Ein hartnäckiger Wanderer: Zur Rolle des Judentums im Werk Franz Werfels." In *Im Zeichen Hiobs: Jüdische Schriftsteller und deutsche Literatur im 20. Jahrhundert*, ed. Gunter E. Grimm, Hans-Peter Bayerdörfer. Königstein: Athenäum. 258-79.

Steiman, Lionel B. 1985. *Franz Werfel: The Faith of an Exile: From Prague to Beverly Hills*. Waterloo, Ont.: Wilfried Laurier University Press.

Tramer, Erwin. 1985. "Der Dichter zwischen den Religionen." *Literat* 27: 171-72.

Wagener, Hans. 1985-86. "Die Renaissance des Schelms im modernen Drama." In *Der moderne deutsche Schelmenroman*, ed. Gerhart Hoffmeister. *Amsterdamer Beiträge zur neueren Germanistik* 20. 53-76.

Gerhard, Cordula. 1986. *Das Erbe der 'Großen Form': Untersuchungen zur Zyklus-Bildung in der expressionistischen Lyrik*. Frankfurt am Main, Berne, New York: Peter Lang.

Lee, Maria Berl. 1986. "Agony, Pathos and the Turkish Side in Werfel's *Die vierzig Tage des Musa Dagh*." *Philological Papers* (West Virginia University) 31: 58-65.

Reffet, Michel. 1986. "Der gelernte Österreicher: Franz Werfel und das österreichische Selbstverständnis." *Literatur und Kritik* 21 (207/208): 353-61.

Jungk, Peter Stephan. 1987. *Franz Werfel: Eine Lebensgeschichte*. Frankfurt am Main: Fischer. Published 1990 as *Franz Werfel: A Life in Prague, Vienna, and Hollywood*. Trans. Anselm Hollo. New York: Grove Weidenfeld. Page references in the text are to the 1990 translation.

Reffet, Michel. 1987. "Musil und Werfel: Zum Werfelismus und zu zwei Essays." *Modern Austrian Literature* 20 (2): 71-80.

Schmitz, Walter. 1987. "'Ein christusgläubiger Jude': Traditionalismus und Exilerfahrung im Werk Franz Werfels." In *Christliches Exil und christlicher Widerstand*, ed. Wolfgang Frühwald and Heinz Hürten. Regensburg: Verlag Friedrich Pustet. 329-70.

Steiman, Lionel B. 1987. "Franz Werfel: His Song in America." *Modern Austrian Literature* 20 (3/4): 55-69.

Steiner, Carl. 1987. "Showing the Way: Franz Werfel's American Legacy." *Modern Austrian Literature* 20 (3/4): 71-79.

Torberg, Friedrich. 1987. *Liebste Freundin und Alma. Briefwechsel mit Alma Mahler-Werfel*. Munich, Vienna: Langen Müller.

Berlin, Jeffrey B. 1988. "March 14, 1938: 'Es gibt kein Österreich mehr': Some Unpublished Correspondence between Franz Werfel, Alma Mahler Werfel and Ben Huebsch." *Deutsche Vierteljahrsschrift für Literaturwissenschaft und Geistesgeschichte* 62 (4): 741-63.

Grünzweig, Walter. 1988. "'Inundated by this Mississippi of Poetry': Walt Whitman and German Expressionism." *Mickle Street Review* 9: 51-63.

Metzler, Oskar. 1988. "Franz Werfel." In *Österreichische Literatur des 20. Jahrhunderts*, ed. Hannelore Prosche. Berlin: Volk und Wissen. 320-41.

Schalk, Axel. 1988. "Franz Werfels Historie *Juarez und Maximilian*: Schicksalsdrama, 'neue Sachlichkeit' oder die Formulierung eines paradoxen Geschichtsbilds?" *Wirkendes Wort* 38: 78-87.

Smith, Jeremy. 1988. *Religious Feeling and Religious Commitment in Faulkner, Dostoyevsky, Werfel and Bernanos.* New York, London: Garland.

Steiman, Lionel B. 1988. "Franz Werfel." In *Major Figures of Modern Austrian Literature,* ed. Donald G. Daviau. Riverside: Ariadne Press. 423-57.

Brown, Albert H. E. 1989. "Franz Werfel am Broadway." In *Deutschsprachige Exilliteratur seit 1933,* ed. John M. Spalek and Joseph Strelka. Vol. 2. Berne: Francke. 1592-1606.

Clark, Georgina. 1989. "*The Eternal Road:* Werfel's Theatrical Collaboration with Max Reinhardt." In Huber, *Franz Werfel,* 1989a, 211-24.

Furness, R. S. 1989. "A Discussion of *Verdi: Roman der Oper.*" In Huber, *Franz Werfel,* 1989a, 139-51.

Halász, Elöd. 1989. "Trauerhaus und rote Laterne: Eine Symbolenparallele bei Werfel und Krúdy." In *Prager deutschsprachige Literatur zur Zeit Kafkas,* ed. Österreichische Franz Kafka-Gesellschaft. Vienna: Braumüller. 59-68.

Huber, Lothar, ed. 1989a. *Franz Werfel: An Austrian Writer Reassessed.* Oxford, New York, Munich: Berg.

Huber, Lothar. 1989b. "Franz Werfel's *Spiegelmensch*: An Interpretation." In Huber, *Franz Werfel,* 1989a, 65-80.

Ives, Margaret C. 1989. "On Teaching Werfel's Poetry: An Interpretation of 'Eine alte Frau geht.'" In Huber, *Franz Werfel,* 1989a, 5-63.

Jungk, Peter Stephan. 1989. "*Die vierzig Tage des Musa Dagh.*" In Huber, *Franz Werfel,* 1989a, 175-91.

Keith-Smith, Brian. 1989. "The Concept of 'Gemeinschaft' in the Works of Franz Werfel and Lothar Schreyer." In Huber, *Franz Werfel,* 1989a, 93-106.

Midgley, David. 1989. "Piety as Protest: *Barbara oder Die Frömmigkeit.*" In Huber, *Franz Werfel,* 1989a, 125-37.

Pasley, Malcolm. 1989. "Werfel and Kafka." In Huber, *Franz Werfel,* 1989a, 81-91.

Reffet, Michel. 1989a. "Franz Werfel and Psychoanalysis." In Huber, *Franz Werfel,* 1989a, 107-24.

Reffet, Michel. 1989b. "Der Golem-Mythos in Franz Werfels Werk." In *Prager deutschsprachige Literatur zur Zeit Kafkas,* ed. Österreichische Franz Kafka-Gesellschaft. Vienna: Braumüller. 136-52.

Reffet, Michel. 1989c. "Die Wandlung des dramatischen Stils in Franz Werfels spätem Theater: Vom *Reich Gottes in Böhmen* zu *Jacobowsky und der Oberst.*" *Jahrbuch für Internationale Germanistik* 21 (1): 93-113.

Ritchie, J. M. 1989. "The Many Faces of Werfel's *Jacobowsky.*" In Huber, *Franz Werfel,* 1989a, 193-210.

Schamschula, Walter. 1989. "Franz Werfel und die Tschechen." In *Die österreichische Literatur: Ihr Profil von der Jahrhundertwende bis zur Gegenwart (1880–1980)*, ed. Herbert Zeman. Teil I. Graz: Akademische Druck-und Verlagsanstalt. 343-59.

Steiman, Lionel B. 1989. "Franz Werfel," *Dictionary of Literary Biography*, ed. James Hardin and Donald G. Daviau. Vol. 81. Detroit: Gale Research. 300-12.

Wagner, Fred. 1989. "'Das herrliche Verhängnis': The Poetry of Franz Werfel." In Huber, *Franz Werfel*, 1989a, 37-54.

Warren, John. 1989. "Franz Werfel's Historical Drama: Continuity and Change." In Huber, *Franz Werfel*, 1989a, 153-73.

Yates, W. E. 1989. "Franz Werfel and Austrian Poetry of the First World War." In Huber, *Franz Werfel*, 1989a, 15-36.

Abels, Norbert. 1990. *Franz Werfel: mit Selbstzeugnissen und Bilddokumenten*. Reinbek bei Hamburg: Rowohlt.

Abels, Norbert, Franz Adam, Peter Becher, and Sigrid Canz. 1990. *Franz Werfel zwischen Prag und Wien*. Munich: Ausstellung des Adalbert Stifter Vereins.

Weber, Alfons. 1990. *Problemkonstanz und Identität: Sozialpsychologische Studien zu Franz Werfels Biographie und Werk, unter besonderer Berücksichtigung der Exilerzählungen*. Frankfurt am Main: Peter Lang.

Bahr, Erhard. 1991. "Geld und Liebe in Werfels *Der Tod des Kleinbürgers*." *Modern Austrian Literature* 24 (2): 33-49.

Berlin, Jeffrey B., and Hans-Ulrich Lindken. 1991. "Der unveröffentlichte Briefwechsel zwischen Franz Werfel und Stefan Zweig." *Modern Austrian Literature* 24 (2): 89-122.

Berlin, Jeffrey B., Donald G. Daviau, and Jorun B. Johns. 1991. "Unpublished Letters between Franz Werfel, Alma Mahler Werfel, and Ben Huebsch: 1941-1946." *Modern Austrian Literature* 24 (2): 123-200.

Binder, Hartmut. 1991. "Im Prager *Kabarett Lucerna*: Franz Werfels Gedicht 'Einer Chansonette.'" *Modern Austrian Literature* 24 (2): 1-23.

Davidheiser, James C. 1991a. "From Premonition to Portrayal: Franz Werfel and World War II." In *Der Zweite Weltkrieg und die Exilanten: Eine literarische Antwort*, ed. Helmut F. Pfanner. Bonn: Bouvier, 1991. 13-22.

Davidheiser, James C. 1991b. "The Novelist as Prophet: A New Look at Franz Werfel's *Höret die Stimme*." *Modern Austrian Literature* 24 (2): 51-67.

Klinger, Kurt. 1991. "'Die Welt wird Blut erbrechen': Franz Werfels Gedichte der Emigrationszeit." *Modern Austrian Literature* 24 (2): 25-32.

Prater, Donald A. 1991. "Stefan Zweig und Franz Werfel." *Modern Austrian Literature* 24 (2): 85-88.

Steiman, Lionel B. 1991. "'Twilight or Dawn?' Observations on Werfel's Exile as Reflected in His Letters." *Modern Austrian Literature* 24 (2): 69-83.

Abels, Norbert. 1992. "Geschichte als Gleichnis: Franz Werfels dramatisches Werk." In Auckenthaler, *Franz Werfel*, 1992a, 39-68.

Auckenthaler, Karlheinz F., ed. 1992a. *Franz Werfel: neue Aspekte seines Werkes.* Szeged, Hungary: Jate.

Auckenthaler, Karlheinz F. 1992b. "Jeremias: Eine Botschaft an die Nachwelt." In Auckenthaler, *Franz Werfel*, 1992a, 81-89.

Beck, Knut. 1992. "Vom Zähmen der Phantasie: Zu Franz Werfels frühen Erzählungen." In Auckenthaler, *Franz Werfel*, 1992a, 71-79.

Binder, Hartmut. 1992a. "Beschwörung eines Kinderglaubens: Franz Werfels *Stern der Ungeborenen*." In Nehring and Wagener, *Franz Werfel im Exil*, 1992, 129-73.

Binder, Hartmut. 1992b. "Werfels jugendliche Umtriebe: *Der Abituriententag* als autobiographischer Roman." In Auckenthaler, *Franz Werfel*, 1992a, 99-151.

Hadda, Janet. 1992. "Maternal Deprivation and Mirroring Needs in Franz Werfel's *Das Lied von Bernadette*." In Nehring and Wagener, *Franz Werfel im Exil*, 1992, 85-98.

Hyrslová, Kveta. 1992. "Franz Werfel und das Phänomen des 'Mitteleuropäertums': Versuch einer Differenzierung." In Auckenthaler, *Franz Werfel*, 1992a, 9-18.

Jungk, Peter Stephan. 1992. "Alma Maria Mahler-Werfel: Einfluß und Wirkung." In Nehring and Wagener, *Franz Werfel im Exil*, 1992, 21-31.

Kiss, Endre. 1992. "'. . .an einem fremden Tisch in einem fremden Land. . .': Franz Werfels dreifacher Hiobsroman *Der veruntreute Himmel*." In Auckenthaler, *Franz Werfel*, 1992a, 153-60.

Koopmann, Helmut. 1992. "Franz Werfel und Thomas Mann." In Nehring and Wagener, *Franz Werfel im Exil*, 1992, 33-49.

Kraus, Wolfgang. 1992. "Weltuntergang und Erneuerung." In Auckenthaler, *Franz Werfel*, 1992a, 3-7.

Michaels, Jennifer E. 1992. "The Reception of Franz Werfel in the United States." In *Die Resonanz des Exils: Gelungene und mißlungene Rezeption deutschsprachiger Exilautoren*, ed. Dieter Sevin. Amsterdam: Rodopi. 80-97.

Nehring, Wolfgang, and Hans Wagener, eds. 1992. *Franz Werfel im Exil*. Bonn, Berlin: Bouvier.

Nehring, Wolfgang. 1992. "Komödie der Flucht ins Exil: Franz Werfels *Jacobowsky und der Oberst*." In Nehring and Wagener, *Franz Werfel im Exil*, 1992, 111-27.

Nikics, Anita. 1992. "Diskussionsbeitrag." In Auckenthaler, *Franz Werfel*, 1992a, 161-63.

Pirumowa, Medsi. 1992. "Die Entstehungsgeschichte des Romans *Die vierzig Tage des Musa Dagh.*" In Auckenthaler, *Franz Werfel*, 1992a, 91-97.

Reffet, Michel. 1992. "Die Strukturierung von Werfels Theater." In Auckenthaler, *Franz Werfel*, 1992a, 19-37.

Schwarz, Egon. 1992. "'Ich war also Jude! Ich war ein Anderer!' Franz Werfels Darstellung der sozio-psychologischen Judenproblematik." In Auckenthaler, *Franz Werfel*, 1992a, 165-76.

Steiman, Lionel B. 1992. "Werfel, Christianity, and Antisemitism." In Nehring and Wagener, *Franz Werfel im Exil*, 1992, 51-66.

Stern, Guy, and Peter Schönbach. 1992. "Die Vertonung Werfelscher Dramen." In Nehring and Wagener, *Franz Werfel im Exil*, 1992, 187-98.

Stern, Joseph Peter. 1992. "Franz Werfels letzte Aufzeichnungen." In Auckenthaler, *Franz Werfel*, 1992a, 177-83.

Strelka, Joseph P. 1992a. "Die politischen, sozialen und religiösen Utopien in Franz Werfels *Stern der Ungeborenen.*" In Nehring and Wagener, *Franz Werfel im Exil*, 1992, 175-86.

Strelka, Joseph P. 1992b. "Franz Werfels politische Utopien." In Strelka, *Literatur und Politik: Beispiele literaturwissenschaftlicher Perspektiven.* Frankfurt a. M.: Peter Lang. 175-88. (Essentially the same as Strelka 1992a.)

Wagener, Hans. 1992. "Franz Werfel in der amerikanischen Literaturkritik." In Nehring and Wagener, *Franz Werfel im Exil*, 1992, 1-20.

Weissenberger, Klaus. "Franz Werfels *Theologumena* als Ästhetik seiner Lyrik im Exil." In Nehring and Wagener, *Franz Werfel im Exil*, 1992, 67-84.

Zeman, Herbert. 1992. "'Dieses Buch ist ein erfülltes Gelübde": Ethos und künstlerische Gestaltung von Franz Werfels *Das Lied von Bernadette.*" In Nehring and Wagener, *Franz Werfel im Exil*, 1992, 99-110.

Wagener, Hans. 1993. *Understanding Franz Werfel.* Columbia: University of South Carolina Press.

Wagener, Hans. 1994. "Von Weißstrümpfen und Motormenschen: Franz Werfel und der National(sozial)ismus." *Literatur und politische Aktualität*, ed. Elrud Ibsch and Ferdinand van Ingen. *Amsterdamer Beiträge zur Neueren Germanistik* 36: 325-345.

# Index